Also by Leo Lionni

between

worlds

between worlds

the autobiography of

Leo Lionni

alfred a. knopf / new york / 1997

Of course, I dedicate this book to Nora,
the keeper, the anchor, the light of my world
for more than sixty-five years

And to Mannie, whom I have known
and loved for almost as long

And to my grandchildren and great-grandchildren

To Frances Foster, who has been the editor of my fables
for children for the past sixteen years, my thanks.
Her collaboration and encouragement, but above all
the deep friendship we developed, have been an
essential factor in the writing of my memories.

And thanks to the many other people who have
encouraged and helped me, particularly Veronica Rauch
and Doogie Morley-Bodle. And finally, I am indebted to
Bob Gottlieb, who guided this book through a
difficult and sometimes painful course.

*Un grazie speciale va a Marcello e Anita Vanni
e tutta la famiglia per essere diventata nel corso di
molti anni insieme, parte della nostra.*

part one
1910–1931

*I*t was the fifth of May, 1910, in a bungalow of Watergraafsmeer, a suburb
of Amsterdam, when I was suddenly
held high, shivering at the center of shifting
lights and an explosion of sounds. It had
been a hectic, scary day, but, in retrospect,
a good one. Two fives and a ten—a small
symmetry within the infinity of numbers.
Two fives—my hands. Ten, my fingers.
I would be making things.

Amsterdam

I am sitting alone in a small wicker chair in the center of a long, rectangular, freshly mowed meadow. It is late afternoon and the immense golden sky is slowly darkening. I have been sitting here a long time with my eyes fixed on the end of the field. Earlier, a skyful of red, white, and blue balloons had slowly risen from the horizon into nothingness. I am waiting for the fireworks.

This is my only recollection of Watergraafsmeer, where I was born and where I lived the first four years of my life. The occasion, I think, was the queen's birthday. Now and then other images from those distant times cross the screen of my mind, but they are hardly visible and too swift to release meanings: the lozenges of a linoleum floor, a woman walking out of a room, a door slowly closing. . . . Yet I recognize the light and the time of day they share, the soft golden light of late afternoon, the varnished light of old paintings. The light that has coated all the memories of my childhood in Amsterdam.

In 1910, the year I was born, Amsterdam was the capital of the world's diamond industry. Many of the workers were Sephardic Jews whose forefathers had been driven out of Spain and Portugal during the Inquisition. Ever since the time of Spinoza, Spanish and Portuguese names like De la Pardo, Enriquez, Pereira, and Lionni were almost as common in Amsterdam's ghetto as the Ashkenazic names Goldberg, Grunbaum, and Rosenzweig.

My father, Louis, was twelve when his father, a diamond trader, died. His mother, ill prepared for the responsibilities that were suddenly bequeathed to her, asked Elie Beffie, her husband's best friend, who held a seat on the London Diamond Exchange, to guide her son into his father's footsteps. Although Louis seemed to be naturally oriented toward more intellectual endeavors, the persuasive Elie succeeded not only in directing the young man toward a promising career in diamonds but in winning his young mother's affections as well. And eight years later, when Louis had finished school and was gainfully employed as a skilled diamond polisher, Elie and Rose Wolff Lionni were married.

My mother, Elisabeth Grossouw, came from a Christian working-class family and was a gifted young opera singer whose music studies had been financed by the father of one of her schoolmates, a rich benefactor who had been struck by her beauty, intelligence, and talent. She had a natural coloratura voice, an impressive presence, and that other quality so essential for a successful musical career: a strong ego.

My parents first met at a party celebrating the Italian Opera Company's performance of Mozart's *The Marriage of Figaro,* in which Mother was greatly applauded for her spirited interpretation of Cherubino. After a few idyllic months of passionate courtship, they decided to get married. But Father, suspicious of Italian tenors and backstage promiscuity, demanded that his fiancée leave the Italian Opera Company. Mother refused, explaining that the word *Italian* referred to the word *opera* and the company was as Dutch as Edam cheese. And so the matter stood. Their two families, however, had more serious reservations.

On my father's side, objection to the marriage was civilized and comparatively mild. My grandmother Rose saw no reason to disapprove of her son's choice. Born and raised in Paris in a strict Orthodox Jewish family, she was a wise and worldly woman, and although her formal education had been neglected, she had developed an original and open mind. Her diplomatic husband gently asked the practical questions. How could young Louis earn enough to support a wife in proper style? And if a baby came, which was probable, how could the young bride continue her singing career?

On Mother's side, alas, the reaction was steamier. Opa Grossouw was a difficult man, given to sudden outbursts of violence, especially when he had been on a drinking spree. When he learned of his daughter's affair with the flamboyant and slightly eccentric young diamond worker who had the nerve to appear with two white Russian whippets on a leash on the very street where the Grossouws lived, Opa exploded. In a fit of fury, he beat his daughter and then threw her headlong into her room. When a few months later he was told that Betty was pregnant, there was another outburst. But this time the abuse was verbal, and it frightened no

My parents, Louis Lionni and
Elisabeth Grossouw Lionni

one, least of all Mother, who said that she had witnessed better performances on the stage of the Italian Opera Company. Much faster than anyone had dared hope, Opa's attitude toward his daughter's marriage mellowed, and on the day before the wedding he gave the couple his blessing and swallowed half a bottle of Extra Oude Jenever to their health and happiness.

The newlyweds were now surrounded by gestures of affection and love from both families, and at the Grossouws' a veritable epidemic of knitting, sewing, and hammering erupted. The living room on the Jan van der Heyden Straat was rapidly transformed into a display of baby goods worthy of a department store. Three months before my entrance into the world I owned not only a complete layette but an avant-garde crib designed by Uncle Piet and an elegant, scaled-down version of a Vliegende Hollander, a Flying Dutchman wagon typical of Holland's northern provinces, built by Opa.

My parents found a small bungalow in Watergraafsmeer, a quiet community not far from Amsterdam with row upon row of bungalow-type houses hidden in the dense foliage of shrubs and trees. Father installed his workbench and his diamond-cutting equipment in the attic, reached by ladder from the second-floor corridor. Mother had her Steinway brought from Amsterdam, and with the help of a Kashmir shawl, some Javanese shadow puppets, and framed photographs of famous conduc-

With my teddy bear

tors, she transformed the small living and dining room into a charming Bohemian living-dining-music room.

As a freelance diamond cutter, Father commuted to Amsterdam, and at the end of each day, he climbed to his tiny attic laboratory and worked late into the night. Although he was now making a fair income, he had lost interest in his craft, and he began to look for other ways to use his fine, orderly mind, which was naturally inclined toward the logic of figures. Prodded by a friend, he enrolled in a night course in accounting, graduated with record grades, and was preparing for the government examinations, ready to begin a new career as a public accountant, when war broke out. It was August of 1914, and Father was drafted into the army. Less than four months later he was honorably discharged because of deafness, a condition attributed to artillery blasts, which was to plague him for the rest of his life.

While we lived in Watergraafsmeer, Mother took me at least once a month to Oma's house in the big city. I called it Oma's house, never Opa's, although it was as much his as hers. Opa worked as the caretaker of one of Holland's best-known rowing clubs, the Amstel Vereeniging, which took its name from the river that flows through Amsterdam, cutting the city in two. The clubhouse, a two-story wooden structure, rested on barges that

With my pony

Oma Grossouw

were moored to the Amstel Quay, only a few blocks from the Jan van der Heyden Straat, where the Grossouws lived. Opa was at the club from early morning to early evening. When he was not in his little office jammed with papers, folders, books, boxes, and empty gin bottles, he might be found on the lower deck varnishing a sleek racing scull, taut as a bow, or readying one of the lazy wherries to be used for an outing to the small lakes beyond the outskirts of town. Or tending to his rabbits, or more likely still, limp in an armchair, loudly snoring fumes of beer or gin.

While Opa was often drunk and unpleasant, Oma was a big, naive, comfortable angel. She could hardly read or write, but she was wise, and I felt that she knew all the things that one should know, neither one more nor one less. I loved the trip to Oma's, through the polders and over the narrow bridges and the trolley ride from the Amsterdam station to the Berlage Bridge, near the Jan van der Heyden Straat. And I loved Oma's house. It was so light, spacious, and gay, and I could run around the living room, climb on anything, and yell as loud as I wanted without ever being scolded.

Oma's kitchen smelled the way a kitchen should, but Mother, who by temperament and circumstances had outgrown her proletarian origins, didn't agree. To her, nothing should smell except purple lilacs and roses

Aunt Mies

and Houbigant's Quelques Fleurs. She was irritated by the whiffs of cabbage or onion that emanated from her mother; I liked Oma that way. The smells were exotic but still reassuring. They were Oma.

My aunt Mies worked as a model in some of the fashion houses in the center of town. If she was between jobs, as often happened, she would be home when we came. Oma would shout, "Mies, they are here!" and Mies would storm out of her little room, loudly slamming the door behind her. About twenty-two at the time, she was an ideal playmate. Good-natured, scatterbrained, and slightly rebellious, she was not ashamed to chase me, first around the house, then down the stairs and onto the street, yelling at the top of her voice and bumping into people with an outburst of giggles. She was quite beautiful, her long blond hair floating behind her, and although I was only a child, I was fully aware of the impression she made when it was a man she ran into. And in the evenings, if Mother and I should sleep over, there were my uncles, Piet, Herman, and Jan. A feast. Perfect happiness.

On my oma Rose's side there were other relatives: her older sister, Trui, with her dour husband, Michel. Tante Trui's house was in the busiest, noisiest part of the center of town. Steep, narrow stairs led to a small hall, from which one could enter the kitchen or the living room, which I remember being filled with oppressive dark mahogany furniture, Persian rugs, Delft vases, brass menorahs of various sizes and styles, plants and flowers, glasses and silver trays with cookies and chocolates, and, towering over it all, an enormous copper chandelier, like the one I was to see in the synagogue in the city of Cochin, on the west coast of South India, more than half a century later. But what I remember most vividly is the frightening sight of my great-grandmother, small and thin, meticulously dressed, combed, and powdered, sitting motionless like a mummy, propped up with four or five pillows, her eyes closed, in a dark, elaborately carved armchair with a white porcelain pot hanging quite visibly under the seat.

Luckily, our visits to Tante Trui were rare, and Father came with us. They happened mostly on the important Jewish holidays, like Rosh Hashana or Yom Kippur. The house would then be crowded with people who, coming and going, would pass each other on the narrow stairs with great difficulty. Most of them spoke Yiddish, and Polish or Russian. The men wore hats or yarmulkes in the house even when they embraced Tante Trui, or the old Ethiopian maid, Rachel, who had grown up with the family like a Gypsy slave and never learned to speak Dutch, only Yiddish. What a relief it was to be back in the Jan van der Heyden Straat! I could never quite believe that Tante Trui was my father's aunt. A blood relative!

In the spring of 1915 my parents moved back to Amsterdam, where both the Grossouws and the Beffies were clamoring for more frequent visits from their only grandchild. The Grossouws agreed to take us in until Father had passed his examinations and could afford to resettle us in the dignified Amsterdam neighborhood required by his new profession.

Father placed his diamond-cutting bench and tools in one corner of the huge Grossouw attic, an immense cage of raw, unvarnished wood, with two small windows that gave onto the flat, tarred roof. I remember the attic like the backstage of a small opera house—the same emptiness, the same bleak disorder. There were brown trunks, dry and dusty, a large gilded frame leaning precariously against a wooden column, a long table, an old broken sofa, piles of newspapers and magazines. For reasons I could never understand, the attic was larger than the apartment; it must have occupied a considerable part of the fourth floor of the building next door. Years before, Opa had sectioned off three small rooms for the boys, but he had never finished the job properly; the rooms did not even have doors. Only Uncle Jan, the youngest of the brothers, still lived at home and slept in the attic.

Oma totally ignored the attic's existence. Not so Opa, who kept his pigeons there. Incorporating one of the two windows, he had built a large enclosure of chicken wire where a dozen or so nesting boxes hung. Access to this mansard cage was through a small, flimsy door of wooden slats and wire. At least once every two days, Opa would crawl into the cage, feed the birds, climb the four steps of the small ladder that was nailed to the wall, open the window, and let the pigeons fly out. He would then climb onto the roof and with a ten-foot pole begin to wave larger and larger circles in the sky. Soon the pigeons would follow, and in perfect formation fly around and around in ever-widening circles. Close together. Around and around. It was Opa's circus act.

Great excitement in early fall when Father became a full-fledged certified public accountant! After much searching he found a large apartment, ideal, he thought, for both office and home. It was in a pleasant upper-middle-class neighborhood, not far from the Concertgebouw, Amsterdam's great concert hall, a five-minute walk from the Ryksmuseum, a stone's throw from the Stedelyk, and a ten-minute stroll to the Vondel School, one of the best elementary schools in the city. This was a part of Amsterdam quite unlike the quaint narrow streets, the dark canals, the spidery bridges, and the black belfries that tourists remember. There were lanes with elegant, high-roofed villas hidden by rhododendron bushes. And even the more modest streets had wide sidewalks where we could whip our tops and roll our marbles.

We occupied what was called a *bovenhuis,* or upper house, the top floors of a four-story, two-family dwelling. In the tile-covered stoop we had a separate entrance door with a little window through which one could see the long, steep stairs that ran up to the living floor. There was my father's study, an impressive, wood-paneled room, heavy with Persian rugs, dark mahogany bookcases, a library with leather-bound books on finance and law, two green velvet armchairs, and a lion-foot desk.

Mother monopolized the living room with her grand piano, a black Bechstein. On it, at one end, stood a silver frame with an inscribed photograph of Mother's mentor, the famous conductor of Amsterdam's Concertgebouw Orchestra, Willem Mengelberg, while at the center stood, noblesse oblige, a crystal vase with a large bouquet of seasonal flowers. There was a small dining room with simple blond furniture and heavy velvet curtains. Beyond that, the kitchen, and next to it were the stairs that led to the corridor of the top floor. There, at one end, were my parents' bedroom and the bathroom, and at the other, the attic and my room. In my memory the corridor varies in length. It was very long when, awakened from a nightmare, I would tiptoe in the dark to climb into the warm safety

Our apartment house in Amsterdam, with my room—the temple of my aloneness— at the very top

of Mother's bed. It became endless when, yearning to be alone and free to live my fantasies, I closed the door of my room.

In the middle of the corridor hung a very large canvas by the French painter Henri Le Fauconnier, one of the lesser-known founders of cubism, a protégé of Uncle Willem, Elie Beffie's brother. It was an enormous turmoil of swirling gray-brown paint that hid the ghost of a man smoking a pipe. I was proud to recognize the man sitting there in the midst of all that turbulence when friends who visited us said they saw nothing but a mess of gray paint and asked me what it meant. But I never liked that painting. I didn't like the grimy fat paint, a dark gray with blue and green reflections, that lay wrinkled upon the canvas, ready to slide off at any moment. I didn't like the dimensions of the figure, which seemed larger than life. Worse. Larger than me!

How much nicer was the painting that hung between the door of the attic and my room! It was a happy canvas with cheerful colors that seemed to flutter like ribbons in an icy wind. When I see one of its variations at the Guggenheim or in the pages of a book on twentieth-century art, I greet the kind, green-faced giant who plays his fiddle on the snow-capped roofs of a rickety Russian shtetl as an old friend with whom I spent my childhood. We simply called it "the Chagall." It was so unlike the paintings in the Ryksmuseum, where distant times and spaces hung frozen in their golden varnish. It was altogether another world, where anything could happen and everything was unexpected—a noisy, busy world, close by and touchable. Perhaps it was the secret birthplace of all the stories I ever wrote, painted, or imagined.

On the other side of "the Chagall" was my room, my ivory tower, the temple of my aloneness. And above all, the place where I made things happen. It was my zoo, my botany laboratory. For there, with the miraculous consent of my otherwise fastidious mother, I was allowed to gather and collect the abundant, varied, and often smelly evidence of my vehement passion for nature. It was there that I could observe, unobserved, the metamorphosis of seeds, caterpillars, and tadpoles, and study the etiology of white mice, orange-bellied salamanders, and gray-green sticklebacks. And it was there that after a sweaty excursion to the white beaches of the northwest coast I would empty my paper bag cornucopias of the driftwood sculptures, the shells, the carcasses of crabs, that I had patiently disentangled from the black garland of algae that lined the ebbing tides.

In my room there were two built-in closets, one on each side of the door; my bed, two tables, and two chairs. Perhaps there were even three or four tables, for when I recall all the things that were arranged or scattered or piled upon them, two would not have been enough to contain everything. One large table held containers of all sorts, shapes, and sizes, each with its lively little tenant: marmalade jars with caterpillars, praying mantises, dragonflies, cans with worms for the diets of fish, frogs, or fowl. There were aquariums, square and round, with minnows, black mollies, snails, and sweetwater shrimps. There was a cage with two white mice forever burrowing in sawdust that smelled sweet of urine. And another cage with a pair of orange-beaked finches, endlessly jumping from rod to rod.

There were long cotton-lined boxes with blown-out eggs—white, pale blue, and green, plain and speckled, big and small—ranged according to color and size, carefully labeled, and registered in a special little black notebook. And larger boxes full of shells, some shallow with removable glass covers, where beetles and butterflies were pinned onto a cork bottom in neat rows, like tiny drum majorettes. And above this jumble, from strings running the length of the room, hung leaves, pods, feathers, dried flowers, and probably a rabbit skin.

But most clearly remembered are the two large terrariums at the center of the table. I have forgotten the name of the person who taught me this Latin word, the first I ever mastered: *terrarium.* Now the word sounds to my ears like the final notes of a marching song, but then, like the little brass scale, the tweezers, the bell jars, the white rabbit skull, and a few *real* books on zoology, botany, and the discovery of the South Pole, it was part of my impersonation of a scholar, a scientist, an explorer. An adult.

Within the glass walls of my terrariums I arranged make-believe oases of sand, moss, and stone. Here and there I planted elegantly twisted branches bleached in the ocean sun, now become miniature trees where little snakes could coil. I dug caves for toads to hide from an imaginary bird of prey. There was a wading pond (an old frying pan lined with gravel) for frogs and salamanders, and even a one-stone island, scrupulously chosen from among many, from which tiny turtles would stare motionless at a drowning fly or a wiggling worm in the water below.

I had bought some of my little animals with my pocket money at Natura, a shop not far from my school which sold tropical fish, exotic reptiles, birds, sand, corals, water plants, and tiny boxes of dried ants. My emerald snake, the baby alligator, and the butterfly boxes came from there, but most of the little inhabitants of my terrariums had been captured by me on outings along the ponds and canals that crisscrossed the polders at the outskirts of the city.

Now and then my athletic uncles and even my sedentary father would take me rowing in one of the comfortable and yet sporty wherries from Opa's club. We would glide along the city quays and past the outlying factories, and then, a few kilometers out of town, we would pull in the oars and quietly slip into the high reeds of a meadow bank. There was a farm where one could drink thick buttermilk and eat freshly baked ginger cookies. There were swings hanging from the knobby branches of a giant oak, a seesaw, and a squeaky merry-go-round. At the back of the barn there was a small pond so thickly filled with algae that a frog, jumping from the bank, would slowly sink through the green surface into the black water I imagined below.

I don't remember the long vistas of the endless polders, the shrinking geometry of the meadows and canals stretching all the way to the horizon, dotted only with black-and-white cows and the occasional verticality of a windmill. I only know those Dutch landscapes from paintings, guidebooks, postcards, and recent memories. Yet even now I feel the fat earth sticking to the soles of my shoes. I hear the rustling reeds as they bend in the wind or under the boat's bow. And in the memory of my wet hand I recognize the pulsating heart of a slimy salamander as I slip it into my green botany box, lined with wet moss and pierced for air with tiny holes arranged, like sunflower seeds, in concentric circles.

As I revisit in my mind those distant scenes of my childhood and relive emotions and feelings so keenly, I cannot help shifting them into the more recent light of awareness, doubt, and understanding, in search of meanings. Love for nature often expresses an obsessive curiosity about life and fear of death. My terrariums were undoubtedly an act of love. But they were first of all elaborate fictions squeezed into the narrow dimensions of a miniaturized nature, artificially arranged. They were theaters for vaguely perceived dramas: dramas about love and hate, hunger, joy, fear, death, and transfiguration. They were metaphors. They were Art.

Next to the nature table stood a smaller one, painted black. It was the Art Table. There I painted, drew, carved, glued, modeled. Uncle Piet had given me the table for my ninth birthday. When Mother saw it she looked perplexed. "Why black?" she asked. I never forgot his answer. "Because all colors look so good on black."

Uncle Piet, the eldest of my mother's brothers, was handsome, tall, and powerfully built and he had the same steel blue eyes as Mother. Unlike his brothers and sisters, whose wavy blond hair betrayed their thoroughly Dutch origin, Uncle Piet had hair that was dark, and he wore it heavily imbued with brilliantine and brushed to a sheen. Dashing and flamboyant, he was linked by a long trail of gossip to many famous ladies of the city's social, financial, and artistic aristocracy.

When I was six or seven, Uncle Piet worked as a draftsman in a builder's office and studied at night to become an architect. On weekends, to earn a few extra guilders, he would paint the emblem of the Amstel Rowing Society on the small flags that Opa sold to club members for their wherries or racing sculls. On many a Sunday, he would ask me to help him, lifting me onto a high stool next to him at the drafting table and showing me what to do. I would stencil the club emblem, a stylized anchor, onto the small triangles of blue cloth; I can still feel the weight of the brush, heavy with gooey silver paint and the reluctant give of the stubby bristles as I pushed them through the cardboard stencil. I was fascinated when, after slightly more than one generous stroke, the stencil was lifted and, as if by magic, a perfect, clean-edged anchor would be there.

Uncle Piet was a wonderful draftsman. He liked to draw portraits and always achieved a surprising likeness. Besides the one that he drew of me when I was seven, I have the telling drawing he made shortly after the

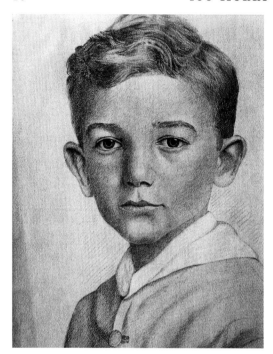

Me, drawn by Uncle Piet

premature death of his first wife, beautiful, mysterious Tante Liesje, who died during the Spanish influenza epidemic that plagued Europe in 1918.

Uncle Piet taught me to draw the shadows of a ball by patiently crosshatching, first with a hard, then with a softer pencil until, round and real, the form would seem to roll on the paper. But most of all I remember my excitement when, a year or so later, he had me trace some architectural drawings for him. No wonder that when I was asked what I wanted to be when I grew up, the answer was always, without hesitation, "An artist." For me Art was a generous word that included painting, sculpture, singing, piano playing, and now architecture. Artists were Le Fauconnier, Uncle Piet, my mother, van Gogh, Rembrandt, Mondriaan, Berlage, Chagall, the person who had painted the calendar that hung in Oma Grossouw's kitchen, and the copyists at the Ryksmuseum.

Since he was intelligent, charming, and adventurous, Piet's success as an architect seemed assured. And so was his success as an eligible bachelor—he was the epitome of the romantic lover of the early movies. A Dutch Rossano Brazzi, he was a champion oarsman, owned big dogs, drove little sports cars, drank and smoked heavily, and lived in one of the first modern houseboats, designed by him, that were moored in an Am-

My copy of Piet's drawing of Oma

sterdam canal. Women loved him. Because of his long, tormented love affair with Fientje de le Mar, Holland's favorite comedienne, whom he eventually married, he achieved national fame, so much so that his life with Fientje became the subject of a musical comedy. When in 1957 Uncle Piet died of lung cancer, the actress grabbed her two beloved cats and, with one in each arm, threw herself from the balcony of her apartment.

Uncle Piet was my childhood hero.

The nature table and the Art Table were symbolic of the pedagogical mood of the times. For those were the years of Froebel and Montessori, and a whiff of Jean-Jacques Rousseau hung in the Amsterdam air. The influential Socialist party was committed to revolutionary educational reforms in the elementary schools, and art and nature study were considered high-priority topics.

At the Vondel School, in a corner of our second-grade classroom, there was a crate where clay was kept under a wet burlap rag, ready for use at all times. The mushrooms we modeled, always three on an oval base, two large and a small one slightly off-center, would be returned to us after a day or two, miraculously hardened and permanent, ready to be painted bright crimson with white polka dots. Was I the small one? The only child?

And on the wall, next to a color chart of all the wading birds of the North Sea, hung two large plaster reliefs. One was an ivy leaf greatly enlarged and the other a giant ear. We learned to draw the veins, the contours, the bulges, and to trace the "outs" disappearing into the "ins." We were taught to judge curves and proportions by moving the outstretched thumb up and down a pencil, and when we had carefully outlined the shapes, we would crosshatch the shadows, gradually building up the blacks and by exclusion reveal the highlights. There was no talk of self-expression then, nor of "creativity." We simply learned the craft of drawing and we tried to draw well. For the first time we experienced the pleasure of performance.

The two great Amsterdam museums, the Ryksmuseum and the Stedelyk, were only a few blocks from where we lived. I had a special permit to draw in the large hall of plaster casts at the Ryksmuseum, and on many a Saturday morning, while my schoolmates met in the park for a game of soccer, I would walk to the museum with a box of pencils, a small drawing board, sheets of paper, and a folding chair. A little van Gogh. There in the great hall, under the benevolent eyes of a guard or an occasional visitor, I would draw, with painstaking accuracy, a nymph's wing, a giant's foot, a gladiator's head. And on my way out I would join a small crowd that had gathered around one of the licensed copiers who, stroke by stroke, with infinite patience, would make his image grow and take shape. I envied him his gray smock, the delicate brushes, and the elegant palette aged to just the right sheen, but most of all I envied him the wooden paint box, so neatly filled with small tubes of oil paint, too small, I thought, for the size of the painting he was copying.

I learned to see and to remember what I saw. While my memory for events, even recent ones, has always been poor, I can still evoke with hallucinatory precision the veil of gray dust on a plaster nipple; the tiny V between the toes; the empty pupil in a sculpture's eye. And the constellations of tiny holes left by thumbtacks in the four corners of my drawing board. I don't need to consult nature books to copy the shapes, colors, and textures of insects and reptiles, rodents and birds, pebbles and seashells. I simply copy them from the images that were stored away in my memory more than seventy years ago. I can evoke the specks of mica flickering in the sand, the fold of lichens on a stone, the hairy edge of a butterfly's wing, the pores in the black shell of an emu egg.

A child's world is a world of parts, of minutiae. For children, still unaware of the weight of meaning, things exist for the mere pleasure of being what they are. Distant spaces lie beyond their mental reach. When for the first time from the top of a dune they see the ocean, they run to the water's edge to pick up a shell that tumbles in the foam of a retreating wave. They do not see the horizon, which like a different world is not as yet in their vocabulary. To children, great vistas suggest frightening prophecies of oncoming evil, for they are the confluence of time and space, the ultimate *ma,* as the Japanese might say. My childhood nightmares were of space, endless corridors with tiled floors that ran into infinity, downhill slopes that never ended.

It was in the Ryksmuseum that I discovered gentle spaces that were no larger than my mind. The paintings there were much like my terrariums but two-dimensional and with the added mystery of total immobility and silence. Their mahogany and golden frames contained friendly horizons, visible infinities, a destiny that was motionless and predictable. Meadows not more than a few feet square faded into a haze that veiled forever the ghosts of towns. In the shade of trees no taller than a cabbage, sheep huddled to wait out a storm that would never arrive. And soldiers the size of beetles were always descending into valleys that were no deeper than the folds of my sheets.

What was there, small or large, was there forever, waiting to be recognized and confirmed. The diamond on a ring, a peony's petal, a cavalier's nostril. And the battlefields, the hefty nudes, the dead pheasants, the flowers, the crystal beakers, the burghers, and, of course, *The Night Watch,* which, oh wonder! did not exist before Rembrandt had given it the last brushstroke!

Secrets I never shared: in a cloud, a bearded giant licking the crest of ocean waves; on the white flank of a grazing cow, the silhouettes of all the islands of Indonesia. I learned to move my eyes through the surface of the canvas, to lift and lower the curtain of paint which was both enclosure and enclosed, means and substance, reality and dream. Magic.

I occasionally have the feeling, absurd perhaps, that nothing of any *real* importance has changed within me since those distant Amsterdam days. There are no terrariums in my studio, no cocoons in the closet, no frogs staring at me through the greenish glass, and no park nearby. But through my window I see the hills of Chianti. A three-foot-long garden snake lives in a bush near the studio and each year leaves me his skin. At night I hear the shrieks of owls. And sometimes a wild boar rushes by. When in summer I walk the path from my studio to the house, green lizards dart off in all directions. And when I go to inspect the rabbit pens or visit Carolina, the small Himalayan goat, I pick some unfamiliar herb or pod along the way or stop to face the swaying immobility of a praying mantis.

Not so long ago I suddenly realized that the dimensions of my children's books are exactly the same as those of my terrariums. I also discovered that the protagonists of my fables are the same frogs, mice, sticklebacks, turtles, snails, and butterflies that more than three-quarters of a century ago lived in my room. And that even the paper landscapes they now inhabit are identical to the ones I used to build with real sand, pebbles, moss, and water. The books I have made, like the terrariums of years ago, contain little continents complete with hills, lakes, islands, beaches, and forests of weeds. My miniature worlds, whether enclosed in yesterday's walls of glass or in today's cardboard covers, are surprisingly alike. Both are the orderly, predictable alternatives to a chaotic, unmanageable, terrifying universe.

On Saturdays, my mother would take me to Oma Grossouw's in the early afternoon. We would catch the Number Two trolley in front of the Stedelyk Museum. The trip took us through a part of town which to me was like a foreign city. Since I had never set foot in those neighborhoods, they unrolled like the pages of a book. Like fiction. We would get off just before the Berlage Bridge, back in familiar territory, and walk along the quay to the Jan van der Heyden Straat.

I don't know how often I asked my mother to drop me off at Opa's club, since we were only two blocks away. The answer was always no and there was always a different excuse. "Not today. I'm already late." "Oma is waiting for you." "I don't want you to miss your snack."

Once she had delivered me to Oma, my mother would disappear for the rest of the afternoon and this other world would be mine. In my memory I see the entrance doors to Oma's house with their edges rounded by too many coats of glossy green paint. I see myself on tiptoes, stretching to reach the little green box with rows of tiny holes, and I can hear my voice shouting happily, "It's *me!*" knowing that Oma is standing on the third-floor landing holding a brown Bakelite receiver to her ear with one hand, while wiping the other, white with flour, on her apron. Now, as then, I marvel at the fact that my words could fly up through three floors of pipe—a greater miracle, perhaps, than today's house phone. I push the door, and I can feel the weight of the brass handle, gleaming from polish

With my mother

and the years. And there I am, tall for my age, running up the long steep stairs, leaving Mother far behind holding on to the wooden railing, panting.

I remember the interior of the two-floor apartment in very vivid detail: the textures, the smells, the shapes of the furniture, the designs of the wallpapers, and the linoleum floors dog-eared at the corners, revealing the gray dusty felt underneath. The short corridor with the crowded kitchen that always smelled of cabbage; my grandparents' bedroom with its cool scent of 4711, and next to it the so-called bathroom, euphemism for an oversized closet with a small window (fortunately open most of the time), which contained the *ple,* a step-up wooden toilet box with a round hole, and a small triangular sink in the corner with a bucket underneath. An indoor outhouse. Was there no other bathroom? There must have been, but I don't remember where. At the end of the corridor there was Aunt Mies's tiny bedroom, all pink and blue, the walls covered with watercolor reproductions of young Englishwomen, their blond hair flowing in the wind, lazily caressing the chestnut-shiny necks of horses.

The living-dining room was unusually large for a low-income housing project and, seen in retrospect, an extravagant luxury. The furniture was an incongruous assemblage of unmatched pieces, mostly Christmas gifts from my uncles. Mother said that it reminded her of a cheap furniture showroom. There was a large dining table with eight uncomfortable chairs, and there were three coffee tables, each with its own sitting arrangement and its own style. One stood in the far end of the room, in front of an Art Nouveau sofa that vaguely matched the dusty honey color of the coffee table. This was the corner where Oma entertained the ladies who came for afternoon tea, or where my three uncles would retire after a rare and noisy family dinner to puff on their cigars in contemplative silence, their minds God knows where, and sip their gin while the ladies were in the kitchen washing dishes and gossiping.

Then there was a small mahogany monstrosity with a center column the shape of an elongated Chianti bottle growing from three lion feet complete with claws. Its oval top carried a lace centerpiece and five or six sepia photographs of ancestors in silver frames, varied in shape and size, reminding one of a miniature cemetery. Against the wall, on the other side of the room, was Uncle Piet's drafting table, where I was allowed to sit on the funny adjustable stool and experiment with pencils, rulers, and a compass. And finally, in the far corner beside a large maroon velvet armchair, obliquely facing the window, stood one more coffee table, on it a huge brass ashtray, which left just enough room for a bottle, a glass, and a pipe rack. Table and chair shared a gaudy Persian rug. This was Opa's island retreat in a linoleum sea. After dinner he would grab his bottle of Bols and a glass from the buffet and disappear behind the high back of his chair. Often the only sign of life was his voice calling the family cat. "Poes! Here, Poes! Pussy, Pussy!" Poes would run into the room from the kitchen straight to Opa's island and jump into his lap.

On weekends everybody left or came home at strange hours. For Opa, Saturdays and Sundays were the busiest days of the week. We all knew that he would arrive home late in the day, sometimes well after dinner. Puffing and groaning, without uttering a word, his eyes fixed on the floor, he would stumble to the sideboard, grab the bottle of gin, retire to his little island, and call the cat. I had learned not to pay attention to him, and the others would ease the general upset and embarrassment by telling stories or faking loud discussions about nothing at all. Those days were always full of surprises: a wherry trip to the watery outskirts of town with Uncle Herman or Uncle Piet, an expedition to the zoo with Aunt Mies, or a walk across the bridge to ancient, unfamiliar neighborhoods, where narrow canals were spanned by drawbridges, bony and light like dragonflies.

Happy and excited as I was with those adventures, I was also perfectly content just to play cards with Oma. We would sit at the end of the dining table in deep concentration, facing each other like two generals at war. Or we would have a wild game of checkers, which always ended with a tremendous flourish of fast victorious moves, mostly mine. Tac, tac, tac, tac, TAC! "Not fair! Not fair!" Oma would shout, dramatically humiliated. Aunt Mies would then come running into the room, her arms raised, and perform her part of the act. "What happened? What happened?" Then we would all hug each other and dance around the room.

When left to entertain myself, I would push Opa's armchair to the window and watch the activity in the street below. The fishman in his uniform—bulky velvet trousers, wooden clogs, and bright red scarf—would stop his pushcart against the sidewalk and yell, *"Verse vis! Verse vis! Verse kabeljouw,"* and little by little the women would gather around him and two or three alley cats would cautiously approach the cart, knowing that sooner or later a bloody herring head would be thrown their way. In summer, I would lean out of the window over the iron balustrade just enough not to scare Oma. Then I could see the river traffic, sculls and wherries from the Amstel Club with the little blue flags that I had stenciled with Uncle Piet and that for a few short minutes had been mine; barges floating by in both directions with little woolly dogs running back and forth the full length of their decks, barking furiously at the cyclists on the quays. And people who, seen from their hats down, just looked funny.

But the main attraction was the windows of the house across the street. I once asked Oma why the curtains were always drawn and who was living there. There was a quick exchange of furtive glances with Aunt Mies, who was standing near the door trying to conceal her giggles behind her hand. "Oh, I don't know. It's like a meeting place, or something," Oma said nonchalantly. I felt ill at ease and never asked the question again.

The curtains became an obsession. I couldn't keep my eyes away from them. Even when I crossed the room to pick up a toy or a book, I gave the house across the street a quick commanding glance, but except for lights being turned on and off, nothing much ever seemed to happen. Now and then a man would enter the portico and disappear. Minutes later, as moving shadows floated over the curtains of one of the rooms, I would desperately try to think the unthinkable. My breathing grew heavier and my ears began to buzz. My mind was blurred. My hand nestled in my crotch. When asked what I was doing or what I would like to do, I invented excuses. "Why don't you go out and play? The weather is so nice," Oma said. "I like to sit here and watch the street." "What is going on?" "Two funny kittens. A black one and a white one."

Sometimes, in my own bed at home, before sleep, I would try to draw the house in my mind. How many stories? Four. How many windows?

Twelve. Was the portico green or blue? I would invent a man and send him to a room on the third floor. When the man enters, the frame of light around the curtain moves slightly. With my mind's magic I can see through the curtains or even stand in a corner of the room, invisible. The man is sitting on the bed and *she* is standing in front of him. She undresses slowly. He is blindfolded. They are both blindfolded. He reaches to touch her. She dances away, out of the room. Into my sleep.

Occasionally, on the eve of a school holiday, I was allowed to sleep over at Oma's. It meant that while Oma was preparing breakfast and the others were noisily getting ready for the day, shaving, washing, dressing, I had a chance to watch the house across the street in the cool, sober light of morning. It was a different world then—solid, hard, sharp-edged. Windows and curtains were open, and women in dressing gowns piled sheets and blankets onto chairs to air the beds. All the rooms appeared to be furnished in more or less the same modest manner, much like the hotel where we had stayed once during a vacation at the seashore. Pictures on the wall, a small armchair, and a freestanding clothes rack near the door.

Directly across from me a woman was brushing her long black hair in front of a mirror. She was heavyset and full-breasted. I imagined her body under the shifting folds of a flimsy nightgown. By the late afternoon the scene would have filled my mind, stormed through my body, raced with my blood. Now a sense of aloneness, of absence, came over me. A sense of failure. I had been robbed of my imagery. I was no longer a secret witness. A protagonist.

A funny little dog with short legs and a question-mark tail stopped to pee against the corner of the portico. Then, in sudden rapture, it ran all the way to the quay and disappeared around the corner. It didn't take long for my mood to adjust. I was now anxious to get out and run on the wide sidewalk, whipping my top. I would ask Opa to take me with him to the club. I would feed the rabbits. Oma came into the room with the oatmeal. Opa was all smiles. "There is my big boy!" I was hungry now. Free and happy. I was going to feed the rabbits.

It was spring, the time when along the sandy coasts of Holland the tulips are cut and the bulbs harvested. That afternoon, two horse-drawn carts loaded with flowers came slowly from the direction of the Amstel Quay. One was filled with tulips, an orgy of colors. The other carried a mountain of bright yellow daffodils. The man who walked next to the cart with the tulips raised his head toward the windows of the higher floors of the buildings shouting, *"Tulpen! Tulpen! Mooie tulpen!"* like a town crier. The other filled in the pauses with a singsong "Daffodils!"

They stopped first near the corner, one behind the other, and then in the middle of the block. Women in aprons gathered around them, filled their arms with gigantic bouquets, bargained, paid, and left with triumphant smiles. Flowers then were as cheap as grass. One of the women had come from the portico of the house across the street. She wore a black skirt and a white blouse. I recognized her as she stepped down from the sidewalk. She was the one I had seen a few weeks before, combing her black hair. She whispered something to the man with the daffodils and then quickly returned to "the house."

In the afternoon, Mother came to have tea with Oma and take me home. Leaning over the dining table they had a long whispered conversation, while I, a glass of buttermilk in my hand, captured stray sentences and watched the street. The weather was unusually warm—the window was open. I put the empty glass next to Opa's ashtray and leaned out over the iron balustrade to see what was happening on the river. Just then a man who looked like Uncle Jan appeared from around the quay corner. He seemed to hesitate, and then he quickly walked in the direction of the blue portico. He looked determined to be going just there. My heart jumped—it *was* Uncle Jan. He gave our house a furtive look over his shoulder. I panicked, quickly pulled in my head, and went back to the chair. I caught him just as he entered the portico, climbed the stairs, and disappeared.

Long minutes went by while the world stood still. Dark clouds had gathered toward the east, and it began raining. A gentle diaphanous rain. I should have told Oma to close the window—I didn't. Across the street one of the curtains of the second floor was open. The lady with the black hair came into the room and switched on a lamp that was standing on the dresser. Now in the new rectangle of red light I saw Uncle Jan enter the room, carefully close the door behind him, and sit down on the edge of the bed. The woman walked quickly to the window and drew the curtain shut. I had run out of silly excuses for sitting there watching and felt guilty. The guilt of witnessing. I was embarrassed by my mother's presence. Besides, I couldn't sit there forever, waiting. Reluctantly, I went to Uncle Piet's drawing table, took a pencil from a little box, sat down with my head in my folded arms, and closed my eyes onto the screen of my fantasies.

Uncle Jan was the tallest, the thinnest, and the blondest of the Grossouws. And his eyes were the bluest, a light shimmering blue. His hair, combed back, disciplined by brilliantine and vigorous brushing, was all neat little waves like a lake on a windy day. It gave out a reddish glow that seemed to expand to his ruddy complexion. He always looked as if he had just stepped out of a hot shower. He was probably the most athletic of the three brothers—he spent far more time at the club than the others— but he did little socializing. Yet everyone liked him. He was a gentle loner. He was a good oarsman. In his spare time he trained with dogged determination. Twice he had taken second place at the national rowing championships, and on the cupboard in the dining room there were five or six gleaming trophies for minor races. With me he was outgoing, gay, and demonstratively loving. He smiled and laughed easily, and when he turned serious, his dimples (oh, those Grossouw dimples!) left two deep scars in his face.

Uncle Jan worked at a general store in the Brede Straat. I think he was ashamed to show or tell me what he did—probably a depressing menial job—because he never took me there. Yet like his two brothers he was a careful dresser. In my memory, all three wore dark jackets and striped trousers, the symbol of class mobility. The Grossouws were determined "to be someone." Jan was the exception. He imitated his older brothers, but whatever he wore was instantly degraded and made him look like a farmhand on Sunday morning. He lacked the strong sense of self that characterized the others. Even Aunt Mies, who was hardly ambitious, had at least the awareness of her beauty. I once overheard Mother, who loved to use Yiddish words, say, "Jan is good but he is a schlemiel." I believe it was the day he announced that he was going to get married.

How many minutes had passed? From the drafting table I gave the house across the street a quick look. Nothing had changed. "Do you want to draw? There is paper right there," said Oma. I had no choice. With a voice that wasn't mine, I said, "I want to see if those kittens are still there." Luck was on my side: I hadn't lied. The kittens were playing in the portico, chasing each other, running up and down the stairs, sideways, tails straight up, tripping over themselves. But my eyes were elsewhere.

Now all the curtains were closed, but only a few rooms were lit. Which window was it? I didn't remember. Then the bell rang. Oma jumped up and ran to the landing. "This must be Aunt Rachel," Mother said. I went back to the drafting table, trying to become invisible.

"Why don't you give Aunt Rachel a nice kiss?" She was a small, heavily built woman. She looked like one of those Russian wooden dolls that have other dolls inside. Her hair was pitch black, and when she had removed her hat she ran her hands over her bun, pressing stray locks into submission. I hated the hairy wart between her nose and her lip. She was not a real aunt, like Mies. For four long months she had been my piano teacher. She believed in strong discipline. "Your fingers must become ten little hammers. That is what piano playing is all about." She gave me painful exercises; never once was I allowed to play a little tune. "Everything has its moment." Perhaps if it hadn't been for the wart, if her hands hadn't been so ridiculously small and pudgy, and if she had used a deodorant, I would now be able to play my favorite Schubert sonata. The other day, I watched Horowitz on TV. *His* ten fingers didn't look like little hammers.

Was Uncle Jan now kissing that woman? "How about a cookie?" Oma said. Everything has its moment. Not daring to return to my observatory of sin, I went back to the drafting table nibbling my cookie, grabbed a pencil, and began to scribble on a piece of paper. I drew a rectangle. I drew it very, very slowly, hoping to hold back time. Or was I speeding it up? Is time ahead of you or behind? I yawned. A numbness came over me, and the busy voices of Mother, Oma, and Aunt Rachel slowly floated away into the distance. I drew a window in the upper-right-hand corner of the piece of paper, and then I must have fallen asleep because suddenly the door of the stair landing banged shut and a few seconds later Uncle Jan stood in front of me. Confused, I tried to focus on the time and my whereabouts. I jumped from the chair and let him hug me. While he held me high I looked out through the window. The sky was black. Aunt Rachel, hat and all, came back from the toilet. "Well, well. You slept like a little rabbit!" she said.

On Wednesdays, Oma would come to our house for lunch. She would stay until dusk and then we would walk her to the trolley stop. When I returned from school I would find her sitting alone at our dining room table with all the silverware spread out before her on a newspaper. Unlike Mother, who seemed to perform all household chores in anger, Oma loved to polish. "It's my solitaire," she said. Mother would be at the grand piano in the living room doing her singing exercises. At other times the two would gossip over a cup of coffee or tea. Sometimes Aunt Mies would appear toward evening to take Oma home.

When the weather was nice I would rush in after school, throw my books on the little entrance-hall table, distribute kisses, and rush out again. But often I would run up the stairs and disappear into my little room next to the attic. Leaving the fun as a prize for good behavior, I would first sit down to do my homework. Was geography more important

in Holland because the tiny country was surrounded by large and powerful nations? The teacher gave us blind maps of Holland and Europe on
which we were to write the names of towns and rivers next to the tiny
dots. Say "Holland" and I still see that pale blue map; but now I couldn't
place more than half a dozen names.

I do remember what the multiplication tables looked like and still
marvel at the patterns of numbers going diagonally across. Compositions
went to the core of things. "An Outing to the Lakes." "Uncle Piet rowed all
the way. We hid in the weeds and saw many ducks. We drank buttermilk.
My uncle and I played with the seesaw." Once I had finished my homework, I would tend to my little zoo—feed the frogs and the sticklers,
change the water in the aquarium, clean the smelly cage while the two
white mice frantically burrowed in the sawdust.

News from the adult world came to me by mysterious means: a
word, a gesture, a wink. A misplaced silence, parallel answers, an inexplicable change of tone. Miraculously, they accumulated in my mind,
forming images of things and events I had never witnessed or experienced. And then, of course, there were the boasting tales of third-year students, full of inflated words and meanings that would not pass through
the sieve of credibility but helped to make suspicions plausible. "Who told
you?" "Nobody. I just happen to know."

The months passed. Through some strange osmosis, early intuitions,
nebulous and hallucinatory as they were, had found their way into the
repertory of my imagination and taken on a certain solidity. Although no
one had ever spoken to me about "the house," I knew enough about it to
consider it taboo. That Uncle Jan had a lady friend there was my most tit-
illating secret. Then one day Mother announced that we would be going to
Oma's house to meet Uncle Jan's fiancée. She had camouflaged herself in
an unnecessary dusting job. I faked my innocence and my surprise. "He's
getting married?" When later that afternoon we walked to the trolley stop
of the Number Two, I mustered my courage. "Do you know her?" "No," said
Mother. I almost said, "I do."

Although we had stopped at the flower shop run by an old high
school acquaintance of Mother's, we were early. Aunt Mies shouted from
her room a girlish "Yoo-hoo! I'm coming!" Oma had just removed her
apron—she had it over her arm as she kissed Mother and me. "Aren't you
nervous?" Mother asked. "Me? Heavens, no. I was nervous when I met
that Jewish husband of yours," and then she added, "Pa was going to be
here on time. He won't be. Sure as hell he'll be soused and won't be here
before dinner." Mother, with one of her better operatic gestures, fell heav-

ily onto the sofa, topcoat and all. Aunt Mies floated in on a cloud of cologne, kissed us, dropped her arms, and lifted her eyes to the sky as if to say, "That's all we need." She gave the room a panoramic look, and in the next few minutes everything mobile, from teacups to chairs, got shoved one fraction of an inch closer to perfection. Nobody uttered a word. Oma was in the kitchen making superfluous noises.

Then the doorbell rang. From below, Uncle Jan, who had a key, shouted, "Hello, everybody!" Mother jumped up from the sofa, removed her coat and hat, and threw them on Opa's chair. Aunt Mies fumbled with her dress and after a second of hesitation went to the landing. I was in a panic. Uncle Jan and that lady had crossed not only the borderline between the areas of sin and respectability but the one between my fantasies and reality. Suddenly the moment of their appearance, expected and precisely imagined, was not more than a floor away. I heard Uncle Jan laugh. "Mia is not a great athlete," he shouted. They were on the first landing. I could hear the woman panting. "Take it easy!" called Aunt Mies as she leaned over the banister. In that very instant, with a sudden spurt of determination, I slipped behind her and ran up the short flight of stairs to the attic, two steps at a time. My heart was pounding. What was I to do? Then I heard someone coming up the attic stairs, and before I knew it Uncle Jan stood before me.

"Don't you want to meet Aunt Mia?" he said. "I came to see the pigeons." "You can do that later," he said in a tone of voice I had never heard from him—a tone of serene authority. Or was it nervousness? "Did your mother tell you that we are getting married?" he asked as we went down the stairs. "Yes." "You'll like Aunt Mia." I had no answer. Just as we passed the kitchen, Oma came out with a tea tray. We almost bumped into her. Then we followed her into the living room. Uncle Jan went to help his fiancée off the sofa. She ran over to embrace me. "So this is our famous Leo! You know, Jan has told me so much about you that I have a feeling I've known you for years." I was embarrassed. I didn't know what to say, what to do. I stood there limp, feeling stupid and sordidly angry.

She was not beautiful, although the word *beautiful* came to mind. She wore a simple maroon silk dress and a big straw hat with a cloud of black feathers down one side. She was even heavier than I had expected, but then I had known her only from a considerable distance. She had a large face. Her complexion, in the shadow of the gleaming feathers, was aggressively fair—its soft, smooth luminosity reminded me of portraits in the museum. Her dark eyes were large, her nose almost too small and pudgy. Her voice was clear and "placed high," as Mother would say.

Her laughter dissolved into a smile, which stayed with her when she returned to the sofa, next to Mother. Luckily, Oma made enough noise with the teapot, dishes, cups, and spoons to cover the heavy silence. Then a hesitant conversation materialized around the plant I had given to Oma on her birthday. Aunt Mia surprised everyone by knowing its name. Uncle Jan looked pleased. Aunt Mies served the tea and slices of Oma's cherry tart.

The secret of Mia's profession was pressing hard against my stomach. I got up from my chair, tiptoed to the bathroom, and just sat there on the wooden throne for a few long minutes. Questions and doubts swirled through my mind in great confusion. One thing was clear: my adventure with the house across the street had come to an unforeseen end, and except for my secret everything was now out in the open. In a way, I felt liberated and much, much older; for I had secretly shared events that I might never have witnessed had fate not assisted me. Of course, I was too young to be able to articulate these feelings, but I seem to remember the swelling sense of well-being that comes when anguish recedes. When I finally returned to the living room, Mother said, "Are you all right? You're pale." Annoyed, I went toward my window, made myself invisible in Opa's armchair, and stared into emptiness.

Mother kept the conversation going by asking personal questions. She was good at that. "Where did you grow up?" "Oh, that is where my husband was stationed. What a coincidence!" "I *love* your southern accent; it's *so* much like high Dutch. Did you go to school in Maastricht?" And on and on. A mean little hook dangled from each innocent question, but Mia didn't bite.

Then the doorbell rang. Expecting Uncle Piet, I rushed to the landing. As I reached the railing, Bobby, Uncle Piet's Doberman, bounced into me, almost knocking me to the floor. Startled, he backed away and then jumped on me lightly with a few happy barks as if to say, "Sorry, I meant it *this* way." Uncle Piet appeared. "Easy, Bobby! Easy!" Suddenly I was back in my own simple universe. I felt the blood return to my face.

When Uncle Piet came into the living room, everyone made a great fuss over him. That was one of his gifts, he was always smack in the middle, radiating vitality and power, and it all seemed effortless and sunny. "First, let me kiss the bride!" "You're a few months early!" said Uncle Jan. "By the way," said Mother, looking at her future sister-in-law, "is there a date?" Mia threw a glance at Uncle Jan and bounced the question to him. He smiled maliciously. "February thirty-first." That was the level of his humor. "Seriously!" Mother insisted. "Shall we tell them?" said Jan, serious this time. He went to his bride-to-be and kissed her. "Mia is pregnant." His voice was a little shaky, his smile triumphant. There was a long silence. Then Uncle Piet suddenly clapped his hands. "Hey! What's the matter with you people? This is a cause for celebration!" He embraced his younger brother, and then Mia. "Ma, get out the glasses and the gin! Unless there's champagne!" Everyone laughed. "I'll get it," said Aunt Mies, happy to have an excuse for not having anything clever to say. As she placed a tray with glasses and the bottle of Jenever on the dining table we all got up from our chairs. Uncle Piet handed me a glass. "Don't you dare!" said Mother jokingly. "He's a big boy now!" said Uncle Piet, while he carefully poured two drops into my glass. Then he handed Aunt Mia a glass. "Thank you. Not for me," she said, with the rhetorical grace of expected motherhood.

To everybody's relief, the future, luminous and clear, had erased the embarrassing past, and although new, painful questions loomed on the horizon, Mia had been promoted to the rank of human being.

A few weeks before the wedding, Uncle Jan asked his parents if they would come to Maastricht for the occasion. Oma had refused at first, but there hadn't been much of a battle. Often, despite her earthy simplicity, she surprised her children with sudden outbursts of originality and sophisticated courage. "Yes, I would love to go. But Opa?" That was a problem. Clearly he would put the whole family to shame. As expected, he had fought Jan's intentions with a rich repertory of curses and many glasses of Jenever before grudgingly accepting the inevitable. But as far as Maastricht was concerned? "Go to Maastricht? I wouldn't dream of it. Tell them I'm sick." That took care of that.

What had been vaguely envisaged as some indeterminate future had suddenly become a matter of great urgency. As the weeks went by, Mia was becoming more voluminous. Once she had taken my hand and placed it delicately on her belly. "Do you feel it move?" she whispered as if she were afraid to break the enchantment. "I think so," I whispered back, hardly audible, desperately embarrassed. Luckily the baby didn't move. Had it done so I would have died.

The preparations for the great Event grew increasingly frenzied. There were lively family deliberations about who would provide what. Mother, being the only one who could boast experience, emphatically took the lead in deciding what a modern baby required. Uncle Piet, who had been retained as architect for a leading pharmaceutical concern and was feeling flush, volunteered to buy a baby carriage like the one in the pages of the latest issue of *Foto Week*. There was a full-page photograph of the queen of England gracefully smiling at the camera while lifting the one-year-old crown prince out of his carriage. The headline read, "Royal Baby's Rolls-Royce." Opa, in a sober moment, volunteered to build a crib—in the club he had the tools to do it. Oma had already started knitting during her rare scraps of leisure. Herman took the easy way out—he would give the neo-parents money. Mother was going to provide a scale, a bassinet, and the implements for feeding she had seen in the window of the elegant Babyshop in the Kalverstraat.

In the meantime, Jan and Mia had moved into their apartment on Schubert Square. The curtains were still missing, but the essential furniture was in place. The fancy baby carriage had been delivered, and the little room was ready for the expected tenant.

With only a few weeks to go, the level of family excitement rose to peaks of happy anticipation rarely experienced before. The Grossouw children had never been close; only the two oldest, Mother and Uncle Piet, notwithstanding their frequent quarrels, seemed to feel comfortable in each other's company. Having experienced the call of passion at an early age, they knew, shared, and respected the feeling of diversity, egocentricity, and aloneness that characterizes those who are endowed with a strong creative urge. They considered themselves the only adults in the family, and they treated the others, including their parents, like a group of innocent and somewhat unruly children. The younger brothers and Mies went very much their own way. They didn't see one another for months at a time, and when they did meet their conversations had a hard, perfunctory tone.

June was already one week old when Mia was to join Mother and Oma for the weekly lunch at our house. I did not relish the prospect of that event; I was sure that pregnancy, birth, and baby care were going to be the central topics of conversation, and I knew that Mother would begin sentences with "When I was pregnant . . ." I felt humiliated at the thought that I, like all the others, had lived nine months in the dark, slimy interior of an extraneous body. No matter how poetic Mother made it sound when she explained it, the idea filled me with disgust and anxiety.

Coming up the stairs, Mia had to stop three times. "I have to climb for the two of us, you know," she said with a forced smile. When Mother saw her she noticed that Mia's beautiful complexion had lost much of its radiance. During lunch, Mia, prodded by her mother-in-law, confessed that she was worried. She complained of nausea, dizziness, weakness, and palpitations. And then, after a long, deep sigh, she announced that according to her calculations the baby was already a week late. Mother gasped. It suddenly occurred to her that Mia had never mentioned a doctor. "When did you last see a doctor?" she asked anxiously. "A doctor? Why should I see a doctor? Until now I was feeling fine. A few weeks ago I talked with a midwife who was recommended by the Schubert Square pharmacy. She's supposed to be excellent." Mother was outraged. "I am going to call Dr. Pimentel," she said as she jumped up from her chair and ran to Father's study. After a few minutes she was back. "He can see you right away. Come on! Let's go!"

From the living room window I watched my mother and Mia disappear around the corner of Van Luiken Straat. Could this have been the precise moment when I recognized the pain of others? Was it like some of the other steps on my way to adulthood, recognition, possession, the naming of things, and the making of images? Or was I simply feeling the anguish of being left alone, the difficulty of seeing my aunt and my mother disappear?

Mia was rushed to a hospital—she wasn't pregnant after all; she had a tumor. A few weeks later, when the baby's toys were carefully packed away and hidden in Oma's attic, I felt something akin to pity—and loss, for fate had robbed me of my only cousin.

After a drawn-out convalescence, Jan and Mia lived a quiet life of easy pleasure, tending their little garden where the pretty plastic flowers could live forever.

Brussels

It took Father seven years after we moved to Amsterdam to finally realize that his illusions about a lucrative career as an accountant had shipwrecked in a sea of mishaps. It was then that his idea of going to America and leaving me (I was twelve then) with my grandparents Beffie began to take shape.

Mother, who had created for herself a presence in Amsterdam's musical world as a concert singer (she had sung the soprano solo in the *Kindertotenlieder* at the first great Mahler festival), did not cherish her husband's plans. When she mentioned her predicament to her mentor, Willem Mengelberg, he told her that he had been planning a series of concerts in America in the fall and intimated that if she and Father decided to go at that time, he would do whatever he could to help her launch an American career. If there were any doubts in my parents' minds, Mengelberg's promise, vague as it was, must have prompted their final decision to undertake the great American adventure. They sold everything they owned and, with the addition of the usual loan from Oom Elie, they sailed for New York in the fall of 1922, leaving me in the custody of my grandparents in Brussels.

I am always amazed to discover new evidence of how deeply the great revolutionary ideologies of our century—psychoanalysis, Marxism, the "modern movement," and feminism—have penetrated popular culture and modified our consciences, our psyches, our taste, our minds. Had I lived only fifty years earlier, before Freud, would I have summoned the courage to question my memory and ask the questions I ask today? Not to speak of suggesting the answers I am willing to risk? Only very recently have I dared entertain the possibility that my parents' decision to *leave me with my grandparents* could be translated, in more dramatic terms, as *abandoning their only child,* a trauma violent enough to leave permanent scars.

I had always thought that mine had been the happiest of childhoods because all my recollections of the early years in Amsterdam are of joyful events bathed in the golden afternoon light of a warm sunny day. Although I am well aware that in Amsterdam such days are almost as rare as snowstorms in the Sahara, I never dared to doubt my memory. I was eager and proud to find the roots of all happiness in the sunny garden of my childhood. Now I suspect that my memory, in one of her gentler moments, systematically refused to accept for storage any adverse weather conditions, thereby giving me the illusion of being immune to the uncertainties of fate and circumstances that rule all our lives.

No matter how meticulously I search among the confused images of my childhood, I do not find a single scene of my departure from Amsterdam, of the trip, or of my arrival in Brussels. They have vanished in the fog of oblivion. But it must have been a foggy, rainy day when my parents told me of their planned departure. I am sure that it rained when someone accompanied me to Brussels, where I was going to stay for an indefinite period. And it must have rained on my arrival. In those wet, nasty days not a kiss, not a last embrace, a waving hand, a tear. Had my childhood come to an end?

My step-grandfather and grandmother,
Elie and Rose Beffie

• • •

Oom Elie and Oma Rose lived in a luxurious town house in one of the most elegant quarters of the Belgian capital, the Square Marie Louise. The square, in reality, wasn't a square at all, but an oval pond almost large enough to be called a small lake. At the center, on an artificial island with a miniature mountain of poured cement rocks, a dozen or so white ducks had their nesting places.

The pond was my personal playground. Hardly a day went by without some sign of the magic of nature. A shoal of tiny stickleback swimming in the perfectly shaped formation of an old carp; little seed propellers shot from the branches of a linden tree; and magic of magic, ten lively miniature ducklings, where only yesterday the nest contained nothing but the static geometry of eggs.

Surrounding the pond was a lawn always neatly mowed, gently sloping toward the water's edge, and spotted here and there by a lilac bush, a Japanese magnolia, a weeping willow, each personally remembered. A walking path with bright green benches facing the pond swerved through the square, sometimes close to the water, sometimes closer to the row of dense trees that hid this little paradise from the hubbub of city life for the benefit of its only inhabitant, young Robinson Crusoe, me.

The Beffie house was situated toward the middle of the long side of the pond, opposite the only spot where there were no large trees to impede the view. It was an elegant three-story town house, which distinguished itself from its neighbors by being almost white, an unusual combination of Carrara marble and sandstone. The style was typical Art Nouveau in the design of the door, a cast-iron composition of intertwining ivy branches, and the iron railing of the small first-floor balcony, and in the sandstone friezes that framed the large vertical windows. The pavement of the first-floor entrance hall and corridor was of white marble and so were the stairs that led to the landing of the mezzanine, my own private little floor where my room and bathroom were. There the stairs made a U-turn and continued in a wooden version to the second floor, where Oma and Oom Elie had their sleeping quarters, in Hollywood proportions and sensually furnished. Apricot, in all its possible hues and textures, was the dominant color.

In memory, my room looks formal, terribly orderly, impersonal, and empty—like a hotel room before the luggage has been brought up. A small desk for writing, two chairs, a closet, and my bed. An interior decorator's sketch. A stage at noon.

I went to a public school only a few blocks from the square. Two years! And yet I cannot muster the face of a single teacher, a single com-

*My parents and I in
Garmisch, 1922*

panion, a single meaningful event. I do remember, however, that I collected postcards of the Louvre masterpieces printed in light blue and sepia, and managed to assemble, from a kit, my first radio—a crystal set that was not much more than a thin wire wound around a cardboard tube and an earpiece, in which I could capture, continents away, all the symphonies of Mozart and Beethoven floating in haunting clarity.

In these two years I not only acquired a fluent use of French but learned enough English to make my later shift to an American school painless. French was my third language, since besides Dutch I also knew some German—though I have no idea when, where, or why I had studied German before the age of twelve. During those years, Mother had gone several times to Germany for singing lessons with a famous Russian teacher and had taken me along. But no recollections have come to my mind except, a few days ago, the name Baden-Baden, a health resort in the Rhineland. No more. A third erasure. Who knows how many moments of panic, despair, anger, fear, jealousy, guilt lie buried deep within my subconscious, never to be exhumed?

My relationship with my grandparents was one of detached affection. The two years I lived with them were like a pleasant family visit that never ended, but in the few images that come to my mind I am, rather than a protagonist, a polite observer, an actor in a Russian play in which from time to time I appear on the veranda, shaking the snow from my shoulders, to remind the audience that the real world still exists.

In my real Brussels world, there were three events that stand out in my memory: the occasional visits of Oom Elie's youngest brother, Willem; my Wednesday afternoons with Mies; and Lilly, my first love.

Lilly

A few years before my intrusion into their lives, my grandparents had discovered the pleasures and benefits of summer vacations in the then fashionable Czech health resort Marienbad. And soon after my arrival in Brussels, it was made clear to me that they had no intention of altering their vacation plans. Besides, they were convinced that I was going to have a great time; there were plenty of nice boys and girls my age at the Heidenhof, and even I would profit from the magical powers of the water.

My feeble attempt to suggest the practical advantages of the nearby beaches, Ostende and Knokke, didn't make a dent in their determination. The seashore was not for them. "Why fight a losing battle against sand, wind, and water," joked Oom Elie, enjoying his own brand of Jewish sarcasm, "when you can enjoy nature in a princely three-star ghetto like the Heidenhof, renowned for its strategically located toilet facilities and scientifically planned walks through the woods?"

Me, Lilly, Oma Rose, and Oom Elie, Marienbad, 1923

He was right; for it was on one of those strolls that I met Lilly. I don't remember how it happened or how my grandparents knew the Loewys. My memory always seems to walk in when the show has already started. I vaguely see Oom Elie lift his hat as we near a middle-aged couple with a girl my age, freckle faced, long red hair, visibly embarrassed, taking a sip from her glass of water. "And this is Lilly," her mother says.

In Amsterdam there had been Tiene, our neighbors' little daughter. She had been my steady playmate there, and yes, she was my girlfriend and we played doctor and patient. And once I wrote her a little letter addressed to "Tiene Lionni." It wasn't the first time I was to equate love with marriage. Nor the last. But my first real love was Lilly. I adored her funny smile, the tiny red freckles, the light blue irises of her eyes, her fragile body, the unruly waves of her long red hair. I loved the way she was always out of breath when we met and mysteriously silent when it was time to go. And I loved her long, weightless kisses.

Too young for the torments of passion, we had an easy, gay time. We were living a bizarre situation, between childhood and maturity. Almost every day she and I would walk to a café in the woods for afternoon tea, be ushered to a table, order tea or fruit juice, dance, go through all the proper rites of paying the check and handing the waiter a tip, and disappear into the woods, all without the slightest embarrassment on our part, or signs of astonishment on the part of adults. That is the way it was. When the vacation came to an end, we swore each other fidelity and embraced with the tacit satisfaction of Lilly's parents and my grandparents.

Back in Brussels, the writing routine began. I wrote one rhetorical love letter a week, and so far as I can remember the answer I received was always disappointing. I expected dramatic, passionate outpourings, but Lilly's letters were simply those of a twelve-year-old schoolgirl, afraid to reveal herself. Little by little the grip of daily events grew tighter; the letters became rare, and finally, after four or five months, our correspondence stopped altogether. The only evidence of our romance was a photograph of us, walking side by side bravely sipping our water, and Lilly's address: Lilly Loewy, Jirassek Platz 1, Moravská Ostrava, which

Me (downstage center) in Marienbad, 1923

remained engraved in my memory. But gradually her image faded from my mind.

Years went by. I came to America, went to live in Italy, studied in Switzerland, got married. We had two children. More years. I was a designer in Milan. Hitler took the Sudetenland. The first stories of deportation and torture began to fill our minds, and somehow the image of the little freckled Jewish girl from Moravia returned vividly in my memory.

With the slow swelling of the news she became an obsession. The victims of the Holocaust were invisible—unimaginable thousands, millions. But she was Lilly. It was Lilly who was pushed into a freight car, stripped of her clothes, dragged to the gas chamber. It was Lilly whose red hair was brutally cut. Who was shot dead on the bank of the Danube. Or near the Dutch border. It was Lilly who managed to escape to Austria, only to fall into the claws of the Viennese Gestapo. And that fragile skeleton I recognized in a communal grave was Lilly. It was always she.

The war ended. Lilly's picture appeared nowhere, nor did her name. I did not recognize her in the gruesome documentaries on the survivors of the death camps. And her little freckle face got lost in the wild stream of events that followed the war.

I had spent the war years with my wife and children in Philadelphia. From there we moved to Connecticut, and ten years later we went back to Europe. For a while we had a farm near Genoa, and in 1971 we moved to Tuscany. One day some years later, I received a telegram from Bratislava, telling me that I had been awarded the Golden Apple prize for one of my fables. The money had been deposited in my name in the State Bank in Prague. I didn't particularly want to go to a Czechoslovakia that was already gripped by the failure of Communism. My wife, Nora, wanted to go even less, but the idea that I had a bank account in Prague kept gnawing at my mind. From time to time I would try to find out how much the sum I had received was worth. The answers varied from $50 to $5,000. Since the crown wasn't quoted on the stock market and crowns were not available at banks outside of Czechoslovakia, no one seemed to know.

Finally I met a friend who had just returned from Prague. He told me that we could easily and comfortably make a two-week trip through Czechoslovakia, stay in good hotels, eat well, see wonderful architecture and museums, and return with nice souvenirs for relatives and friends, all without spending a dollar more than what I had in my account at the State Bank in Prague. We decided to go the following summer.

We did it all. We saw the splendid city of Prague, without any doubt one of the most beautiful of Europe, and unlike other large European cities, not yet touched by Gucci/McDonald's glamorization. We saw the Black Theatre and had supper with a group of actors in the Rathalle. We traveled to the Tatra Mountains close to the Polish border, and in a bungalow restaurant hidden in a dense forest of evergreens, ate roast chicken to the sound of Gypsy violins moving imperceptibly from slow, whining laments to a mad frenzy. Near Bratislava, on a barge in the not so blue Danube, we had an elegant dinner with the director of the Bratislava Museum of Fine Arts. We got lost on our way to Moravia but had lunch at a town that is nameless in my memory but might have been Ostrava. We returned home to Porcignano, triumphant and happy with our trip. Surprisingly, I hadn't spent a single thought on Lilly.

Then one night, in 1990, it happened.

Our friends Natasha and Hansa Fisher were at a small and lively dinner party at our house. After Nora's celebrated dessert of dried fruit with a curry cream, we got up from the table and moved to the living room. I sat down on the sofa next to Hansa with a glass of grappa. "Oh, Hansa," I said, "did I ever tell you about my first love? She was Czech, all of twelve and I was thirteen . . ." And I told the story. Hansa was moved.

"Where was she from?" he asked. "What city?" "Moravská Ostrava," I said, showing off my Czech accent. "No! That is my town!" shouted Hansa. "My whole family is from Ostrava!" "Then I'll tell you more," I said, as shivers crawled up my neck. "I have never forgotten her address. To this day I remember it: Jirassek Platz One." Hansa leaped to his feet. "Jirassek Platz One? I know that house! It's on the corner of the Klassek Strasse. What was the girl's name?"

"Lilly Loewy." "Lilly Loewy? So far as I know, she is in London!" I also sprang to my feet. How many beats did my heart miss? "I don't know her well," Hansa went on, "but a good friend does. I'll call him tomorrow and see what he can tell me."

Two very long days later, Hansa called. "Are you seated?" he asked, and continued in a voice that promised news. "Lilly Loewy is no longer in London. Two years ago she and her husband moved to New York. His name is *Leo*—Leo Kronenstein. They live on West Ninetieth Street and run a picture-frame business. Lilly is in fine shape, but her husband has a rather serious heart condition."

Two weeks later we made our annual return to New York, and then the phrase "I think I'll call Lilly" formed in my mind. I found the number. I dialed. Two rings. A woman's voice answered. "Hello!" "Hello. May I talk with Mrs. Kronenstein?" "This is she. Who is speaking?" "Lilly, this is probably the oldest friend you have. Guess." How I hated the stupid, rehearsed words. "I have no idea." "Think back . . . 1923, Marienbad." "Who are you?" I had to end this ridiculous game; I regained my normal voice. "I am Leo. Leo Lionni." "I don't remember." "Let me try to remind you."

I told her. Slowly and only the essentials. She must have noticed that I had some difficulties toward the conclusion. Conclusion? My heart was bare. She had filled my brief hesitations with a painfully whispered, "I don't remember." The conversation ended with a gentle but perfunctory exchange of addresses and telephone numbers, regrets on both sides, and a vague promise of lunch in the ambiguous future. I dropped my head onto my crossed arms and cried, deeply disappointed. It was as if the ground of history had collapsed under my feet. Abandoned by my memory, or Lilly's, I was on a foreign island, alone.

The next few days were so densely packed with making calls, rearranging furniture, paying bills, filling the refrigerator, hanging or placing the art loot brought from Europe, and recovering from jet lag, that the conversation with Lilly lost much of its drama. And when it reentered my mind, I found excuses for Lilly's lack of memory. Would *I* have remembered *her* had it not been for that photograph of us that every few years floated to the top of a drawerful of old documents and letters? Was it surprising that the memories of a child's vacation adventure were wiped out by the anguish of a young Jewish woman during the Nazi years in Czechoslovakia?

Four days later the telephone rang. "Hello, Leo." I immediately recognized Lilly's accent, but her voice had a different tone to it. It was clear, happy, and astonishingly young. "Yesterday something strange happened. I talked to my sister in California. I told her about your call and, you know, she remembered everything about that vacation in Marienbad and you. She said that she was very jealous because you always danced with me and never once with her!" "When can you have lunch with me?" I asked, elated. I had found Lilly.

On Seventy-first Street between Fifth and Madison was the Pleiades, a French restaurant where I liked to take guests for special occasions when conversation and privacy were important. I had reserved for half past twelve, and to be certain to be there when Lilly arrived I got there about five minutes early. In the empty dining room, two waiters were going through the motions of moving a napkin or a glass as they slowly went from table to table, checking details. Another one stood leaning against the wall in the rear corner, napkin draped over his arm, his mind in God knows what Paris bistro. Another step and then, in a corner that had been hidden from my view, at a table for two, squarely facing me, was Lilly. It was unmistakably she, the thin-boned, fragile, red-haired, freckle-faced she. We exchanged embarrassed smiles. She got up from the bench on which she was sitting, and as I came closer I realized that she was the same Lilly, virtually unchanged except for the tiny wrinkles that covered her smiling face, and the hair dyed dark red. We embraced and sat down in silence, searching each other's eyes for fragments of the distant past.

And before we knew it we were feverishly talking. Lilly told her life and I told mine. We cried and we held hands, as almost seventy years of joys and horrors rolled by, crucial years in which fate had dragged us along in the wild swirls of a stream of events that had no precedents in the history of our civilization. I experienced an overflow of emotions I could hardly contain, a density of awareness I could no longer bear. It was very much like being desperately in love. And yet I realized that the woman who was sitting across the table, bent toward me in order not to miss a single word, was a total stranger.

It was almost three when I hailed a cab for Lilly, and we held each other in a long, silent embrace. I walked home in a daze, knowing that I would never see Lilly again.

Mies

On a misty November day in 1991, five months before what would have been her one hundredth birthday, my aunt Mies was buried in the small cemetery near the Coltibuono Abbey, a five-minute drive from our house at Porcignano. The Giorgi brothers, two young undertakers from Siena who, in their black suits, looked like actors in a Strindberg play, were now on their way back to their headquarters with the empty hearse; our caretaker, Marcello Vanni, who had dug the hole, was quietly moving from grave to grave reading the names and dates on the tombstones, some almost illegible, others shockingly new with passport-size plasticized portraits in color. In the west corner, next to our son Paolo's grave, was our plot, the last unkempt patch of earth, stones, and weeds. It was large, like a king-size bed—extravagant, I thought, for the two small jars that would hold our ashes. But then we had always lived big.

My mind wandered off to other cemeteries we had visited around the globe, the time capsules that hold the bones and the belongings of the human presence on earth. I thought once more of the Egyptian desert and the small encaustic portraits that were hidden for more than two millennia, and discovered less than a century ago in the cemetery dumps of Fayum and Hawara. I felt a pang of nostalgia for my white Greenwich studio, where those small marvels triggered my seven-year-long series of imaginary portraits. I gave one more look at the long heap of black, freshly raked earth that covered Mies's wrinkled body and in vain searched my soul for a touch of pain or tenderness. Or love. But to no avail. "Let's go," I said. And suddenly, at the hard sound of my voice, I burst out in an uncontrollable spell of crying.

Ever since she had suffered a displaced hip at the age of ninety-three, Mies had been living at the Ricovero della Misericordia, a modest home for the aged in the Gaiole valley with an ample view of the Chianti hills. Since it was only a twenty-minute drive from Porcignano, we went

Aunt Mies, my father, me, René Gaffé, my mother

to see her at least once a week, but I always returned home disappointed. My efforts to extract from her confused mind fragments of her life with René Gaffé and the stories of their love and divorce never produced more than the tales we had heard over and over again, ever since René suddenly walked out, leaving her. But from that day on, her memory, which even in her youth had been poor and strictly limited to gossip about the world of fashion, film stars, and royalty, slowly began to fade. And of late, even when a name like Cardin or Delphine or Prince Charles reached her consciousness, it was acknowledged with little more than a grunt and a feeble smile. Her hearing, too, had deteriorated to a point where every single word had to be accompanied with gestures and repeated five or six times.

A few months before she died, I tried to tell her that Pippo's son Luca, our great-grandson, age four, was an exceptionally beautiful child. I was speaking Dutch, but no matter how I shaped my lips or how hard I yelled in her ear, I could not get her to understand the key word *mooi* (beautiful), to the delight of the feebleminded inmates who sat along the facing wall and followed my struggle with intense interest, mimicking my unsuccessful grimaces. I had repeated the word four or five times when little by little they joined in, first in a self-conscious whisper and then louder and louder until finally the word echoed through the building like the howl of a cosmic cow. *Mooi! Mooi! Mooi!*

Madame Lecour, Mies's only friend from her Brussels years, told us once that Mies began complaining about deafness soon after she had moved from the luxurious building where for more than ten years she had played the role of glamorous wife to one of the most sophisticated intellectuals in Belgium to the modest one-room apartment a few blocks away. She also told us that no one really understood Mies's relationship with her husband. Since it seemed highly improbable that a man as sharp and witty as René would have knowingly chosen for his life's companion a woman as uneducated and naive as Mies, the legend spread that her ignorance and superficiality were a clever act, that in reality she was a superb actress, an enchantress who knew how to play the secret chords that excited the Professor Higgins side of her sophisticated husband. It is true, she added, that Mies blamed her lack of understanding on her deafness and her lack of art appreciation on her eyesight, but she never explained why she could not pass a mirror without throwing a quick glance its way.

During her last years at the Ricovero, one would usually find Mies bundled up in a collection of old scarves, sound asleep in an armchair in the corridor that led to the Ricovero's squalid backyard. She shared this improvised hiding place with three or four inmates who, like her, preferred solitary boredom to the rowdy communal life in the large living room where, like an evil spirit, the ever-blasting television would set off endless discussions on subjects that no one knew anything about. Italians are good at that sort of interaction.

Not that the corridor was a haven of bliss. While throughout most of her life Mies had remained the innocent and good-natured woman I remembered from my childhood days, during her later years she could unexpectedly and without the slightest provocation explode in anger, insult the nuns and the nurses, threaten her corridor companions with her cane, and generally carry on like a stubborn child until the Mother Superior would take her to her room. Sometimes when she woke up and saw us standing before her, she would stare at us as if we were a sizable part of her own anatomy that she had never noticed before. But then the following week she would welcome us with all the mannerisms of the enigmatic, beautiful, and elegant Madame Gaffé. And then again on the next visit it could happen that she would burst into tears when she saw me, grab my hands, bring them to her lips, and in that easy, slightly vulgar Amsterdam Dutch of hers mumble with the voice of a teenager in love, "Oh, Leo, I am so unhappy."

Although I had known each of these impersonations, and had witnessed her gradual decay, I always marveled at the way she stumbled from one role into the other. Mies was the unfinished sketch of a woman, never quite ready, but if you squinted your eyes, the overall effect was that of a woman of rare elegance. She was able to keep her few dresses and her coat up to date with a few stitches and some pins, and judging by the way she checked them in the mirror you knew that she had been a pro. All the other things in life—people, love, money, work, art, politics—confused and bored her.

I wish I could erase from my memory the Mies I saw a few weeks before she died, when for no reason at all she suddenly rose from her chair shouting Dutch vulgarities and waving her cane under the noses of her frightened companions. I could not believe that this person was the meek, submissive ninety-nine-year-old lady I had seen only a week before, still miraculously blessed with occasional flashes of beauty, and now suddenly transformed into an angry hag, her few remaining white locks, inexorably tamed by almost a century of obsessive brushing, in wild disarray; her face, disciplined to perfection by a thousand mirrors, in a grimace of wild anger.

In my memory people don't age, they live like mummies suspended in time. Close friends and relatives may have two or three ages or even more, depending on how old they were at each last meeting. I would like to remember Mies as the splendid young woman she was—free, still untouched by the distortions of time and circumstances, an angel in a night blue, sequin-studded sky.

Although I was an only child, I had a multitude of aunts—young and old, Jewish and Christian, Dutch and foreign, nice and horrible. Aunt Fre, Aunt Flossie, Aunt Rachel, Aunt Cato are but a few remembered. None of these aunts was a relative—their aunt status derived mainly from embarrassment. How else should little boys and girls address their parents' friends? Mies was the only exception. Not only because she was the youngest of my mother's siblings but because it took her longer than her brothers and sister to become an adult. And besides, she was the only real aunt I ever had, and my favorite playmate. And she was beautiful. For all these reasons, I called her Mies. She was taller than Mother, and slender, with the fashionable figure of the times. With blond curly hair, light steel blue eyes, and a fair complexion, she was a prototype of Nordic beauty. At eighteen, she began working as a freelance fashion model, and five years later she was hired by Maison Hirsch, the most elegant store in Amsterdam, as their number-one model. But a more important career was lying in wait.

One late afternoon in 1916, a Belgian officer walked into the shop with a lively young woman happily clinging to his side. He asked to see the dark blue evening gown shimmering with sequins that was displayed in the window facing the City Theatre. Mies, at her coquettish best, modeled the dress, and to everyone's delight the sale was made, the gown fitted, and the officer promised to pick it up the following day. When the couple had left, Mrs. Hirsch asked Mies, "Do you know who that woman was?" "No," said Mies. "That was Mata Hari!" The next day shortly before noon the Belgian officer picked up the gown and took Mies to lunch at Trianon, and three months later the two were married.

Once Mies told me that she was not really in love with René. She was flattered and impressed by his attentions, but she said, "He was too much for me." René Gaffé was ten years older than Mies, twice divorced, and ran a successful perfume business. He was a brilliant conversationalist, a witty journalist, and as an art critic he was well known for his fiery advocacy of modern art.

Since René had no relatives except an old aunt, the wedding was celebrated in Amsterdam at the Café Schiller on the Rembrandt Plein, where Piet was a celebrity. For their honeymoon, the newlyweds were the guests of the sultan of Morocco, and when they returned to Brussels, where René had his elegant apartment near the Palais de Justice, Mies discovered that her eclectic spouse had assembled one of the largest,

Mies

liveliest, most outrageously modern art collections in the world. Ignorant and naive as she was, she was bright enough to ask no questions and make no comments about the strange, ugly paintings that covered every square centimeter of wall space. By now she knew that the world was full of mysteries beyond her comprehension. Art was one, René had explained to her, adding that she herself was an unexplored universe and that this was the quality that had so attracted him to her.

During the two years I was in Brussels, I spent every Wednesday afternoon with Mies, and Oom René would often join us for lunch. While my familiarity with modern art had its roots in Amsterdam, my conversations with Uncle René, and above all my many hours alone with his masterpieces, gave me the unique opportunity to get acquainted intimately and directly with that mysterious world, bypassing the lectures, the books, and the criticism that never once point out that the only possible explanation for so many things is their simply being there. I am convinced that René's shifty but sharp dialectics, his very French love of the absurd, and his clever games with the imaginary, as if it were all made of tangible stuff, must have been an important factor in my later development as an artist. Although at the time I was too young and ignorant to judge the quality of paintings, the fact that I remember with mind-boggling precision the details of almost every painting that hung on Uncle René's walls means that I examined them passionately. I knew that the collection was praised, as was Uncle Willem's, for its coherence, which in those early years of rebellion and experimentation meant that it was "modern" throughout.

Six Picasso cubist portraits hung on one wall of the living room, opposite one of the most beautiful of De Chirico's *Piazze d'Italia.* Next to it, from the floor to the ceiling, hung Miró's *Chien qui abboit a la lune.* There was Miró's earlier series of small farm landscapes, *La Terre labourée,* which is now at the MoMA. A large, mysterious Delvaux, a gray nightmare of an abandoned station with middle-aged nudes, ancient locomotives, and a clock. Paintings ran along the walls of the corridors and of the other rooms. Out of all those paintings there were two that I loved in a very special way. One was Modigliani's *Petite Laitière,* a subtly romantic, delicately painted canvas of an adolescent with her chemisette open over one breast, and the other was a Max Ernst landscape of red cliffs under an oversized full moon in a dark blue sky, flat like the running of time.

Uncle Willem

What was extraordinary about the six Beffie brothers was how much they had in common: the love of language, the speech mannerisms, the frothy sense of humor, the taste for intellectual small talk. Their curiosity was all embracing. While only two had graduated from college and the other four had been in the diamond business in one capacity or another, they all shared in equal measure an encyclopedic knowledge of the world, which voracious reading and endless discussions had kept conscientiously updated and alive. Aware of the risks of dogma and belief, the brothers had the wisdom and self-irony of those who reach maturity with more doubts than certainties, more questions than answers. Early in life they had rejected the Jewish religion, but while they were outspoken agnostics, they recognized in their Jewishness a prodigal source of wisdom and humor.

Except for Philip, who had married a few years after graduating from medical school, and Oom Elie, who married my grandmother eight years after her husband's death, the Beffie brothers had lived most of their lives all together in the spacious, comfortable family house on the Gruenburgwal, one of the opulent canals in the historic center of Amsterdam, not far from the house where Rembrandt had lived.

It was a simple, no-nonsense brick building, quite elegant in its rigorous symmetry and proportions. The facade, with its large, white-framed windows and green front door with gleaming brass trimmings, was typical of the eighteenth-century patrician houses of Amsterdam. Flanked by two smaller buildings of earlier vintage, the Beffie house gave the impression of standing defiantly alone on the tree-lined quay. In fact, the brothers referred to it simply as "the Burgwal."

From time to time, Father or Oom Elie would take me along on one of their pilgrimages to the Burgwal. Never once did I go there with Mother or Oma. It was strictly a man's world, warmly alive with a permanent disorder of deep leather armchairs, books, ashtrays, newspapers, green-shaded reading lamps, and Persian rugs. And on the walls, paintings of all sizes, with or without frames, with or without recognizable subject matter, but all sharing an indefinable aura of importance.

Even when I was still a small boy I was fully aware of the privilege of being a junior member of that exclusive club, of having been considered and accepted not only as a man of sorts but as some kind of Beffie. While Father or Oom Elie took part in the discussions, I would proudly sit in a dark corner of the living room, sometimes for a whole afternoon, mesmerized by the endless manipulation of ideas, puns, stories, metaphors, quotations, hypotheses that flew through the air with the speed, elegance, and lightness of Ping-Pong balls.

The discovery of this exotic arena, where intellectual confrontations were every bit as spectacular as the rowing races on the Amstel River, must have been a dramatic experience for a sensitive ten-year-old at the shaky threshold of self-awareness. Not to speak of the discovery of thought as an instrument of pleasure.

When I try to remember the six Beffie brothers, they usually appear on the stage of my memory merged into one vaguely shaped personage trailing a heavy scent of newsprint and tobacco, and behind him I see a large, dimly lit room filled with brown leather armchairs each facing a different direction. Perhaps it is a scene from a childhood dream, perhaps an unconscious metaphor for six brothers, so remarkably close together and yet so strongly marked by their personal uniqueness.

Salomon was a big, bulky man who was always busy organizing his brothers for trips, games, dinners, and special events at one of the small avant-garde theaters or cabarets nearby.

Jakob, a secretive loner among his gregarious brothers, seemed to be dedicated to the art of discerning the essential. A shrewd diamond merchant, he knew the importance of "holding back," and regardless of the temperature of the debate he was able to withhold his remarks until the most propitious moment. His ironic comments with their perverse choice of words and gestures never failed to provoke irrepressible outbursts of laughter.

I don't remember Bernard, because when he deserted the Burgwal to settle with his wife in a perfectly normal small villa not far from the Ryksmuseum, I was not yet born. Perhaps I never met him, but I do remember that more than once, when we passed his house on a walk to the museum with Mother or Father, I questioned them about the sign on his front lawn that said: "Dr. Bernard Wolff Beffie—Urologist—Venereal Diseases."

And then there were Uncle Willem and Oom Elie, who at the Burgwal went under the joint name the *kleintjes,* the "small ones." The term, however, did not reflect their age, as would be customary in Holland, since Oom Elie was the oldest and Uncle Willem the youngest of the brothers. It was clearly meant in the physical sense of the word, for while the others were all of a certain bulk, Willem and Elie were small and thin-boned.

Often the *kleintjes* were targets for their brothers' sarcastic comments on their tax-free status, their travels, and their dandyism. But it was all in good humor, part of the verbal horseplay, the innocent rhetoric that characterized their repartee. Brought up with the warning that emotions should be felt but not shown, the brothers found sarcasm and irony easy and painless ways to express the inexpressible: their profound affection for Uncle Willem and Oom Elie, and their secret envy of the one quality they lacked, "style." There was a certain heaviness about them, a provincial clumsiness that was accentuated by the suits they wore, a bit too large or too small, often in need of some major alteration, always of a good pressing. They probably knew better, but just didn't care.

The *kleintjes* had style. Their gestures and stance, their ways of speaking, their attire, even their manners and mannerisms were blessed with a light, natural grace, a quiet sobriety free from superfluous ornamentation.

Like his elder brother Elie, Uncle Willem managed to avoid the greedy reach of the Dutch fiscal authorities by spending not a day more than six months of each calendar year in Holland; during the remaining months, he played possum beyond the Dutch border. But rather than follow his brother's example and leave Holland for good, he chose to travel six months around the world, taking temporary residence here and there. Occasionally he would visit friends or family in Antwerp or Brussels; that was as close to home as he would come during his months of hiding, and that was where, during my two years at the Square Marie Louise, I would see him. The moment the six months of voluntary exile came to an end, he would take the first available train to Amsterdam, where he would immediately join his Burgwal brothers for a round of bridge. Only at the conclusion of the game would the clan move noisily to the library to celebrate Willem's return, and often it was deep into the night before he would retake possession of his room.

Besides his full share of Beffie idiosyncrasies, Uncle Willem held some remarkable peculiarities of his own. During his long, lonely travels he had developed three serious hobbies that took up much of his energy and money: fencing, dancing, and, more passion than hobby, collecting modern art. In the fencing societies, ballrooms, and art galleries of the major European cities, he was known as a gentle, generous eccentric. When he arrived at a hotel, his first visit was invariably to the telephone operator. Not until he had made his appointments in the three areas of his interest would he talk with the receptionist and register.

I liked Uncle Willem. He was one of the very few people who talked to me as if I were a normal human being. The fact that I was only thirteen did not make him change his tone of voice, facial expression, choice of words, not even the subject matter. If I asked him about his latest adventures in his quest for paintings, he would narrate them in the same manner as he would to his brothers.

With few exceptions, the paintings Uncle Willem collected were the works of young artists who were committed to challenging not only the traditional values of the artistic establishment but—as in futurism, dadaism, and surrealism—the very foundations of the bourgeois traditions and institutions. The collection covered the full range of modern painting, from expressionism to abstraction, including many of the names that less than half a century later were to become status symbols of enor-

Uncle Willem

mous worth—Chagall, Klee, Kokoschka, Kandinsky, Mondriaan, Mark. By the time I was in Brussels, the works of these painters were as familiar to me as those of Rembrandt, Hals, or Vermeer, and I could recognize them at a glance. I liked to pronounce their names the way Uncle Willem said them. "Kandinsky" gave me real physical pleasure; it had the taste of salted licorice drops. "Chagall" was a dog. "Here, Chagall!" "Kokoschka" a dessert. "Have another Kokoschka." "Mark?" Nothing.

Had it not been for a banal conflict of schedules, Picasso (a swearword?) would surely have been among them. A Parisian acquaintance had told Uncle Willem about the young Spanish painter, who was the talk of Montmartre. Uncle Willem tried to contact him in Paris but was told that Monsieur Picasso had just left for the French Riviera. Stubbornly, Uncle Willem went to Nice, only to learn that Señor Picasso had just left for Spain. Discouraged, he went to Bern to see Paul Klee, from whom he bought three exquisite watercolors and two drawings, which I acquired from him many years later for the now ridiculous sum of $1,500.

The Beffie collection, which today would probably seem eclectic for including such widely diverse painters as Kandinsky, Mondriaan, and Klee, during those early years of the new art was lauded for the coherence of its underlying ideology, for its artists, while acknowledging their formal differences, were bound by an important common goal, the Modernist Revolution. Ever since the Cubists had taken virtual space out of painting, there had been a frantic turmoil in the art world. To bring the imagery, whatever its nature, from an illusory depth onto the surface of the canvas was perhaps the most important break with tradition in the whole history of Western art. There was a fever in the air, a revolutionary zeal, that yearned for radical changes in all values. From that stormy point of view and considering the times, Uncle Willem's collection was not only re- markable but also "politically correct."

Furthermore, in a more subtle sense, it bore the unifying imprint of Uncle Willem's taste. The paintings he chose, though polemic in content and form, also reflected the gentle side of his character. Despite all their Sturm und Drang, they were generally low key, and while they were obvi- ously experimental in nature, they still seemed to obey many of the tradi- tional canons. As I now see those paintings in my memory, compared with the wild, kaleidoscopic canvases of the later decades and with the more recent breakdowns of the few remaining traditional values, the overall character of Uncle Willem's collection reveals the comparatively sober, gentle means and schemes of the Impressionists and Post-Impressionists. In the warm, woodsy Dutch living rooms of Uncle Willem's friends and relatives, his revolutionary paintings conducted themselves as neatly dressed, well-behaved guests, and with their traditional brown, ocher, and sienna dominance and carefully arranged color chords they faded in with the general gemütlichkeit.

The period in which "everything happened"—the ten years that shook the arts—was then too close and too dense with isms to allow for the subtle distinctions which we now demand. There was one unifying ism: *modernism,* a term well suited to appease the growing popular hos- tility toward the revolution. No one could then have predicted that the art which filled the short span of my early youth would have been the shaky pedestal for all the isms of our turbulent century. The pictorial arts de- fined their goals, claimed their independence, and then shaped the new, cluttered, but energized map of the continent of all the other arts.

Uncle Willem did not have a place of his own to hang or store the many paintings he acquired on his trips around the world. After having filled the walls of the Burgwal, he began to fill those of his friends' and rel- atives' houses with the understanding that the works would remain on permanent loan. But many of the recipients of this generous art bonanza were terrorized when in their mailbox they found still another notice from a shipping agent announcing the delivery of works of art, especially since size was not one of Uncle Willem's worries. Some, too embarrassed to hide paintings that "my four-year-old could do better" in their attics or closets, hung them in the darkest corners of their houses or apartments. Others placed the least offensive ones in the children's room, claiming that they were good for their art education. Father, fascinated by all that was new and provocative, was one of the few relatives willing to hang Uncle Willem's paintings throughout the house. He openly admitted that although he didn't understand them, he was willing to judge them for the appeal of their colors and shapes, for their "abstract qualities" as well as for his respect for his uncle's taste, intelligence, and expertise.

On each of the walls of our house hung at least one painting of Uncle Willem's collection. Father gave preference to the large, lush watercolors of Le Fauconnier, a French painter with whom Uncle Willem had established a close personal relationship—so close that at the beginning of the war, when Le Fauconnier fled to Holland to escape induction into the French army, Uncle Willem financed his and his wife's stay there for the duration. I have no idea how this strange friendship had come about, for Uncle Willem was secretive about his personal life and his actions were often unpredictable. Le Fauconnier, whose long red beard and easily aroused temper had made him one of Montmartre's tourist attractions, was known in Parisian avant-garde art circles as a very gifted but ambitious, arrogant, and somewhat corrupt Bohemian, whose work now and then would touch astonishing heights as well as dismal lows.

Uncle Willem wrote in his will that his paintings, regardless of their value, would belong to the persons in whose houses they were at the time of his death. Nora and I own a dozen or so Le Fauconniers, most of them inherited from my parents and grandparents. When in 1960 we moved back to Italy, they came with the rest of our belongings, and some ten years later they found a place in my storage room in Radda without ever having been uncrated. A year or so ago, while we were in Italy, I received a catalog from my friend Walter Bareiss, together with a note telling me that the Salander and O'Reilly Gallery in New York had shown a collection of Le Fauconnier paintings. The catalog had a few black-and-white photographs and a long essay, which I read with voluptuous concentration.

Since I had been sure that no one in America had any interest in Le Fauconnier, this unexpected piece of news aroused my curiosity, and I decided to take a fresh look at the paintings I now owned. We opened the crates, and as we took the canvases out of their wrappings, we placed them around the whitewashed walls of the storage room. I couldn't believe my eyes. . . . In all those years not only had I changed but my memory, perversely determined to play into the hand of my prejudices, had gradually distorted my recollection of the paintings to such an extent that now I could hardly recognize them. I had even forgotten that among them were several oils, almost cubist, painted with thick impasto and gutsy, en-

Solea Polichroma, oil on canvas, 1970

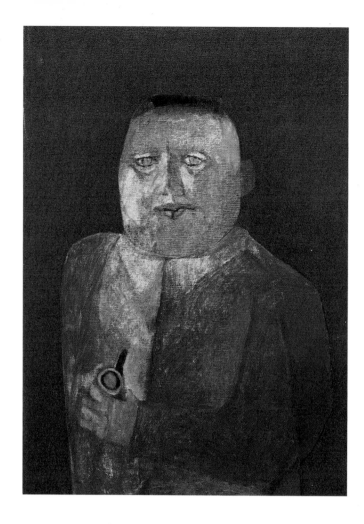

LEFT: *Marzo,* 1962

BELOW LEFT:
Easter Parade in Baena,
1965

BELOW RIGHT:
Imaginary Portrait, 1962

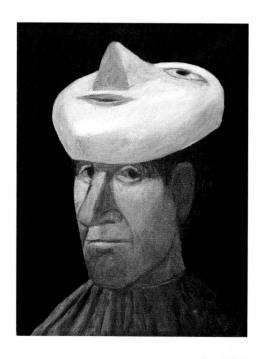

Profile, oil on wood, 1967

ABOVE: *Protorbis*,
oil on canvas, 1970

LEFT: *Siguria*,
bronze, 1974

OPPOSITE: *Dorodeme*,
oil on canvas, 1970

Project for an Imaginary Garden, in the real garden of Verona's Castelvecchio, bronze, 1978

LEFT: *Parallel Botany*,
pencil drawing and assemblage,
1974

BELOW LEFT: *In Three Skies*,
oil on canvas, 1985

BELOW RIGHT: *Olé*,
from the Black Table series, 1992

ABOVE: Menorah, handblown glass
with ribbons, 1986

RIGHT: *Annona edula*, bronze, 1971

BELOW: *For Kukai*, pencil drawing, 1980

One day, when there was no one in the house, Alexander heard a squeak in Annie's room. He sneaked in and what did he see? Another mouse.
But not an ordinary mouse like himself. Instead of legs it had two little wheels, and on its back there was a key.

"Who are you?" asked Alexander.

Illustrations from children's books   ABOVE: *Alexander and the Wind-Up Mouse,* 1969
BELOW: *Cornelius,* 1983

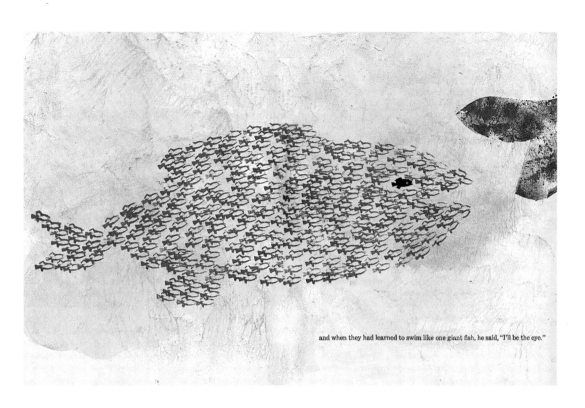

and when they had learned to swim like one giant fish, he said, "I'll be the eye."

ABOVE: *Swimmy*, 1963

BELOW: *Matthew's Dream*, 1991

The inchworm measured the neck of the flamingo.

Inch by Inch, 1960

ergetic brushwork. Among these, one winter landscape in particular impressed me to such a point that I carried it to the house and hung it on the wall opposite my personal armchair in the living room, where it still hangs. I have yet to understand why it fascinates me, and to find the key to its mystery. Without doubt it is a beautiful and profound work, and it has forced me to reexamine and reevaluate all the other paintings by Le Fauconnier, including the much maligned watercolors.

Of all the paintings Uncle Willem had "stored" at our house, my favorite was the Chagall that I call *Fiddler on the Roof.* Unfortunately, he sold this painting a few years before his death. It is one of four or five variations that now hang in museums in Europe and America. But, as I have said, when I was six or seven, the painting hung in the top-floor corridor of our Amsterdam house, between the attic door and the door to my room. I don't believe that Father had put it there for my educational benefit; I can easily imagine that for him the painting was too buoyant, too folkloric, too raw in color to give it an official position on the living floor.

I loved it. Although I knew that it belonged to the adult world of the Arts and the Intellect, with all the sacrality that those words implied, when it presented itself to my fading mind in that no-man's-time between wake and sleep, I would switch its components around, rearrange the colors and composition, move the characters, and invent stories of muzhiks and music, of donkeys and cows, of thunder and snow, and a singing moon—the ancestors, no doubt, of all the fables I was to dream, write, and illustrate fifty and more years hence.

Of course *Fiddler on the Roof,* while describing the picture accurately, is not its real title. I borrowed it some years ago when, through a strange string of circumstances, the musical got tangled up with my life. An invisible silver thread was to hold our two destinies joined forever.

One day in the late forties I got a call from my friend Ben Shahn, inviting Nora and me to a reading in New York of the dramatization of a group of Sholem Aleichem stories with the working title "Tevya and His Daughters." The draft of the play would be read by Howard de Silva, a Hollywood actor famous for his impersonations of Jewish characters. We went and enjoyed the people who were there, and we liked the Sholem Aleichem stories, but I could not imagine them as a full-fledged play. At the end of the evening the guests were asked to invest in the production. It was the first time Nora and I had been to a reading; we had never even heard the word used in that sense. Taken by surprise and slightly embarrassed, I made the grand gesture of writing a check for four hundred dollars, a large sum of money for the underpaid employee of a conservative Philadelphia advertising agency.

A few months later we received an invitation, designed and illustrated by Ben, for the premiere of "Tevya." The production was charming, but, as we had foreseen, the play, too delicate for hard, noisy midtown New York, lasted not more than two performances, and Ben told me that I could deduct the four hundred dollars from my taxes as a business loss.

The years went by, and "Tevya" lay buried in a dark corner of my memory, when one day I received a letter from a New York law firm announcing that the rights to it had been sold. It was being turned into a musical with the working title "Fiddler on the Roof," and our share was 0.15 percent. We thought that this was probably good news but had no idea that "our" musical was to become one of the most successful Broadway hits of all time. A year or so later, we saw a triumphant performance of *Fiddler on the Roof* in New York, with Zero Mostel as Tevya.

I have often asked myself how Uncle Willem, who came from a family almost entirely involved with the world of words and ideas and clearly indifferent to the visual arts, came to direct his attention with such intense, passionate zeal toward the abstruse products of the revolutionary avant-garde of painting. What magic confluence of genes and circumstances had given him the turn of mind and an eye so precisely focused on painting—an art whose inner secrets are usually reserved exclusively for its high practitioners in rare moments of intuition?

Not that Uncle Willem was unique in this. I've asked myself the same question after encounters with critics, historians, dealers, collectors, museum curators who "couldn't draw a straight line," let alone paint one, and yet possessed that specific sensibility which I had always believed to be a painter's exclusive privilege, and which alone, I thought, gave one the right to evaluate and judge a painter's work.

I love music with a passion, I have been exposed to it since I was an infant, I have heard the best orchestras in the world, I know the history of music, I have perfect pitch. Is that enough to qualify me as a music critic, a music director of an opera house or a concert hall, a professor at a music school? Isn't identification with the creative process of an art essential to its complete understanding? Without ever having held a brush, faced a white canvas, smelled the scent of Venice turpentine, chosen between two brands of Mars yellow, can I know what painting is all about?

And I haven't mentioned the very act of painting. Nor the endless soliloquy that accompanies it.

One evening in the fifties when we lived in Greenwich, Walter Bareiss, a passionate and fine collector of modern art, and his wife, Molly, invited us for dinner. When we arrived, the German housekeeper, who knew us well, told us that the missus had called to say that they had been delayed and invited us to have a drink while waiting in the east living room—the small modern wing that had recently been added to the large Bareiss villa. The reason for this seemingly extravagant addition to a house that had become far too big for the two of them was to accommodate their expanding collection of modern paintings and sculptures.

We had just sunk into the sofa facing the fireplace when I noticed that one of my favorite pictures of the collection, the splendid vertical Bonnard, which I remembered hanging in the master bedroom, had been moved to the wall next to where we were sitting. Nora was turning the pages of a book on Mantegna; it was a unique occasion for me to be alone with the great Bonnard painting for at least half an hour and let my thoughts and senses float freely over the paint. I got up, took a chair, and sat down squarely in front of the large canvas. Seen close-up, the chromatic intuition which had guided the painter's touch to immerse the most ordinary things and spaces in a light vapor of mystery and beauty was sheer magic. One had the hallucinating illusion that the pigments, instead of hugging the canvas, were at times slightly in front of and at other times behind its grainy surface.

Following the brushstrokes from the light, airy top of the canvas to deeper shades, I reenacted the painting process as if I were the artist. I closed my eyes and faced the empty canvas. I summoned to my mind's screen the painting I had just seen, then I picked up an imaginary brush from the table next to me, crowded with bottles of turpentine and linseed oil, damar varnish, and smaller ones with powdered colors. I dipped my brush in the small container of turps that was clipped to the palette, and with the tip of the brush touched the canvas here and there, just enough to leave on the white linen the reminders of the critical places where the forms joined. Then I began to apply light dabs of color moist with turpentine to the top of the canvas, and from there danced my brush gradually downwards, shifting colors and hues as I followed the lazy curves, the rising slopes, the sudden accents. I was painting now, but the words that accompany all creative acts were rapidly fading. Unaware of space, time, and circumstances, I painted and painted, lost in rapture. The whole canvas was now covered and I was ready to step back to compare it with the image that still hung motionless in my mind when a sudden clash of voices reminded me where I was. I had no idea how much time had passed. Molly and Nora were hugging each other affectionately, and a smiling Walter was coming toward me with outstretched arms, saying words I did not understand.

That night I couldn't sleep. As a painter I could reconstruct in my mind a reasonable analogue of Bonnard's actual painting process and accompany it with its probable interior monologue, the lonely dialectics that always move parallel with the physical creative act. I tried to imagine seeing a painting without reference to this experience. It was of course absurd—by removing the memory of performance, I ceased to be a painter. What was left? The aesthetics of the subject? A woman sitting at a kitchen table? A picture of a woman lying in an old bathtub? The painting's historical significance? Without assigning the object an intrinsic value, it was meaningless.

Having fantasized and tested all the various possibilities in my mind, one proposition became more and more convincing: there must be human beings whom Mallarmé's dice have blessed with an exceptional, incomprehensible gift—the means to read signals that others cannot perceive. Much like the ones that guide a frog to a distant water hole. Perhaps there are ways of seeing art that are accessible or comprehensible to only a chosen few. Uncle Willem must surely have been among them.

> "Willem Beffie, a noted diamond merchant and art collector, a
> Dutch citizen, died of a massive heart attack while dancing at
> the Roseland ballroom in New York. He was seventy years old."

To America

The blooming years of my adolescence in Brussels should have been a thundering event that would leave deep traces in my memory. I had witnessed Van Kampen's midnight victory in the six-day bicycle race, landed a big carp in a fisherman's competition at the pond of the Square Marie Louise, and been taken by my open-minded grandfather to see the musical *Pas sur la bouche*. I find nothing else until the day Mother made her dramatic appearance to come and fetch me, to take me to America. Exploiting both her difficulties with the written word and her familiarity with the stage, she came, unannounced, from behind the Japanese magnolia in the park, shouting, "Surprise! Surprise!"

I remember it as an exceptionally balmy day for Brussels in June. The freshly mowed lawn around the pond was dotted with clouds of tiny daisies, dandelions, and forget-me-nots. At the sound of Mother's bellowing voice, three ducks followed by a flotilla of bobbing ducklings, the size of tennis balls, peacefully paddling around their small cement island, shot off in all directions, hysterically chasing one another, quacking wildly. Mother, in the shortest act in her stage career, reaching way beyond her emotional means, immediately broke down in tears as she embraced me. "Oh, darling boy, how you have grown! A man!" she said, holding me at arm's length.

It is clear that for me the event must have been one of great importance, for it meant not only that I would rejoin my family, small as it was, but that my life was going to shift to a newer and altogether different gear and take me to what was going to be the Fatherland of my Future. It was like a cosmic somersault; the world had made a full turn on its axis. I was going to America.

One cluster of images rises to the surface of my memory. I remember walking around the deck of our ship, and I see a very tall American girl, from Kalamazoo. We danced cheek to cheek, and later, standing hand in hand on the top deck, united by the cold, salty spray, we exchanged promises for an indistinct and probably nonexistent future. I had expected to read real liberty in the statue we floated by, but instead I seem to remember a heavy, melancholic malaise. Was it the fog hanging over New York Harbor or an intuition of the empty rhetoric of the statue, heavy with the tears of millions who unknowingly invented America?

Stunned, only half conscious, I felt limp in my father's embrace, not unlike the way I had responded to Mother's pantomime at the edge of the pond, and when we had finished with the immigration authorities and I had run ahead toward the taxi stand with the porter, Father shouted, "We'll get rid of all that fat, you need to do a lot of gym. America will be good for you!" The only defense I had was that I was wearing a European suit that no American boy, who thought that plus fours were a homework assignment, would be caught dead in!

The crumbs of a much later occasion drift into my memory. I was made aware of the hardships of my parents' first year in America when they showed me, with pride, as if it were Buckingham Palace, the weird apartment house in Philadelphia that was to be my new home. The best I could do was to judge it an interesting freak, typically American.

Of course I was happy to be with Mother and Father, but everything was strange, starting with the street where we lived—an industrial area that had turned residential in a hurry. The facade of our building, like those of most buildings in Amsterdam, was made of red bricks. The entrance was like that of an office building, but there was no elevator. The house to our left was painted gray. The one to our right was made of cement, but the facade, all the way to the top story, was made with white painted steel columns that looked a little like the columns of the Parthenon.

After the "column house," as we called it, there was an empty lot shut in by a high fence covered solidly with small posters. A mostly hidden apple tree waved a few branches in the cold wind. One branch leaned over the fence, offering to the few strollers three bright red apples. They hung there undisturbed. In Amsterdam they wouldn't have had a chance, but here no one seemed to care.

Past the fence there was one more building, on the corner of Twenty-third Street, where the trolley ran. The noise reminded me of the Hoofd Straat, and at times in my daydreams I walked to the stop on my way to Oma's house in the Jan van der Heyden Straat. Our address was 2210 Walnut Street. We were between Twenty-second and Twenty-third streets.

It was a second-floor, three-room apartment. There was a dark, windowless entrance hall, which got its light through glass doors that opened onto a spacious living room. The first oddity I was introduced to was a big, flat, wooden box leaning against the wall in the entrance hall. "That," said Father, who had opened the door and pushed me inside, "is your bed. Watch." He pushed a button, and slowly the box swung down and settled with a brief shudder on the floor, a neatly made bed. "Welcome to America," said Father.

Against the opposite wall stood an upright piano and next to it a small coffee table and a chair. While we were watching the bed ceremony, Mother had grabbed from the coffee table a porcelain pot holding a cactus, which had obviously died from darkness and drought. "Sorry," said Father when he noticed. "I forgot to water it while you were away."

I liked the living room, which fully deserved the qualification "living" but could barely be called a room. It was as long as Oma Grossouw's living room, but Father and I were never able to figure out why the wall where the stove, the sink, and the Frigidaire stood—the "kitchen"—was a good three feet narrower than the other end. To fit regularly proportioned furniture in it was impossible. The whole year we lived there, not a week went by that Father and I wouldn't try another place for the large table around which our daily lives revolved. In the late afternoon when Father and I had returned home, the three of us would settle around the table, and while Father would read the paper and Mother consult her cookbook, I, half hidden behind my schoolbag, would do my homework. Perhaps it was because of the room's odd shape and because it contained the irregularities of the kitchen that the place had a warm, informal air about it that I had never before experienced. Could it previously have been a sweatshop? I was excited by this romantic idea, and it did have a feeling of hasty and ruthless improvisation that was truly American. I swore that I would find out, but I never did.

I soon discovered that Philadelphia, like Rome, abounded with historical buildings. Penn Charter, the Quaker school Father had chosen for me, founded by William Penn, occupied half a block on Eleventh Street, smack in the middle of town. It was attached to the old Quaker meeting-house, where our teachers took us every Wednesday afternoon to debate religious and moral issues, Quaker style. This was its last year, because the construction of a brand-new school in the fancy suburb of Queen Lane was just about finished. In the meantime, the new gym and all the outdoor sports facilities were ready, and a bus would drive us every afternoon to Queen Lane. I don't remember how it was found out that I had a natural predisposition for basketball, because our doctor in Amsterdam had written a letter to "whom it may concern" asking that I be excused from any form of gymnastics and athletic activity because of "water on the knee." Miraculously, Dr. Pimentel's diagnosis had been respected throughout my entire school career, from the very first years in Amsterdam's Vondel School to the uncompromising Istituto Tecnico in Genoa. But this didn't prevent me from playing basketball, and before I knew it I was on a regular training schedule, a proud member of the Penn Charter Basketball Team. (I ignored Dr. Pimentel's warning only one other time. After my hip replacement in 1975 in Zurich, I was trained to walk up and down steps and to board a crowded trolley with or without crutches. But by then I was considered an adult with a naturally shaped six-foot body, and never once in those years did I feel the urge to do a single push-up.)

School took up most of my time. I made fast progress in English, and as the headmaster testified on my report card, "In a few more months he should be speaking like an American." On the days when there was no basketball practice, I spent the afternoon at home. I enjoyed being there when Mother studied her songs. Without knowing it, I learned the words of some of the things she sang, and these have stayed in my memory. They ranged from sweet French shepherd songs of the seventeenth century to the arias of Mozart's Queen of the Night. The first year of Mother's American adventure had been more successful than Father's. I found a clipping that reported her having sung the "Mia Speranza Adorata" aria by Mozart in a performance with the Philadelphia Orchestra. Father got his own back the following year, when he was hired by the foreign department of the Atlantic Refining Company. All of this while my mind was full of the triumphant moment in yesterday's wild basketball game against Germantown High, when I had slid to a sharp stop at the end of a mad dash that had brought me almost directly under the basket and simply heaved the ball into it.

I had been in Philadelphia a year when Father announced that he had been asked by the president of the firm to take over the management of its Italian branch in Genoa. Both Mother and he were ecstatic about the idea of returning to Europe, and this at double the salary he was then making. I spent a good part of that night reading about Italy, Genoa, and the Liguria region in an old *Britannica* that Father had bought. I had never heard of Genoa and was surprised to learn that it had more than half a million inhabitants, was the third most important harbor of Europe, had several splendid museums, elegant hotels, an extraordinary cemetery famous for its marble sculptures, an early Gothic cathedral, and a first-rate opera house. But no matter what I read about Genoa, what I saw in my mind was an assemblage of photographs of Naples: narrow, slummy streets with clouds of laundry floating between the houses, sweaty families wrestling with their spaghetti under the pergola of an outdoor trattoria, a barefoot old fisherman asleep on a heap of fishing nets, and a couple of helpless American tourists assaulted by a horde of half-naked *scugnizzi*.

We would have to study Italian, of course. The three of us would do it all together. "My fifth language!" I shouted, excited. Mother got up from her chair and embraced Father and me.

Thus the second chapter of my life as a transient came to an abrupt but happy ending. Perhaps it is true that I don't remember much of my years in Brussels because my parents abandoned me at a critical moment of my adolescence, but this doesn't explain why the American year, which was a happy one, suffered the same fate. Perhaps the fact that I did not have a room of my own was more important to me than it might seem. The Walnut Street apartment was not pleasant. Everything about it—the

What Some of the American and European Critics Have Said of MADAME BETTY LIONNI:

Philadelphia Public Ledger, January 30, 1924 (Fullerton L. Waldo):

"Mme. Lionni, a discovery of Willem Mengelberg, gave Mozart's 'Mia Speranza Adorata' with lyrics of Strauss and others. She is a singer who makes her gifts effectual because she commands acquired and natural resources of her art in its technical as well as its spiritual phases. Insight and moral earnestness combine to enforce the appe_l _f t_n__ th_t h___ _m_ti_n_l quality and are forcefully projected. Her

Philadelphia North American, January

"Mme. Lionni, the soprano, featured in Club in the ball-room of the Bellevue-Strat reputation that preceded her when she d completely under control. Her first num Adorata' by Mozart, that furnished her flexibility and range of her voice. She can

Philadelphia Record, January 30, 1924:

" 'Hitch your wagon to a star' used t who aspired, and it would appear to be Musical Club when giving its fortnightly figured in the program of yesterday's conce Lionni, Dutch soprano, was the bright sta

Philadelphia Evening Bulletin, January

"Mme. Betty Lionni, the Dutch sopra artist with the Matinee Musical Club at i Bellevue-Stratford yesterday afternoon, ar was enthusiastically applauded for her art 'Mia Speranza Adorata' and a group of s and Doret."

Het Vaderland, The Hague:

"Madame Betty Lionni sang the solos soprano I may welcome an addition of t life of the Netherlands. She has gifts of liant vocal material, and her singing gives which brings out that splendid material to talent which will add to the national musi singer, after all, constituted for me the p

Nieuwe Rotterdamsche Courant, Rotter

"Madame Betty Lionni, soprano, cha fairylike quality of timbre which is too enunciation, too, are remarkably fine."

MADAME BETTY LIONNI

"The Eminent Dutch Soprano"
—Public Ledger

Studio: 2210 WALNUT STREET, PHILADELPHIA
TELEPHONE: LOCUST 5556

Mme. Lionni is available for appearance in Concert, Oratorio and Opera

Telegraaf, Amsterdam:

"Madame Betty Lionni has a sensitive voice of beautifully tender quality, which is particularly adapted to the songs of the modern French repertoire (the songs of Roussel at this concert, for instance)."

Algemeen Handelsblad, Amsterdam:

"Madame Betty Lionni possesses beautiful and voluminous vocal material which has been trained excellently. The voice sounds round, brilliant and free. In her interpretation she reveals an especial talent for the characteristic, the roguish and humorous. The Wolf songs were given splendidly."

Nieuwe Arnhemsche Courant, Arnhem:

"Mengelberg gave evidence of being thoroughly satisfied with Madame Betty Lionni, the soprano soloist, and no wonder. She delighted the audience with an interpretation which made Mahler a blessed benefactor to the spiritually inclined listener. She seemed to inspire the orchestra, the chorus and all around her."

spaces, the colors, the light, the furniture—was ugly, shabby, and frightfully impersonal. It failed to give me what I so desperately needed—the sense of having a permanent home, a secure point of reference. For a young adolescent at a stage when a dramatic existential crisis could be expected at any moment, it was not a desirable habitat. And yet from other points of view 1925 had been a fruitful year. Without much effort I had managed to perfect my fourth language. This meant that I now possessed a true multilingual vocabulary that allowed me to make linguistic comparisons and cross-references, weighing shades of meaning and formulating useful generalizations. The groundwork had been laid for the kind of literacy I would need to develop the analytical internal monologue that was to accompany and guide my creative work throughout the rest of my life.

Genoa

Genoa was a magnificent, exotic city built like an immense, steep amphitheater embracing the harbor. The sober elegance of its ancient palaces and churches testified to a rich past. The first weeks after our arrival we lived at the Miramare, a luxury hotel spectacularly situated on a hill in the midst of terraces and gardens with a full view of the ancient city. It had a large, impressive lobby, cozy reading rooms, a lush American bar, and a three-star restaurant, not to speak of amenities like a billiard room and three real slot machines in the lobby. Most of the Miramare's guests were businessmen, some on a last European stopover on their voyage to the Orient, others there for meetings with the local merchants. Genoa had centuries-long traditions in international trade. Sometimes during the day, when the ground floor of the hotel was deserted, Mother and I, alone in the lobby and its adjoining halls, struck by a sudden fit of foolishness, would chase each other wildly around sofas, armchairs, and potted palms. Those first months in Italy stand out in my memory as the happiest times I ever spent with Mother alone. For once she was not afraid to lose her composure, to let go, to risk her dignity. Her mood reflected Father's elation at the discovery that his job had turned out to be far more challenging and important than he had dared anticipate.

The Atlantic Refining Company of Italy had its headquarters in Via Balbi, one of the most elegant streets of Genoa's historic center, in an almost solid row of seventeenth- and eighteenth-century palazzos. Father's office, which before his appointment as manager had been the company's *salon d'accueil,* was a huge room on the first floor with a Baroque white marble balcony that gave onto the street. It had a fifteen-foot-high ceiling with a Tiepolo-style fresco from which a dozen chubby cupids, armed with bows and arrows, seemed to meditate on the promiscuity of art, business, and love. The first time I visited Father in his new quarters, I found him stretching his neck to greet me from behind a mastodonic desk—an important period piece, no doubt, but so high that it made Father, who was not a tall man, look like a midget. When I told him, we both got the giggles, and Father seized the occasion to call his assistant and ask him to provide an ordinary American gray steel desk, which was delivered the very next day.

It was then that I first met Ragionier Boni, a bright, charming young man who looked like someone who knew that he was launched on a successful career. Not only did he help Father find his way through the intri-

My father's office in Genoa

cate antics of the Italian private and public bureaucracy and find us *the* ideal apartment in Genoa but he was also instrumental in providing me with a tutor to whom I owe most of my mastery of Italian.

L'appartamento ideale was in Via Maragliano, a quiet residential street in the center of town, two blocks from the Via Venti Settembre, the busy thoroughfare famous for its porticos, mosaic sidewalks, and elegant shops. We liked the street. It had a quiet, simple dignity about it which even in the bustling center of town gave one a sense of ease and clarity. Our building, Number Ten, was the last on its block. From there, Via Maragliano curved to the left, following the contour of the rising terrain of the higher part of town, which could be reached on foot by climbing a series of steps that began right in front of Number Ten. Since the steps were flanked by greenery and an occasional palm tree, the front rooms of our building had a pleasant view that no other building in the street could boast.

The first time Boni took us to see the apartment we looked at each other worriedly when the porter opened a door on the third floor and turned on the light of the entrance hall. Boni noticed and immediately put us at ease. "Don't worry," he said. "I know it looks gloomy because the curtains and shutters are closed, and the wallpaper is dark and there are no good lamps. Just look at the space."

He was right. The living room, even though crowded with too many sofas, armchairs, and little tables, was huge. Boni tried to open one of the windows, but the mechanism was stuck and neither he nor the porter could move the handle. "OK," said Father. "Don't bother." We moved to the corner room. "This room faces those steps," said Boni. "Good," said Father, who seemed to be in one of his single-syllable moods, which indicated that his mind was clear, his reactions quick, and that he was anxious to make an important decision regardless of the risks involved.

Next was a slightly smaller room with a door that led to the entrance hall. When I walked in I felt something pressing against my heart. "Could I try to open this window?" I asked with half my voice. "Go ahead," said Father. Opening the window was easy, but hard as I pushed and pulled I couldn't move the shutters. I yanked once more, and suddenly a stream of light burst into the room. I had expected more dark walls and black furniture; instead, everything seemed to swim in a bright yellowish pink magma. I recognized the color—apricot, like Oma Rose's bedroom. "This is the *salottino*," Boni said. He then explained that the *salottino* is the room where guests are received before going into the dining or living room, and where tea is served. "Most *salottini* in Italy never see the light of day, for the wallpaper and the furniture are more delicate and expensive than those of the other rooms, and for walls and furniture the sun is enemy number one." I was terribly excited. I knew that the *salottino* would be mine. My studio.

We crossed the hall and continued the tour on the other side, where some of the shutters were half open. We saw the master bedroom and the bathroom, the maid's room and the kitchen and the dining room, where Father looked out the window and said, "Boni, you are a devil." Boni forced a coy smile. That side of our building faced an empty lot in which a few cars were parked, and there was a small gas station with all the Atlantic products on display. "Prepare the lease," said Father.

I had never considered that one day the time would come when I would have my own room again. The only room that had been really mine was my room in Amsterdam, but that had been almost four years before. A century. I was still a child then. And now the *salottino* was to be mine, and my parents were letting me choose my own furniture. How do you begin? A bed? No, simply a mattress on the floor and an assortment of suitcases. A table? Four legs and a top—the black table Uncle Piet had given to me in Amsterdam for my ninth birthday. There should be an easel, yes, a real easel with a crank for moving paintings up and down. Isn't that what a painter's room would look like? That evening in bed, just before disappearing into sleep, I saw myself standing in front of an easel scrutinizing the canvas I had just finished painting. Firm in my determination to become a painter, I must confess that I had never painted before. But now I would.

One afternoon I walked to the corner of the Via Venti Settembre and then with the crowd under the *portici,* uphill to Piazza de Ferrari, the true center of the city. Here was the starting point for most of the trolleys, here both the horse-drawn carriages and the so-called auto cabs were stationed, and here, all around the square, were the Opera, the Palazzo Ducale, the Exchange, the Post Office, the Public Library, and in a corner under the *portici,* the Caffè Grand Italia, where presently a five-piece all-woman jazz band was elaborating on one of the latest foxtrots to hit the still half-deserted Italian airwaves. Quickening my pace, I crossed the square, circling twice the equestrian statue of Garibaldi, turned left along the Palazzo Ducale, and, following the trolley tracks, began the descent toward the harbor until I was standing openmouthed and deeply moved before Genoa's finest monument, the Cathedral.

Then I turned around and crossed the street. There at the corner was a storefront with a glass entrance door totally covered with pages torn from an art materials catalog and a small, dusty display window chock-full of paint tubes, paper samples, erasers, pencils, pencil sharpeners, T squares, triangles, palettes, bottles—large and small with labels that said Damar Varnish, Turps, and Venice Turps—and sticking out of three large bowls, dozens of brushes of various shapes and colors. And in the middle of all this hodgepodge, straight and strong, solid on its four black steel casters, was a professional pinewood easel, complete with cranking mechanism and two handy side drawers for carbon sticks or other special use.

For a few minutes I stood there, and then before I knew it I was inside the shop, pointing to the easel, and with a voice higher than normal and hardly audible I asked, "How much does it cost?" The elderly gentleman in the gray smock looked at me, amused and somewhat perplexed. "For you?" he asked. I nodded. "Look, we have many other easels, just as good as the one in the window, less expensive and more practical for you . . ." and on and on in rapid Italian. When he finally stopped, I managed to say, "I understand very little Italian. How much does that one cost?" The man went to the counter, pulled some papers out of a drawer, and handed me a sheet with a picture of the easel and a German text underneath. "The list price is twenty-eight lire, but I'll give you a discount." Then he pulled a pencil out of his pocket, crossed out the price in marks, and wrote: 25 lire. I mumbled a swift "*Grazie,*" took the paper, and ran all the way home.

I was the son of an important foreign industrialist, I had reached an age that entitled me to opinions, and now I had a beautiful room of my own with Renaissance furniture and a real German easel. Clearly I was no longer a transient. This was home, and everything seemed to have conspired to make me feel secure and happy. But at the crucial moment when I was expected to choose the direction of my education, I found myself having to grapple with scholastic requirements that limited my options to a career for which I had neither the talent nor the slightest interest. If in Holland, Belgium, and America, high school would have given me access to an unlimited choice of college careers; in Italy, unfortunately, things were more complicated.

Italian high schools were then of three types: the Magistrale, whose diploma entitled one to teach in elementary schools but opened no college doors; the Istituto Tecnico, which eventually could lead to a university degree in economics and business administration; and the Liceo Classico, the only school that left all options open. Obviously my choice would have been the last, but its requirements for admission turned out to be impossible. For my entrance examinations not only would I have had to confront math, physics, chemistry, Italian history, Italian literature, Latin, and Greek but, of course, I was expected to have perfect command of the Italian language as well. The only possibility left was the Istituto Tecnico, whose entrance requirements, while not quite so demanding, still included a heavy dose of Latin and, of course, all the Italian subjects, not to speak of Italian itself.

The upshot was that for ten months I was to have a private tutor to prepare me for the examinations and for a profession which, despite Father's shiny example, represented a world that was frigidly alien to me and in some ways outright hostile. And yet it was not an unhappy year. Boni had produced a tutor who had a surprising knowledge of all the required subjects.

Professor De Amicis was a small, gentle man, always dressed in a black, ill-fitting, threadbare suit. Nearsighted, he wore a pair of small silver-framed spectacles perpetually balanced on the point of his nose, and when he raised his head from a book he was reading to answer my questions, he would lift his eyebrows as high as they would go and look at me with his long-lashed, bulby eyes as if he had never seen me before in his life. He was a grandson of Edmondo De Amicis, famous in the history of Italian literature as the author of *Cuore,* a sentimental, moralizing tale of a little boy.

Despite such distinguished ancestry, *il professore* was a shy, modest intellectual, and he would, like many Italians of simple origin, become self-deprecating and overly ceremonial when confronted with "important" personages. In the presence of people like Father, who in his eyes was an important American oil magnate whom he owed respect and deference, he would fall prey to an attack of questionable Italian rhetoric, and the simplest words and gestures would become banal, pompous, and subservient. Nevertheless, *il professore* turned out to be an extraordinary tutor. A man of vast culture and a fine literary mind, he gave me far more than the correct answers for the entrance examinations of the Istituto Tecnico. By firing my love for Italian literature and art, he opened my eyes to a world that soon would be mine.

With a full-time study schedule, vacations in Holland and Switzerland, and a membership in the International Country Club, where I met other young foreigners, time flew by. And then, thanks to *il professore* and the leniency of some of the examining professors, I was admitted to the four-year course at the Istituto Tecnico Superiore Vittorio Emanuele Terzo, with the prospect, if all went well, of becoming a licensed business administrator, euphemism for bookkeeper, in four years.

Adda

My first days at school could not have been more of a culture shock had I been in Libya or Thailand. Unlike my three previous schools, not only was Vittorio Emanuele a mixed school but the girls were in the majority. Discipline was strict, the girls had to wear black uniforms, and all so-called

My parents and I in Venice, 1928

excesses of familiarity with the opposite sex, such as walking arm in arm or even holding hands, were strictly forbidden. We were not allowed to address the girls with the familiar *tu* form or even by their first names. Many students wore the Fascist uniform, and the Fascist salute to the Duce was the day's opening ceremony. Thank God, being a foreigner, I was excused from both. The first two weeks were no joyride. I felt like a cat in a strange warehouse—as the Dutch would say—and were it not for a totally unforeseen event I would probably have quit.

Adda Maffi appeared at school a week after classes had started and was assigned a desk not far from mine. She wore glasses, still an exception in those years. She was quite tall and seemed slow and slightly awkward in her motions, and she hardly dared raise her head. While the current feminine fashion was bangs, à la Colleen Moore, she wore her dark hair in long braids, yet she seemed far more mature than her giggly, restless schoolmates. There was an air of mystery about her, and although I could see no more than the back of her shoulders and her chestnut-colored hair, I couldn't take my eyes off her.

When the class ended I committed what in Italy at that time was considered an outrageous act of transgression. As we walked out of the classroom, I edged up to her and asked if I could walk her home. The girl gave me a surprised and somewhat ironical look. "Sure, if you don't mind going as far as the Circonvallazione." Too embarrassed to utter another word, we walked in the direction of the *funicolare,* which was to take us to the high parts of town. When we were about to enter the long entrance tunnel, I stopped her and asked abruptly, "Why do you look so sad?" She looked me defiantly in the eyes and said, "Because my mother died a few months ago, and . . ." She hesitated a moment, and then she added, "and my father is in jail." Tears sprang to her eyes.

It was a warm autumn afternoon. We talked and talked. From a bench near the *funicolare* station we moved to a café on the Rotonda, a lookout point that, like an eagle's nest, dominated the white city below. Her father—a prominent physician, a Communist, and a member of parliament—had been arrested by the Fascists along with the other Communist and Socialist parliamentarians when Mussolini took over the government. Since he was in jail in Genoa awaiting trial, she, her brother, and her two sisters had moved from Rome to Genoa, in order to be able to visit him once a week. They lived in a boardinghouse on the Circonvallazione, the wide avenue lined with eucalyptus trees that traces the arch of the high part of town.

I was profoundly shocked and felt almost ashamed to tell the young woman about my own life, which by comparison suddenly seemed insignificant and banal. But I did my best to dramatize my story, describing with gusto some of my eccentric aunts and uncles and my year in America.

The sunset had paled when I left her at the door of the building where she lived, and although Via Maragliano was on the opposite side of town, I walked all the way home, trying to repeat and remember every word that had been said. A few days after the encounter with Adda I met her older brother, Mario, one year older than I, a student at the Liceo Classico, and her younger sister, Nora. Bruna, the oldest of the four, was working in Milan and would come down to Genoa occasionally on weekends. Friendship with all of them was instantaneous. Often I would go to their pensione to do my homework or join them for a meal.

In the weeks and months that followed that fatal day of October when Adda and I opened our hearts to each other, we became inseparable, causing no end of scandal in school. My life had taken on a drastically different rhythm and style. Until that moment, spoiled by the privileges of my only-child status and a generous imagination, I had lived passively and pleasurably in a well-protected vacuum and had felt no need for permanent relationships beyond those with which I had been endowed at birth.

I believe it was a Saturday afternoon when, after a several-hours session at the library on Piazza de Ferrari, I walked down the Via Venti Settembre toward home. I had stopped for an espresso at the bar under the Carignano bridge and was just about to turn into Via Maragliano when I realized that a small crowd had gathered at the corner. I decided to force my way through to see what they were watching with such intensity when a stern voice ordered them to move on. *"Avanti! Muovetevi!"* Obediently, they began crossing the street. I, instead, was turning the corner when a young man in Fascist uniform grabbed me and yelled something I didn't quite understand. "My house is there," I ventured, pointing my finger in the direction of where we lived. The man released his grip, and said, "Go ahead, then, but be quick about it."

In the middle of the street there was a big pile of garbage smoldering in a dense, slowly rising cloud of smoke. And as my eyes moved up with it I saw three or four young men standing on a third-floor balcony. One leaned over the balustrade and through his cupped hands shouted something to a similar group near the burning heap. They were all wearing the same Fascist uniform as the young man who had just stopped me, except two or three who wore the long, pointed cap modeled after the Renaissance student headgear that was the official hat of Italian university

Class picture: I'm the tall one in the back row; Adda is just below me.

students, a different color for each faculty. Theirs were gray, the color of the School of Economics, ironically the one I was slated for.

As I began walking toward home, hugging the walls of the buildings to make myself as invisible as possible, it gradually became clear that what was burning was not garbage at all but books, among which were many big ones with stiff bindings that burned along the edges with little dancing flames.

Now I was near the grocery store, the only store on our street. Instinctively I jumped into the entrance, where three people, two women and an older man, had already taken refuge. "Come!" they said, as they pulled me closer to them. "What's going on?" I asked. "Ah, Signorino," said the old man with an unsteady hoarse voice, "it's awful. A lawyer lives there, a Socialist."

A truck carrying a dozen or so students hysterically waving clubs at imaginary enemies to the sound of "Giovinezza," which they sang at the top of their voices, had driven in from the side of our building. It stopped in the middle of the street just behind the small crowd of Blackshirts who were already there. The students jumped down from the truck, and some of them improvised a wild dance around the fire.

"For shame," mumbled the old man behind me. The older of the two women, white haired, hushed him. "Shut up!" Then a deep, mysterious silence set in, interrupted only by the occasional screeching of the trolleys in the Via Venti Settembre as they struggled their way uphill to Piazza de Ferrari. I leaned out to see what was going on. All eyes were now turned to the balcony, where two students were trying to heave a huge black box onto the marble balustrade, while others, half hidden in the dark inside, appeared to be pushing. For an interminable instant the box seemed to grow as it leaned farther forward until it reached its balance, and then it suddenly seemed to fold over and came sailing down in a twirling motion, crashing onto the edge of the sidewalk, where it exploded with a monstrous choral noise of cracking wood and metal strings followed by an obscenely rhythmic "*Eja eja alala,*" the official cheer of the Fascists.

The woman behind me began crying. And the old man repeated the same word over and over again: "Barbarians! Barbarians! Barbarians!" I began to tremble all over and suddenly jumped into the street and ran home without ever slowing down or stopping. Stefano, our concierge, was at the door. "Stefano!" I shouted. "The Fascists have thrown a piano from the third floor! A piano!" Stefano looked at me with an expressionless face, shrugged his shoulders, and said, "Eh, Signorino, you wouldn't understand. You come from a different world." Some months later I was told that most doormen were informers for the police.

Although I knew vaguely what Fascism was, I had not imagined how politics could affect the fate of real living people and have a stranglehold on the destinies of their daily lives. My tutor, mildly anti-Fascist, had explained to me the meanings of the word *ideology,* but I had ignored its inevitable translation into action. The sudden awareness of my responsibilities for a world that until then had remained scandalously unnoticed called for a radical change in my values. I was yearning to find confirmation for the new ideas that were storming my mind. Feverishly I devoured Tolstoy, Pushkin, Gogol, Turgenev, and the other Russian greats, many of which, forbidden by the Fascists as Communist propaganda, I had bought at a secondhand bookshop near the harbor. In no time at all I developed a love for the working class, hatred for all bourgeois values, and, more important, passion for the written word. Obviously I declared myself a Communist, and as a budding artist I was ready to join the Futurists, if only for their contempt of bourgeois institutions. At the few art galleries in town I met other rebellious young artists who had joined Marinetti's Futurist movement. One was Gaudenzi, whose widow still runs one of the best galleries in Genoa, where in 1993 I had a retrospective of drawings and other works on paper.

My reading stimulated all sorts of related side interests, and so while I was going through the perfunctory tasks of studying bookkeeping and statistics, business writing, and banking practices, in reality I was acquiring a modern humanistic education. After the Russian period came the momentous discovery of *À la Recherche du temps perdu* and works by other contemporary French authors. I had become a habitué of the public library in Piazza de Ferrari. I went there mostly to consult works that were out of print or too expensive to buy, but I couldn't resist the temptation to leaf through heavy, parchment-bound tomes with odd woodcuts and madly elaborated initials, laying the foundations for my bibliophilia.

The world of books and ideas held excitement for me, but all was not smooth sailing in my school career. At the end of the first year, I was flunked by our Italian literature teacher, not so much because of the obvious weaknesses in my command of the language but for my refusal to wear the black Fascist shirt and to raise my arm in Fascist salute when he made his entrance into our classroom. When scolded the first time, I politely and, I thought, diplomatically explained that as a foreigner I should be excused from actively showing my allegiance to a foreign regime. His angry answer was that I should do it to express my gratitude to the nation of which I was a guest, and my solidarity with my companions. It was well known at the time that Professor Bergamini was an ardent Fascist, a temperamental hothead who knew that I was courting the daughter of a Red revolutionary.

Having to pass Italian literature in the fall exams, I not only prepared myself thoroughly for the specific examination requirements but with gratuitous passion went way beyond them. My readings included the complete works of poets I loved, like Papini and Leopardi, as well as critical works at the university level. Although my discussions with my former tutor could have testified that my knowledge of the subject was well above that of the average aspiring bookkeeper, Bergamini flunked me again, and so I was forced to repeat the first year. It was perhaps out of rage that I decided to try for admission to the third-year courses. On that occasion, the head of the school, a pedantic, authoritarian, but reasonable man, called me into his office a week before the examinations and informed me that he had given orders that I take my exams with a different professor.

This time I passed with ease and was able to rejoin my original school companions. Encouraged by the results, I decided to try to prepare for the final exams during the third year; that would entitle me to skip the fourth-year courses and to enter the Scuola Superiore di Commercio. I passed all the tests successfully, but once again the course of my life took a sharp turn. After skipping two years, I had become overconfident, and when I had heard that one could enter the University of Zurich as *Auditor mit Uberstunden* (with extra hours), even without regular entry examinations, and have the courses and relative exams validated later, after regular admission to the university, I persuaded Father to let me try my luck in Zurich.

If my school life had followed a tortuous path, often difficult, even painful, but then again exciting and sometimes rewarding, the map of my sentimental life during those first Italian years was not much simpler. My love affair with Adda had been intense but short-lived. She was an extraordinary young woman, intelligent, strong tempered, romantic, and for her age—she was one year younger than I—her insights could be astonishingly profound. She shared my sudden passion for reading, and much of our pleasure of being together lay in discussing what we had read and the ideas and feelings it had provoked.

Adda had grown up in a family that was addicted to the game of dialectic confrontation, and she, too, a perpetual transient of sorts, had had a checkered school career. Neither of us had the slightest inclination to become bookkeepers, but alas that was where the system had channeled us, and since we knew that there were no reasonable alternatives, at school we struggled passively through the boring technicalities, knowing that eventually we would get our true education through avid reading.

I spent most of my time with Adda at her pensione, where we would lazily lie across the beds reading or telling stories of our childhood. Sometimes she and her younger sister, Nora, would visit me in my room in the Via Maragliano, where I would help them with their homework, draw their portraits, or play English jazz records on my portable Victrola. Nora would then lure me into dancing with her, while Adda, physically lazy and somewhat awkward, would grab a book, fall back onto my couch, and pretend to be deeply absorbed.

Nora

Nora was physically quite different from Adda and their brother, Mario, both thin boned and tall. Like a Maillol sculpture, she had an elemental beauty; she stood solid on her legs, and her body was smooth and firm. Less intellectually inclined than the rest of the family, she was gregarious and outgoing, anxious to please and be helpful. While Adda struggled to keep her long braids in place, Nora's daringly short hairdo and fringe would fly in the wind. In contrast to the rest of the family, furiously committed to causes and ideas and the rebellious rejection of all current values, she embodied, unknowingly, the popular image of a girl of the twenties. She preferred magazines to books and was disarmingly honest about her likes and dislikes. When discussions at the luncheon table became violent, as they often did, she would run out of the dining room crying. She loved to have fun, the sillier the better. I was enchanted by her directness, the clarity and simplicity of her soul. We danced the Charleston and talked foolishness. And one day we discovered that we had fallen in love.

This new situation brought painful complications to our lives. For a while Nora and I were careful not to show our feelings. Because of the bonds of friendship, the ideas we shared, and my love for Adda still smoldering beneath the ashes, I was thoroughly confused and hesitated to take this turn of events seriously. The complexities of my character had been challenged before, but this time they involved the happiness and pain of others.

My feelings for Nora were as different from those for her sister as the differences between the two young women. While Adda played the romantic chords of devotion and passion, Nora stimulated my natural lust for life in the high, syncopated notes of her essential, elemental vitality. But much as I tried to talk myself into the theory that the two complemented each other in a morally acceptable unity, it soon became obvious that a crisis was inevitable.

Had Nora and I been hit by a *coup de foudre,* a minor tragedy might have been risked. But if our awareness of love came as a sudden revelation, my deeper feelings for her had developed gradually, gathering strength and definition as those for her sister were slowly losing their

Nora and Adda

original fire. The transition was all very civilized, and despite an occasional scene of jealousy and some sarcastic remarks, the profound sense of solidarity which had bound us together did not abandon its hold. Adda was heroic throughout, Nora somewhat bewildered and self-effacing, Mario and Bruna sarcastic but tolerant. I was desperate in the beginning, but then by earnestly swearing that my love for Nora would last forever, I felt that I had cleared my conscience. Adda and I would still get lost in the twelve volumes of the NRF edition of Proust's *Recherche,* while Nora and I soon discovered how to get lost in the high, bushy hills just above the city, not far from the last stop of the *funicolare.* We knew the naked, narrow paths that wound like the snakes of a labyrinth through the shrubs. That year winter was slow in relinquishing its privileges, but wrapped in our woolen scarves we knew how to find the gray, snow-washed, and now sun-drenched bench where other lovers' names had been carved.

The fact that the Maffis and I met at a moment when none of us, if for unrelated reasons, had a single friend can probably account for the enthusiasm with which I was admitted into their midst. For one thing, I was a foreigner, and that freed them of the ever-present suspicion that an intimate relationship might be politically dangerous. And then there was the fact that we shared the uncomfortable sense of not belonging. Having changed country, school, and language three times in the previous three years, I had never yet enjoyed the possibility of establishing lasting friendships. Nor of any continuity in my studies. While Brussels and Philadelphia had been little more than temporary abodes, the Amsterdam of my childhood was still home base, and the target of all my nostalgia. Now I had found new symbols of permanence. With an elegant apartment, Father's important job, and friends I vowed to love forever, permanence was here to stay. And just in case . . . Amsterdam was on the same map as Genoa, only fifteen centimeters away.

After I had met all four Maffis—Adda, Bruna, Nora, and Mario—hardly a day went by that either in pairs or in larger combinations we didn't meet. In different circumstances, my courting two sisters simultaneously would have exploded and left an unsurmountable abyss. What pains, jealousies, or resentments it may have provoked were dealt with within the privacy of each of us. It would have been considered immoral to have it reflect on our basic communal friendship.

One day in late April I was told that Father Maffi (Papà) would be transferred to Milan toward the end of May. I was destroyed. Now, each time Nora and I stepped out of the *funicolare* at the last stop, I felt with terror that we were stepping into the dark void of a last time. When spring came, Nora discovered the first, tender wild daffodils, and over and over again she marveled at how much they looked like minuscule cups and saucers. I thought that her clear, high laugh echoed through the hills and the city beneath us, and as I saw it glide softly onto the golden tremor of the sea far below, I prayed that the whole world would hear, for I knew and feared the fragility of love at a distance.

Cavi

Contrary to what we had expected, Papà Maffi did not want Mario and his sisters to move to Milan before the fall. They would spend the summer in Cavi as they always had, at the pink villa originally bought by the grandfather as a summer house.

Cavi then was just a secondary railroad stop that had not yet gained a name as a beach resort. Only twenty or so families of farmers and fishermen lived there all year round. On the narrow, hilly grounds that stretch from the station to the rocks of Sant'Anna between the railroad and the highway, there were half a dozen villas, hidden in the evergreens, pittosporum bushes, and high palm trees. Except for the Maffis' house, the first one after the station, and Villa Spinola, the last, where the Baccan, the Maffis' eccentric uncle lived, these villas were closed up during the winter months. At the rocks of Sant'Anna, both railroad and highway disappeared in their respective tunnels to reappear at Sestri Levante, a charming little harbor town with a real station, a boat-building yard, a small fishing fleet, three restaurants, and two internationally rated hotels.

My original image of Papà Maffi was, and still is, a fusion of two snapshots that Adda had shown me when we first met. In one, Papà Maffi is standing, in a long nightgown, on the balcony of the house in Cavi. In the other, he is in the garden in front of a half-opened venetian blind, which is probably shielding one of the glass dining room doors from the hot southern sun. He appears to be laughing heartily, throwing back his head so that his Adam's apple shows in the shade of his beard. Or perhaps he is singing, for he is holding a guitar and his right hand seems ready to touch the strings.

The summers in Cavi are among the most carefree and happiest in my memory. On weekdays especially, the beach was practically ours. It is hard to believe that where now stands an almost solid row of noisy, ugly bathing establishments with thousands of Milanese and Parmense bodies frying in the gray sand, and where thousands of cars with license plates from every Italian province are parked tightly all along the highway that flanks the railroad and the beach, and where hundreds of cafés and bars are blaring their brand of rock and roll, there was once, and not so long ago, a five-mile strip of gentle desert, where in the midst of summer only a few groups of families would gather to swim, play, talk, or make love.

The summer seemed endless. Except for a vacation in Sils Maria with my parents and the time studying at the library for my exams, I spent most of my days on the beach between Cavi and Lavagna. Often I would sleep over, and in the evening after dinner we would be picked up by friends who had a car and drive to Santa Margherita, where we would dance at one of the beach clubs or hotels. Later we would drive into the hills for a special wine and focaccia treat. The focaccia had brought fame to a dark-skinned, curved old woman known as *la sporcacciona,* who lived alone in a decrepit barn hidden in the woods and whom we would wake up by banging on the door until she opened it, grunting like an angry pig, staggered to the furnace, lit the fire, and without uttering a single word, produced what was without doubt the most delicious focaccia on the whole Ligurian coast.

These were happy times. To be accepted by a family of friends as a full-ranking close relative is surely one of the greatest, most pleasurable feelings one can hope for. The fact that I "owned" a permanent place and my own silver napkin ring at the Maffi dining table gave me a sense of utter well-being. It was the ceremonial confirmation that those with whom I shared my meals were more than just close friends or connections, they were brothers and sisters through reciprocal choice, not through circumstances officially sanctioned and totally beyond our control. I was free to reinvent my life, and yet I was surrounded by affection and a structured human environment that gave me the limits of my freedom.

Though Papà Maffi was not with us that first summer in Cavi, his presence was strong—or it might be more accurately said, his absence was almost visible. And as I think back to those early Cavi years, it is the times he was there, under house arrest, that most vividly come to mind. The nicest moments in Cavi were when Papà, instead of eating in his study on the third floor, as he mostly did, would come down and join us in the dining room. It was always surprising how much he—after all, an intellectual, a politician in exile, a doctor, a figure of importance—seemed to be thoroughly enjoying himself with whatever was going on around him, including the banalities of small talk. In this we were very much alike, and instinctively we knew it. Yet from time to time I would sense something artificial in his seemingly hearty laugh, when he would throw his head back as in Adda's snapshot of him and then would suddenly regain his dignity, his awareness of being a public figure. Did he, like me, have a secret observer with him, a "third man" constantly watching over him?

Sometimes when there were no patients waiting or expected and the light lay soft on the silver-green olive groves that covered the hills, Papà would say to his man Friday, "Paolo, bring me my paint box, et cetera." Paolo knew what the et cetera were: a folding chair, a new canvas, a parasol, and the combination easel–paint box of Papà's own invention. Paolo would then hastily announce to the cook or whoever else might be in the kitchen quarters, "We are going painting." If Papà had a place in mind with a particularly difficult perspective, Paolo was told also to bring the "grid frame," a light metal frame in which thin copper wires had been stretched in both directions and at equal distance from each other, to form a grid which from a fixed vantage point would guide the painter in drawing the landscape on a canvas with an identical grid already sketched in.

Notwithstanding these amateurish inventions, Papà was a better than average Sunday painter with a remarkable sense of color and composition. The final results of his expeditions were often pictures well worth framing, in which a happy combination of talent and poor eyesight would produce some truly pleasurable, evocative impressions of the Tigullian Gulf at its haziest, dreamiest best.

Sometimes, Papà would remain with us after lunch to tell us about a particularly interesting medical case or to play his guitar and sing for us. He had good pitch and a powerful voice, and although he had mastered little more than the basic chords on the guitar, they served him well. The songs were mostly workers' songs, many of them from the district in Piemonte which had been his constituency during his early terms in the Chamber of Deputies. The rice fields of Piemonte, where he fought his first important parliamentary battles in the interests of the *mondine,* the women who worked in the rice fields, were shamefully and tragically untended breeding grounds for malaria and tuberculosis. In his songs, some comical and some tragic, his "third man" would occasionally allow Papà to reveal some real emotions. In those rare moments, especially when he was quite old, when his voice had become raspy and his range limited, his feelings would erupt with great intensity. When that moment came, we would listen with tears in our eyes. Papà probably never knew that our tears were not for the beauty of the song but for our anticipated nostalgia for him and for the happiness we were now sharing.

The freedom and irresponsibility that are typical of beach life soothed my despair at the prospect of the Maffis leaving Genoa, and in the heat of the summer sun the obsessive image of Nora boarding a train for Milan evaporated with my anguish. But one day autumn arrived unannounced. Nora's departure fortunately coincided with my preexam jitters. In the confusion of feelings and fears, and with the general excitation that young people bring to such occasions, the event even had something festive about it, and only hours after Nora's handkerchief had disappeared with a curve of the tracks did the full impact of what had really happened take hold of me. Until early morning I sat at my table writing a long and desperate love letter. The answer came a week later. It was a hastily written note, acknowledging my letter without comment. The sentences were short, but they had the ring of her gay vitality. She wrote something about school and complained of being bored. She mentioned the weather and said that she was nostalgic for Cavi. She asked about my exams and closed with an ambiguous impersonal use of the word *abbracci.*

The letter threw me into a panic. I read and reread it, hoping to find the clue to a secret code, but there was not the slightest hint of a second level; her words were as clear as when she spoke. Instead, I recognized in her unsteady, large handwriting her mannerisms, the tone of her voice

Dueling beards: Nora and Adda's father and uncle, Fabrizio and Fabio Maffi

when she was embarrassed, that nervous gaiety just a bit too daring and loud. I had expected to read a passionate outpouring of her commitment to our eternal love, of her despair at our separation and words of nostalgia and hope. None of this.

That is the way our letters remained, mine long and passionate, hers as if some mysterious censor organ, hidden in the dark of her body, eliminated from her writing all reference to her feelings. Once a few months later, when I thought that her letters were becoming less frequent, I tried to call her on the phone. Out-of-town calls were still a special event in Italy. One had to go to the Central Telephone Office in Piazza de Ferrari and book the call. Sometimes the wait for a call to Milan would be as long as two hours. There was no telephone at the pensione where she was staying, but I had sent her a telegram saying that I would call her at her uncle Attilio's house at a certain hour of a certain day. When I got through, however, her uncle sounded hostile and said he knew nothing about the call.

And so, with alternating moods and rhythms, our correspondence staggered on until, three months or so after her departure, I stopped receiving answers to my letters. After a few miserable weeks I decided to go to Milan, and one day in the early hours of the morning I boarded the Lombardy Express full of dark forebodings. When the train finally rolled into the great glass-domed Milan station, my legs could hardly carry me. I staggered to a taxi and fifteen minutes later got out in front of a gray, ill-kept six-story building whose entrance was hardly noticeable in the midst of a row of cheap, overcrowded shop windows.

I stood on the sidewalk gathering my thoughts and my courage when my eyes caught Nora, fresh as a wildflower in spring, as she hastily exited the building and almost bounced into me. I grabbed her by the shoulders and, incapable of uttering a single word, looked her straight in the eyes. She lowered hers and shaking loose from my grip mumbled a hardly audible "I am sorry." She then threw a frightened look in the direction of a tall, handsome young man who was leaning against a showy car. Without so much as a parting glance at me, she ran toward him, the two settled in the car, and with a strident shriek of tires it pulled into the traffic and disappeared.

I don't know how long I stood there, paralyzed, totally dejected and confused. Then Mario came out and held me in a long embrace. He slowly guided me into the entrance hall of the building, and there we sat down on a bench. "What happened?" "You won't believe this," Mario said, "she has a crush on that idiot who's in Adda's class. You know how wild she is about fancy cars. Well," he added after a long pause, "you know how she is."

At Father's insistence, I registered at the Scuola Superiore di Commercio in Genoa, although I was certain that I would never set foot in that building. The following week, age nineteen, I left for Zurich.

Zurich

It was one of those bright autumn days in Zurich, when no matter where you were you had the impression that the mountains and the lake had moved somewhat closer to the city. I don't remember who had given me the name of the Pensione Doberli on the Bussinger Strasse, where I was going that morning. The pensione was on the second floor of a four-story building half hidden in the trees and bushes of a neglected garden—an impenetrable piece of rain forest. There was a certain charm about this wild fragment of nature in the midst of the obsessive orderliness of a Swiss city.

I had to ring the bell four times before it was answered. For a moment I had feared that everything in this place had gone the way of the garden, but the very moment I stepped into the small entrance hall of the Pensione Doberli I knew that I was wrong. The smell of wax and the sheen on the door handle told me that I was very much in Switzerland. And so did Mrs. Doberli herself, in her spotless white apron, her light blue eyes sunk deep in a wrinkled, sun-burned skin, and her gray hair forcefully gathered into a tightly bound bun at the nape of her neck. There was something comical about her vigorous up-and-down handshake, and her smile instantly reminded me that I had run out of toothpaste. "Did you have to ring long?" she asked apologetically in perfect German. "I was showing a charming Italian student the two rooms that are still unrented. Please forgive me." "Well, I am also an Italian student of sorts," I said as we walked into a cozy, sunlit living room with simple blond furniture and lots of framed photos on the walls.

A young man lifted himself awkwardly from a sofa. He forced a smile. "*Buon giorno*. Did I hear that we are both Italian? What a coincidence!" I didn't know whether there was irony in his voice or not. While we shook hands he introduced himself as "Giorgio Cacciapuoti, Politechnicum, naval engineering, third semester." Once he had straightened up, he was the tallest Italian I had ever seen. "I have problems with my back," he added. "I had a bad fall in Gstaad." "My name is Leo Lionni, Universitat, National Oekonomie, first semester." It was the first time I had introduced myself that way. "Well," I added awkwardly, "it's not quite that way, but I'll explain later." Mrs. Doberli, who had been waiting during our strange introduction, said, "Gentlemen, why don't I show Mr. Linni the rooms? Perhaps you can strike a deal." "Lionni," I corrected. "*Ach ja,* Lionni. What a nice Italian name!" "Well, actually . . ." and I suddenly realized that everything about me was complicated. It was a sickening feeling. "Come," said Mrs. Doberli, suddenly impatient, "come with me."

Giorgio, who had made the tour before I arrived, nevertheless came along. The first room had an unusual shape. It was very long and very narrow; it looked like a hospital room, with its white metal bed and white painted wardrobe and table. "Where would I put an easel?" was my initial thought. And for the first time I realized how absurd this was. I had hardly used the easel I so desperately wanted in Genoa. It had been little more than a decoration and an embarrassing conversation piece. Wasn't my life ambiguous enough?

The other room was much larger and of normal proportions, and with its blond furniture it was like a small version of the living room where Giorgio and I had met. It had a spacious balcony that gave onto the rain forest. A bird's nest. "I have an idea," said Giorgio. "If you don't mind sharing a bedroom, we could share the two rooms. We could put another bed in the long room and have this as a study and"—he winked—"invite some young ladies for tea." "Naughty naughty," said Mrs. Doberli, laughing. "But that would be all right with me, if you want it that way."

I was cornered. "Well, it's fine with me." And so it happened that Giorgio Cacciapuoti and I became lifelong friends, almost brothers-in-law, and that I became a French poetry addict. For a while.

Colette

It was a strange year. For the first time in my life I tasted the light, inebriating pleasures of being free and independent, although now and then I was surprised by my indifference. I had expected to be haunted by the loss of my first great love, but only in rare moments of solitude did the specter of jealousy and nostalgia roam through my nights.

I knew that I was on a path that was taking me somewhere—where, no one could know yet. I assumed that Father knew, or thought he knew, and he must have believed that I knew. I played the part of a student in economics at a university where I had not even been formally admitted. My modus vivendi with Giorgio was the only satisfactory aspect of this new rehash of previous failures. Our initial mutual sympathy grew into a solid friendship. Giorgio turned out to be a kind, even sweet companion, who regarded his roommate as a slightly mad intellectual, a charming, innocuous dreamer who needed an intermediary between him and the hard, practical, boring world, to solve the endless little contingencies that all human beings must unfortunately face.

In our beds before falling asleep, we would talk and talk about our childhoods, our loves, our ambitions, our convictions, and our doubts. If, as an only child, I had little to tell him about my family, and egocentric as I was, preferred to talk about my own problems in defining an identity for

Me in my college years

myself, Giorgio always seemed eager to talk about his mother, his two sisters, and his aunt, who ran a *pensionnat de jeunes filles* on the lake not far from Lausanne, and he proposed that I join him during the Christmas holiday. Like most young men in similar situations, he hoped his best friend would fall in love with his sister and eventually marry her. This not only would be a guarantee against the ugly possibility that some stupid, pimply, unknown stranger might enchant his beloved Colette and carry her away but would secure our friendship forever as well.

When Giorgio tore the last November page from his calendar, his excitement about our approaching vacation began to sizzle. He showed me photos of the various family members, especially of Colette, his favorites being postcard-size shots of her sitting or standing or lying on the flat dark rocks of a resort hotel on the French Riviera. With the anxiety and intensity of an Indian marriage broker afraid that the deal of a lifetime might slip through his fingers, he brought out photos of Colette in a succinct bathing suit and without the slightest sign of embarrassment pointed out her most salient features and held forth at length on her beauty, intelligence, and wit. Although at the time I still firmly believed in the objectivity of photography, I was skeptical. If Colette was all Giorgio

said that she was, why would she be standing at the door waiting for me?
Why wouldn't she have a beau?

Just when the Christmas frenzy in Zurich became almost unbearable, we left for Lausanne. Except for Cavi, which had become a home
away from home, I had never spent more than an occasional night in a
friend's house. I was excited and a little scared. What if the whole project
didn't work out and I hated every single member of Giorgio's family, what
would I do then? What was I doing here in this train, rushing to visit people I didn't really want to meet? What was this love affair with a girl I
didn't know? How was I to get out of it and take a train home to Genoa
without offending my best friend? Was Nora now sitting in a similar train
going to a similar nowhere?

At the station we were met by Giorgio's younger sister, Yolanda, and
a young woman named Natasha, who was introduced as "our Russian
guest." Yolanda looked quite different from the way I knew her from photographs. She was taller and thinner than I had expected and far more social than Giorgio had described her. I knew that she was quite deaf, but
trained as I was by my father's deafness, I had no problems talking with
her. Her long face, fair complexion, large, distant eyes, and long, loose
blond hair looked strangely familiar: they reminded me of the watercolor
illustrations of a Swedish children's book I must have owned at one time.
Yolanda was two years younger than I, the same age as Nora, but she
looked and acted like a very talkative but much younger girl. Natasha
was well into her twenties. I remember her as small and somewhat plump
in the Cacciapuoti world of giants, a quiet, soft-spoken young woman with
a hard Russian *RRRRRR,* always wrapped in large woolen shawls.

To my disappointment there was no sign of Colette when we drove
into the Cacciapuoti garden. Instead, I saw a smallish, red-haired woman
come running out of the door toward us. It was impossible to imagine her
as Giorgio's mother, and yet I knew that was who she was. Except for the
cobalt blue eyes, noticeable even at a distance, there was nothing that
even slightly resembled the features that Giorgio and Yolanda shared.
After she had embraced Giorgio, she embraced me as if she had always
known me.

We were hardly settled in the large living room when in rushed Colette. She jumped into Giorgio's lap with a shout of joy, kissed him, leaped
up again to stop motionless in front of me, and with a deeply serious expression and a melodramatic half whisper of femme fatale said, "And who
is this enchanting creature?" to which I answered with equal irony, "The
man you love, darling." "Don't mind her," said Giorgio, "*e un po' matta.*"
Then we all went upstairs, and she showed me my room.

While everything so far seemed very different from the mental images I had formed from Giorgio's descriptions, Colette was almost exactly the way I had imagined her. Completely unexpected, however, was the vigor of her presence, the extraordinary way she claimed center stage. And Giorgio had been right—she was quite stunning. But her beauty defied explanation and description. One might have said that her nose was too prominent, her stance too stiff, but no one would disagree that she was exceptionally beautiful.

At dinner I couldn't keep my eyes off her, but this was fine since during the entire meal she calmly dominated the conversation and made me feel at home. She obviously adored her brother even if she did not spare her irony whenever he expressed an opinion or a feeling. Despite his size, she treated him as if he were not quite grown up and wanted to make it clear that that was what she loved about him. But more than once during the dinner Giorgio was embarrassed by their rapid skirmishes when obviously for my benefit he had been the victim of her sharp humor. Noticing this, she would then muster all her charm to repair the momentary damage she had done and bare her love for him.

Mother Cacciapuoti did not talk much during that first dinner. She let the young have the floor, knowing with ancient instinct that her moment would come whenever she decided to claim it. After dinner we moved to the living room, where Natasha, whose position in the household was never quite clear, was rearranging the furniture. When I asked Colette what was going on, she whispered, "This is Mother's great night. We are getting a special performance in your honor." "Performance of what?" I asked, puzzled. "I don't know. Sometimes it's theater, sometimes her own personal philosophy, and sometimes poetry. Maman is quite something." Suddenly I noticed that we were speaking French. And that the guttural R which in Giorgio seemed a class affectation was in reality part of a slight French accent in the otherwise perfect Italian they all spoke.

Colette sat down on the sofa, which had been pushed against the wall, and motioned me to sit next to her. She placed Yolanda next to me on the other side. Giorgio had sunk into one of the two armchairs in the corner near the window and was reading a magazine. Mother Cacciapuoti had settled into the other armchair, directly facing us. She was turning the pages of a book; next to her, on a small table, were more books and a large silver ashtray. Natasha was fussing with a wall-bracket lamp with a small red silk shade. It was pointed in the direction of Mother C, and when it was switched on, a red glow spread over her.

No one said a word. Not having the slightest idea what was going to happen, I felt ill at ease and didn't know where to look. Was it going to be a séance? I hated any situation in which I might lose control—hypnosis, et cetera. Colette had her hand under my arm and almost imperceptibly hammered her fingers as if she were thinking a quick march. Suddenly all the lights went out except the little red lamp.

In the near dark, Mother C's hair seemed a fiery torch. "Here we go," Colette whispered in my ear. And then Mother C raised herself out of her armchair, took one slow step forward, and with a slightly timid and uncertain voice announced that she was going to recite a poem by Albert Samain, a little-known French poet, a contemporary of Baudelaire and, she thought, equally great. She took one more step forward, and now, in the middle of the room, directly in front of me, her large blue eyes fixed on mine, she began in a sure, dramatic voice to declaim what was the first poem that ever gave me cold chills from beginning to end.

> *J'ai secoué du rêve avec ma chevelure. Un long frisson me*
>   *suivant*
> *comme un bruit de feuilles dans le vent*
> *et ma beauté jetais des feux comme une armure . . .*

It was a long poem, and when the last word died in silence, I wanted to applaud but couldn't raise my hands. All I could manage was a hardly audible *"Incroyable."* I had heard poetry for the first time. Mother Cacciapuoti knew. She fell back into the armchair with a happy smile and her eyes closed. Then, after a few moments she said, with her normal voice, which suddenly seemed to come from another world, "Now I would like to read a few short poems by Samain and tell you a little about his life."

This magic evening happened more than sixty years ago. I wrote down the words of Samain's poem from memory, though memory may not serve me perfectly. I know that there are better poems in the world, but this one led me into regions of my mind and heart where I had never walked before.

Crisis

I cannot explain what motivated me to write the letter I wrote to Father less than a month after my return from Lausanne. There must have been a specific impetus for the sudden realization that my life was making no sense whatsoever. The preposterous notion that in a single year I could have mastered the entire Liceo Classico curriculum, as intended, while studying economics and constitutional law at the University of Zurich was pure folly. I should have known it when, after the second chapter of the organic chemistry book, I had "temporarily" put it aside. I should have known it when in an entire year my knowledge of Greek had gone not much further than the genitive of *anthropos*. I masterfully succeeded in avoiding all summing up, all confrontations between goals and achievements. I was living in the illusion that I was accomplishing, as if *to accomplish* were an intransitive verb.

And in a way, of course, it was true. It wasn't all time wasted: I learned many things that cannot be taught. In the long run, the discovery of French poetry was probably more important to me than three years of Greek grammar. Learning to live alone was probably more useful than two years of organic chemistry. Losing Nora and knowing a young woman like Colette had ultimately been more maturing than a course in world history. And then, I had been living. I had tasted *Rösti* and white sausage; I had danced to the music of Jack Hylton, run through the bluish highlights flickering in a woman's hair, floated in the scent of linden trees in bloom. I had seen the walls of a Bierhalle, huge as the Milan station, buckle and bend to the clinking of jugs, and I had thrown my voice to the highest Alp in Engadin . . .

The Letter, as it was called thereafter, had been as much a surprise to me when I finished writing it as it must have been to Mother and Father. For writing, as often happens, had forced me to structure the confused picture of my confused mind, torn between loyalty and self-interest, between passion and reason, between utopia and tomorrow's breakfast. The outcome was an old compromise that had been lying in wait ever since my friendship with Claude Martin, a mad Swiss cinéaste who had introduced me to the works of Viking Eggeling, René Clair, and Walter Ruttmann, and now, finally, had its short moment of triumph in the rhetoric of a proposal that, if accepted, might have changed the entire course of my life.

My proposal to Father was that I renounce the idea of preparing for a Liceo license, quit Zurich, but instead of jumping off the deep end into the uncertainties of a career as a painter, which Father would surely object to, try to enter the Centro Sperimentale di Cinematografia in Rome for their three-year course in film directing. My main argument was that while some of my many talents would be wasted if I chose a specialized profession like architecture, the combination of a great variety of interests was the main ingredient for a sucessful film director's career. Diplomatically, I thought, painting was never mentioned. A week after I had sent The Letter, I received a telegram from Father saying that he would arrive in Zurich the following morning and stay two days to "discuss situation."

From the moment we embraced each other on Platform Four of the Zurich Haubtbahnhof, I knew that everything would work out. I knew it when in a quick glance I caught Father's eye, as clear and precise as an enlarged photo of the eye in a scientific journal. I shall never forget the absolute perfection of the iris, the luminous beauty of the gray-blue rays that from the edge radiated inwards toward the deep black of the pupil. This was the way all of Father was, the clarity and sharpness of his mind, the elegance of his logic, the quiet self-assurance, his measured temper, and the sureness of his taste.

Father looked surprisingly gentle, and he relaxed as he broached the subject right after we had settled in our armchairs in the lobby of the Baur au Lac, where he was staying. What he said was in substance this: look, it is your life we are going to talk about, I came only as adviser, financier, and last but not least, because I am your father. I think I know what you really want to do, we have discussed that in the past. It will always be nagging at you. On the other hand, life often dictates its own needs, and this is why, instead of jumping into a situation like that thing in Rome, where you would have to make a three-year commitment, three of your most precious years, it would be wiser, I believe, if you took advantage of the fact that you have a comfortable place at home that would allow you to quietly think things over, and if around autumn you still feel the way you do now, go down to Rome and look the situation over. Until then, you could give some time to painting, to your friends, and perhaps do some reading and traveling.

I was astonished, and literally speechless. My feeling of relief can only be compared with the way I felt on regaining consciousness after my stomach operation a few years ago, when I suddenly awoke from the longest, most intricate, and most frightening nightmare I had ever experienced to find, looking at me from above, the healthy, smiling, reassuring faces of Nora and our granddaughter, Annie.

It was ironical that it should have been Father who made a suggestion that I had never dared consider, certain that he would violently oppose my not completing some kind of formal education, no matter what. He later explained his lack of enthusiasm for a cinematographic career. Since filmmaking requires so much capital and depends so heavily on private investors, competition at all levels of the industry was frightening.

*My father and I—
two Dutchmen
abroad*

It was only when the Gotthard Express with Father aboard had left the Zurich Bahnhof, puffing its way to Genoa, that I suddenly felt as if Father had taken all my excitement with him in his new pigskin city bag. I stood on the platform quite a long time staring at the empty tracks, wondering if it was humanly feasible to think about nothing. And then I found myself sitting at a little round table at Rumpelmayer's, facing a monumental coupe Denmark. But it was not until I woke the next morning that I was able to sum up what the decision implied and to establish priorities among things that had to be done.

I had told Father that it would probably take me a week to straighten out my affairs. I believed that. And yet the very next day I was ready to leave well before dinner. I had miraculously managed to have an improvised farewell lunch with Giorgio at the Kronenhalle, settle my position with the university, pay Mrs. Doberli, close my account with the Schweitzer Bank Verein, pack my suitcases, buy my ticket, and be ready to join Giorgio and some of our friends at the Basler Bierhalle at eight. That this had been possible was the measure of both my excitement and Swiss efficiency. In Italy, a similar enterprise would have taken two weeks.

When the taxi left me off at the Bahnhof the next morning, it had just begun snowing. Across the Station Square the veil of mist that had hung lightly in front of the gray office buildings and the cafés in the Bahnhofstrasse was now becoming an opalescent screen on which clusters of neon signs imperceptibly vanished into light puffs of yellow, green, and red. I boarded the train and found a seat, and when a slight jolt told me that we were on our way, I swiftly wiped some of the steam off the window with the side of my hand. I wanted to give the town a last look, but all I could see was a blank, white wall. I hid my face in my cupped hands, still cold and wet from the steam. The tears felt soft and soothingly warm against my skin.

I woke up when the train rushed out of the Gotthard Tunnel, down into a deep cobalt Mediterranean sky. The green trees, the neat gardens at the outskirts of small towns, the cafés, garages, stores, and parking lots of factories were smoothly floating by. It all looked surprisingly real. After Chiasso and Como some passengers began to put newspapers in their briefcases, lower suitcases from the racks, disappear into the corridor for a hasty smoke, consult railroad guides, comb their hair, or simply adjust the expressions on their faces. We were nearing Milan. As the first rows of apartment buildings zoomed by, my heart gave a thump. What if I were to get out in Milan, take a taxi to Viale Monza, and simply present myself at the door. "Is Signorina Maffi home?" "Signorina Adda or Signorina Nora?" "Signorina Nora." "Whom shall I say is calling?" "Tell her . . ." It was all very silly, of course, but why was I suddenly shivering?

Two hours later we pulled into Genoa's Stazione Principe. As a gesture of both love and defiance I hailed a carriage instead of a cab. Carriages were a bit more expensive and of course much slower. *"Via Maragliano dieci, per favore."* I hummed an old Dutch song that fitted the clappety-clonk rhythm of the horse. *"Ik heb myn wagen volgeladen . . ."* I recognized the languid late-afternoon sun, and the sudden silence as we turned the corner of the Via Venti Settembre into "our" street.

I wasted a few days calling on friends, doing some shopping, and just hanging around adjusting to the sudden shift in lifestyle, getting used to the continuous presence of my parents and finally to the idea that this time I had no excuse for not rolling up my sleeves, buying some canvases, and getting down to some serious work. From the back of my wall closet, where all my things had been stored, I pulled out my heavy paint box, weighed down by the full range of Windsor and Newton "professional quality" oil paints, of which only white, black, and blue had been touched, the bottles of turpentine and linseed oil, the wooden palette, a package with my brushes, and *Warwinds,* the only real oil painting I had ever painted.

I remembered that at one point I had talked myself into believing it would be immoral to try to make a beautiful painting about so ugly a subject as war, but soon after I began laying down a first rough sketch of the idea, it became clear to me not only that I had plunged into my painting career without the slightest knowledge of technique but that, unknowingly, I had ensnared myself in one of the thorniest problems of Art: the ambiguous relationship between means and expression, subject and form.

In the early forties Saul Steinberg brought this up when, shortly after arriving in the United States from South America, he visited us in Philadelphia for a few days. I had commissioned him to do a drawing for an account I was art-directing at the time, and he also had to draw some sheep for a magazine. Still unknown in the United States—these were the first drawings he had been asked to do—he was a bit nervous and complained that he was not able to detach himself enough from the inno-cent sweet-sheep syndrome and draw them the way he felt about sheep, which he said he hated. His drawings became more graceful and cuter with each try, until he finally concluded that it was impossible to deliber-ately make an ugly drawing.

Warwinds refuted his theory. Its surface was an ugly, greasy, slimy mess of gray-black paint, the excrement of someone possessed by the devil. The painting was so repulsive that no one in his right mind would have wanted to look at it long enough to discover a meaning or a motiva-tion. Uncertain and confused as I was, I did not have the courage to de-stroy *Warwinds* and returned it to the deepest corner of my walk-in closet. For some mysterious reason the painting disappeared, but a snap-shot of it survived the war, our intercontinental movings, and the chaos of my photo files. From time to time it surfaces, probably to remind me that messy art leaves no message.

I was now ready for a second, less ambitious beginning. And during the weeks that followed my return home, I became so deeply involved with painting, and with thinking, reading, talking, and writing about it, that I lost all sense of time, to the point of ignoring the growing evidence that spring was here and Easter was approaching.

In the windows of bars, cafés, and confectionery shops, there was a proliferation of spectacular eggs of all sizes, colors, and materials. They ran the full gamut from the enormous chocolate egg that filled an entire window of Caffè Kleinguti at the corner of Via Roma and Piazza Corvetto, which, with its colored-sugar silhouettes of the seven continents, was an obvious comment on the fragile state of our globe, to the strings of vividly colored blown chicken eggs which decorated the podium of Caffè Grand Italia, where every afternoon, in clear defiance of the Duce's order to avoid all references to British and American culture, "five o'clock tea" was served to the music of the "Wiener Women Jazz Band."

What all this extravagant Easter promotion failed to achieve was successfully performed by the particular quality of the first balmy air, suddenly rich with the scents of growth and decay that exuded from the flower and vegetable market three blocks away, on that wider stretch of the Via Venti Settembre that ran from Via Galata to Via Maragliano. It brought back rich memories of days and events that seemed to have faded away in the chills of winter: the endless checkerboard quilt of tulips, daffodils, and the reds and yellows and greens and whites that now covered all of the eastern part of Holland, the names of villages and flowers long forgotten; the *Bloemenman* with his pushcart heaped high and dense with daffodils, from which with Chaplinesque elegance he would pluck romantic bouquets for only one florin twenty-five, *meneer.* The ten little balls of yellow down, diving and bobbing in the bottle green water of the Square Marie Louise's pond in Brussels, around the great white ship of Mother Duc; the first baby turtle I ever saw, not larger than a silver dollar, fearlessly raising its hard little head to the light of a cloudless morning sky near the muddy bank of the Wissahickon Creek, right in the city of Philadelphia, Pennsylvania. And finally the empty gray beach and flat gray sea slowly gaining substance and color and motion in the rising day, not of high waves rolling in and crashing onto the stone-hard sand but of water gently nibbling at the ribbon of algae that stretches all the way from the black slate rocks of Lavagna to those of Sant'Anna, where, after having shaken the wet sand from the blanket that kept us warmly wrapped during the long, enchanted night, and from your skirt and sweater, we walked hand in hand. In silence.

"What is the matter, *Jongen?* I haven't heard a word out of you." "Mother, I was thinking that Thursday or Friday I'll go to Cavi. The last time I saw the Maffis was two years ago. Now that I'm back here, I miss them. They should be there for Easter vacation." "Couldn't you call their uncle and find out?" "Oh, I may as well just go, and if they're not there I'll spend the night at Villa Spinola."

Marry Me

I took the three o'clock local for Sestri Levante from Brignole Station, which was only a ten-minute walk from our house, and at a quarter past four I stepped down onto the platform in front of the little station of Cavi. "*Buona Pasqua, Capo,*" I shouted against the noise of the departing train as I saw the stationmaster wave his green flag. He was standing at the end of the platform, too far to hear or to recognize me. I knew that, but I felt an irrepressible need to reaffirm formally my possession of a place which in so many ways had been mine.

"Well, well," said the capo as he shook my hand. "We haven't seen you for quite some time. Where have you been? Back in America?" "Oh no! I was in Zurich studying. Tell me"—I was too anxious to engage in long conversations—"are the Maffis here?" "You didn't know? Even the *professore*! With a whole army! They're all there."

If I hadn't known that feelings, unlike images and words, cannot be retrieved from memory, I would have been shocked to discover that in my recollections I walked the few hundred feet to the Maffi villa without the slightest emotion—like an automaton. But my memory, lazy and approximative, knows that the right words will always be there with the necessary fictional support for the crude images she produces. Of course, as I neared the house my steps grew faster and somewhat unsteady, my breathing failed me, and as I climbed the steps to the entrance my heart pounded wildly.

The door to the house was closed. On the stone bench under the two giant palms sat two carabinieri in sleepy silence, and as I walked around the house toward the kitchen, I noticed that when I passed what had been described to me as Papà Maffi's waiting room there were two or three people inside. But the kitchen door was locked. Although it was close to five, no sign of life came from inside the house. I finally decided to ring the bell. I heard a venetian blind being slowly opened, and when I looked up there was a loud shriek and then someone came running down the stairs. It was Adda. We had a long embrace. *"Quanto tempo!"* Then Bruna and Mario came down. Now it was instant *festa*. We moved from the hall into the living room. "You know, Father was released and is now under house arrest here. We've been here a little over two weeks." Each one of us was eager to tell something—about Milan or school or plans or *il Papà*. It was a typical Cavi reunion.

"And Nora?" I finally dared to ask. "I believe she's in her room," said Mario. "There is also my German friend, Kathe," said Bruna. "Goffredo and Canepin are supposed to pick us up at five-thirty with their cars. We have a table at the Savoy at Santa Margherita for six o'clock. They have a good little English band." Bruna's friend Kathe entered the room. She was very large and heavy and seemed quite a few years older than any of us. Unfortunately when she heard that I spoke German she wouldn't let go of me.

Then the bell rang and the two motorized friends came in and there were more embraces. And finally, just as we were all in the hall ready to leave, Nora came slowly down the steps, her head lowered. As she passed by me she gave me a swift, furtive look and whispered, *"Ciao."* "God," I thought, "how well I know you," as a shiver ran up my spine. With difficulty I too managed to say *"Ciao."* Luckily the embarrassing exchange was lost in the general happy noise.

Adda and Nora boarded Goffredo's coupé, Bruna, Kathe, and I climbed in Canepin's convertible, and off we drove to Santa Margherita. When we entered the large, brightly lit gala room of the Savoy there were two more old friends waiting for us, and more celebratory embraces. Nora was now radiant and beautiful.

We had two tables. Nora was sitting, her back toward me, at the other. Kathe, who was at my right, kept on talking German, but I could give only the vaguest answers to her questions. From the corner behind me came the first notes of a tune, imported from the States, that was popular at the time: "You Are My Lucky Star." Here and there couples stood up and began dancing. No one from our group did—they all seemed to be talking at the same time, involved in the excitement of this first reunion after the dreary winter months.

And then it happened. Suddenly emptied of will and mind, weak on my legs, I stood in front of Nora and, hardly audible, I must have mumbled something like "Let's dance." She rose from her chair, came toward me, I put my arm around her, and we danced. We had always been a good dance pair, naturally coordinated. We had circled the floor without uttering a single word when I put my lips near her ear and whispered, "Will you marry me?" Nora straightened, looked me quickly in the eyes, and without hesitation, echoing the simplicity of my question, said, "Yes." Then she leaned her head against my shoulder, and so we danced until the music ended, when, emotionally exhausted, we both plunged into the pillows of our white wicker armchairs, absurdly alone.

We were married by the mayor of Lavagna on December 23. The year was 1931. Together, as Nora used to say, we were forty years old.

part two
1931–1948

The day of our wedding, after the festive luncheon prepared by Annetta, the long-time Maffi cook, starting with the traditional Annetta-made ravioli and ending with a generous shower of rice at the Cavi station, we left for Florence on the Rome Express. It was a beautiful but cold winter day. The sky was dark blue, and a pearly gray Mediterranean lay shimmering like a sheet of frosted glass beyond the sliding landscape. We looked and felt like two mannequins that had just escaped from a show window of the Rinascente. From my haircut to Nora's shoes everything was brand new. And so were we.

Our arrival at the three-star Hotel Baglioni turned out to be an embarrassing event. After a hushed conversation with the splendidly uniformed doorman, the clerk at the reception desk called his supervisor, who called the director, who asked for our passports, gave us a critical going-over, and finally, after another consultation, told the "boy" to take our suitcases and show us to our room. For fear of Russian agents, subversive terrorists, and offenders of the *"buon costume,"* the Fascists had forced hotels to exercise a rigorous control over their guests. Those two Italian teenagers with their immaculate Dutch passports fresh from the press and their clothes fresh from the store racks surely could have been anything but run-of-the-mill foreign tourists.

Like movie stars, we had dinner brought to our room, and like real newlyweds we didn't venture out until late afternoon the following day. While waiting for Nora in the lobby, I discovered a decorative map of Italy that was frescoed on one of the walls, and the name Viterbo—halfway between Florence and Rome—suddenly reverberated in my mind. Wasn't it in Viterbo that Nora's cousin Bruno was incarcerated? Bruno had been arrested in Milan in April 1931 for having hidden a suitcase full of subversive leaflets in his room, and after a much publicized trial by the Tribunale Speciale, he was sentenced to two years' detention. When Nora, stunning, finally came down the wide marble steps, I had my plan ready. "How about going to Viterbo tomorrow to see Bruno?"

There was no train to Viterbo. At the desk I was told that the only way to reach the town was to take the Rome local to Orte and from there a taxi to Viterbo. And that is what we did.

At Orte there was no taxi in sight, but the stationmaster, apparently intrigued by the elegant pair of teenagers, phoned for one, and a rickety old Lancia eventually pulled up in front of the station. The driver, who looked more like a pig farmer than a taxi chauffeur, asked if we would mind giving his brother a lift. We didn't, of course. The man then brought his cupped hands to his mouth, and no sooner had he shouted "Daniele!" than a gray-bearded Franciscan monk, round like a robin in winter, came running toward us, his brown robe flying behind him. Puffing and snorting, he climbed into the seat next to the driver, and settling down with a long, deep sigh, he turned around to face us, smiled, and said all in one breath, "May the good Jesus bless you; you wouldn't have a cigarette for a poor monk, would you?"

An hour later we rang the bell of the Viterbo jail, an enormous, windowless building, part of an ancient abbey. Only after we had tried three or four times and banged on the door did a grumpy voice ask what we wanted. When we told him, the door opened and a uniformed guard let us in. "The *permesso?*" he asked, holding out his hand. When I told him that we had no permit, that we were passing by on our honeymoon and wanted to visit our cousin, he looked at us as if we had just landed in a spaceship. "You have to present a request on a one-hundred-lire official request form," he said, "mail it to the Ministry of Justice in Rome with the necessary information pertaining to you and your cousin and the reasons for your request. You will then, if accepted, be notified by the superintendent of the Viterbo jail if and when, within the usual temporal limitations, you will be granted a ten-minute visit on the specified day and hour."

As we listened our hearts sank, and Nora pulled a handkerchief from her bag and began to cry. The man gave her an embarrassed look and said, "Wait. I'll be right back." He returned five minutes later with a triumphant smile. "I talked with the superintendent. You can see the *professore* at two o'clock." Despite everything, Italy was not Germany.

At two we were at the door of the jail. This time the guard greeted us as old friends. "Everything has been arranged," he said as he guided us proudly to a small waiting room. "You'll have half an hour."

From where we were sitting we could see down a long, wide corridor to a large door at the end. We presumed that Bruno would come from there, and we found ourselves staring anxiously in that direction. A minute? Ten minutes? Time had shifted gears. Then suddenly the door

Nora and I, 1931

opened, and coming toward us, arm in arm, there they were: Bruno, dressed in gray-striped prison pajamas, two sizes too large, his head shaved to zero, and a broadly smiling guard. "Here he is, our beloved *professore*!" said the guard.

With the big round clock above us ticking away, we talked and talked. Bruno surprised us with his accounts of jail. "My life isn't all that different from the one I lead in town," he said. "I manage to get the books I need. I'll probably be able to finish my thesis, and besides," he added, "there are several other *politici* here besides me. We've organized a sort of miniuniversity in which each of us teaches what he knows best. I have finally decided to study Russian. The days are too short for it all."

No one could imagine what a happy half hour it was. Our laughter must have echoed through the corridors, and occasionally a guard looked in to see what was going on. After forty minutes or so the guard who had brought Bruno returned to take him to his cell. Our farewell was as joyous as our meeting. "Time will fly," we said, full of optimistic conviction as we held each other in a long embrace. Outside, the Lancia was waiting for us. "What about your brother?" I asked. "Oh," said the driver, smiling, "he'll find his way back."

"You know," said Nora as we were nearing Orte, "here is where it all began," and seeing my puzzled look, she added with a sigh, "the March on Rome." I suddenly felt a sense of emptiness in my stomach, a vague nausea. I was still a foreigner, a transient. An outsider.

The first months after our wedding would have been idyllic had it not been for the promise that Papà Maffi had extorted from me when I had asked for his daughter's hand: the promise that I would get myself a "real" job. He must have had anxieties about the boy who was courting his daughter, whom he seldom saw wearing more than swimming trunks. He never explained exactly what he meant by a job, and I'm sure his ideas were more confused than mine, but I had accepted his condition as a temporary transition from celibacy to the career of a freelance artist.

Although Papà Maffi came from modest origins, where money had always been the direct counterpart of work done or things made—like bread or clogs—he himself had never had to deal with the vulgarities of real money. From school through college his studies had been financed by scholarships and the help of his older brothers, and after his marriage to Milly Baldini, then a nurse at the sanatorium he had founded, the bills were paid by the administrators, lawyers, and bankers. Totally involved as he was with his profession and in the affairs of the Communist party, he could hardly have been expected to understand how, day after day, month after month, a healthy young man could squander his time on the beach, alone or in the company of girls, talking about abstract art, cinema, or American dance music.

What Papà meant by a "real" job, I believe, was one that would get you out of the house in the morning and back for dinner, and pay for the groceries. The inner workings of a wealthy Protestant bourgeois family like the Baldinis, whose dealings with money were always mysteriously indirect, were incomprehensible to him. It was his wife, Milly, in fact, who dealt with financial matters.

Strongly recommended by my father's aide, Boni, I had no problem getting a job at the Società Foltzer, an Italian petroleum concern with headquarters in Genoa, at eight hundred lire a month—a "real" salary then, and a substantial sum for a beginner whose mind, most of the time, was on leave of absence on some other continent. All I remember of the "real" job during the five months I worked as assistant cashier at the Foltzer headquarters are the mechanical adding machine with its long, rotating mahogany handle, a medieval contraption that for each entry made the triumphant noise of a coffee grinder, and the three enormous books in which I had to register all incoming payments with a fine calligrapher's pen.

Not only was 1932 the first year of my marriage, the year of my first real job, my first abstract paintings, and my discovery of Beethoven's String Quartet opus 135 but it was also the year when Claude Martin, my Swiss friend and mentor, whom I hadn't seen since 1928, reappeared. Claude was a sensitive and well-informed observer of the rapidly changing art scene. A born activist, he was usually to be found on the side of the rebels threatening to shake up the status quo. A brilliant and daring polemicist with a prodigious wealth of information at his fingertips, he made me feel like a provincial dabbler. Yet he was respectful of my enthusiasm and curiosity and enjoyed his role as mentor.

When Claude showed up at our apartment a few months after Nora and I were married, his passion was the cinema—he had seen every avant-garde film ever made and had met many of the people who were engaged in the field in Paris and Berlin. From him I learned enough about the work of Ruttmann, Eggeling, and Len Lye, and enough cine-slang to be able to hold my own in endless café discussions and to write a series of four articles on the German avant-garde film for the *Giornale di Genova* without ever having seen a single one of the great films Claude talked about. But at Foltzer, hidden behind my gargantuan bookkeeping volumes, I wrote surreal film treatments on the backs of old checks in a handwriting smaller than my present Parkinson's script. I felt that I had finally found my medium, and totally forgetting that I was supposed to be a painter, a student of economics, and last but not least a married man who soon would be a father, whenever I could I tried to gather information on Rome's Centro Sperimentale di Cinematografia, with the conviction that sooner or later fate and passion would lead me to it.

But fate was no amateur gambler. Having invested heavily in my future as a painter, she manipulated circumstances in such a clever way that one fine day Claude brought Marinetti, "the father of futurism," to our apartment to show him my paintings. I remember his smug I-told-you-so smile when Marinetti exclaimed, "But this young man is a great futurist!" Marinetti must have meant what he said, for a few days later I received an invitation to show six of my paintings in an exhibition of *"aeropittura"* in Savona, a picturesque industrial town on the coast west of Genoa, near Albisola, where occasionally I still make my ceramics.

At the official opening of the exhibition, Marinetti read some of his new "aeropoems" and explained that our perception of the world had changed radically since man had taken flight. He described me as the typical young artist determined to fight for the new vision, and finally introduced me as an *"aeropittore."* For me, who had never been in an airplane, and who panicked at the mere idea of standing on a kitchen chair, it was a moment of great embarrassment.

Briefly, I thought of arguing my case for pure abstraction and the language of cinematography, but I resisted the temptation. I had great re-

A gathering of futurists. The central figure with bow tie and mustache is Fillippo Tommaso Marinetti. I'm fourth to the left of him.

spect for Marinetti's genius as a provocateur, promoter, and poet. For at least two years I had been active with the young futurist groups in Turin and Genoa; Fillia, one of the leading futurist painters, had become a close friend. To argue would only point to my own inconsistencies. What had attracted me to the futurist cause had been not my enthusiasm for painting clouds but rather my sharing its disdain for the bourgeois mentality. To me, to be a Futurist meant simply to be committed to the permanent freedom to reinvent.

After a noisy dinner offered by the Savona township, we, the exhibiting artists, were asked to reconvene in the hall of the hotel where Marinetti was lodging, to meet with him to discuss some urgent problems that concerned our German colleagues. That very afternoon Marinetti had received a telegram from Mies van der Rohe, then director of the Bauhaus in Weimar, informing him that the Nazis had decided to close down the Bauhaus and asking us to express publicly our dismay and our solidarity. After an emotional discussion, we agreed to offer hospitality to a Bauhaus colleague, hoping secretly that Klee, Kandinsky, or Schlemmer might come to stay with us in Cavi, but unfortunately no one in our group ever received an answer to our invitation.

Mannie

The baby was expected around the middle of November, but although we had known this all along, we panicked when we suddenly discovered that the event was only a week away. It was then my parents suggested that since the maternity clinic was within walking distance of Via Maragliano, we move in with them for a few days. And a good thing it was that we did, because as the due date approached I became a nervous wreck, incapable of making the simplest decisions. Bruna joined us a few days later.

To avoid risking an emergency, Nora had arranged that she and Mother would sleep at the clinic from the tenth on. And so during that time the two women would leave home after dinner with their little suitcase, only to return the next morning in general hilarity. I plunged into one of my typical reactions to an impending crisis, sleeping almost uninterruptedly for two entire days, until right on the predicted date I was awakened by a telephone call from Mother, who with a shaky voice informed us that Nora was in labor and that the baby could be born at any moment. Father, Bruna, and I threw ourselves into a taxi and in a few minutes were at the clinic, where a nun led us to a waiting room. There she told us to be patient, that all was going well, and that it would be a question of an hour or so, not more. We sat awkwardly in the small armchairs, motionless and in heavy silence, until about half an hour later the door was vigorously yanked open and a nurse stood smiling before us, announcing that a beautiful, healthy little boy had been born, and that the father could come up with her. We jumped to our feet, and I automatically stepped back to let Father go up.

Any dreams and plans we might have made for the near and distant future vanished with Mannie's arrival in our lives. And when Father announced a few months later that the Atlantic Refining Company had been sold and that having refused their offer of a job in Jakarta, he and Mother had decided to go and live in Amsterdam, I clearly saw that our unstable little world was near collapse. Nora and I realized that we had passively slipped into a fragile situation with no future of substance in sight. But unable to take courageous, dramatic steps toward a drastic change, and with the arrival of summer and the temptations of our sheltered life on the warm beach of Cavi, the future was temporarily shelved. And for the moment I decided—once again—to give all my time to painting, and I resigned from Foltzer.

Like many of its predecessors, this resolution vanished in the diversions of an easy, lazy summer season, with Mannie pampered by a horde of real and improvised aunts and nannies and Nora, smooth, dark skinned, and serene, until one day the pang of guilt and restlessness caught up with me. For lack of other ideas I arrived at the easy solution that thousands of confused and discouraged young men had invented before me; *coûte que coûte,* I would finish work for a university degree and then we would see. This was the one time I would surely have fulfilled my promises had it not been for unforeseen pressures from unexpected quarters.

From Amsterdam came ecstatic letters about the cozy two-floor apartment my parents had finally rented, after a three-month stay at the American Hotel. Father held forth about the modern architecture in the part of town where they were now living, while mother waved the Vondelpark flag and raved about the concerts at the Concertgebouw nearby and casually mentioned the Amsterdam Film Society. Little by little, I began to fantasize that perhaps emigrating to Holland would give us a unique opportunity to start from scratch and, in a totally new environment and new circumstances, reinvent our lives.

It was one of those ideas that from an occasional appearance develops imperceptibly into a permanent guest, and in the spring of the next year we began preparing for our exodus. At the same time, I organized a study program which would make it possible for me to get a university degree without going to classes. Toward the end of August 1933, we left for our Dutch adventure.

Amsterdam

The Hacquartstraat was situated in the brand-new housing development Amsterdam South, which stretched from the back of the concert hall all the way to the outlying polders. That entire section of Amsterdam was a veritable collection of modern row-housing projects designed by young Dutch architects. Still today, after sixty years, it looks new and civilized.

The first weeks I was enchanted. The large windows, the careful brickwork, the polished brass knobs, the spotless sidewalks, the long white aprons of the housekeepers, the fishmongers in their wooden clogs, even the long-haired caterpillars on the linden trees . . . they were all there, as if waiting for my return. On long walks, pushing Mannie's carriage, I tried to make Nora live the vibrations of my early youth. I showed her my room, still towering over the nearby houses, the Vondel School, the museums, and of course Natura, my favorite nature store. And often in the evening I would take care of Mannie while Mother and Nora went to a concert, an occasion for Father and me to have one of those mad, very fast chess games which for both of us always ended in a severe headache. But once the excitement of rediscovering my beloved city and being a guide to Nora began to wane, the old problem reemerged: what now? I tried to study, but I felt displaced in the totally Dutch environment. Italian seemed as remote as Sanskrit.

Then one evening Alfred Beffie, a nephew of Oom Elie, came by on a courtesy visit. An energetic young man with no particular qualifications or talents, he had an air of accomplishment and inevitability about him which explained his rapid success with a stationery-supply business he had recently acquired. Having begun with seven salesmen on his payroll for North Holland and Brabant, he now, only six months later, had twelve, who covered the entire Dutch territory. Before the evening was over there were thirteen.

I was now a traveling salesman. It said so on my calling card. Every morning at around seven-thirty you could see me standing in the Central Station, my eyes closed, the black-leather sample case between my legs, waiting for the train that would carry me to some small town with an unpronounceable name. There I would visit the two or three stationery stores, patiently wait until there were no customers, engage the owners in conversation, and at the strategic moment open my sample case to display the latest in pencils, fountain pens, desk sets, and whatever novelties Alfred had managed to import from China or Japan or some underdeveloped country. I would show the items, slowly take out my notebook, and wait for the order. Sometimes I managed to have an interesting conversation that might end with a cup of coffee, but generally the people I met were curt, suspicious, and narrow-minded.

Occasionally at some local station I would enter into conversation with a colleague, and playing the part of a real traveling salesman, I would invent shocking gossip about the customers we shared. I would surely have become a pro if one lucky day someone hadn't asked me what my military status was. One thing led to another, and I discovered that if I stayed in Holland for another two weeks, I would be drafted into the Dutch army. That did it. Thirteen days later I was back on a train to Milan, leaving Nora and baby Mannie behind in Amsterdam.

Milan

With my profession still undefined, and our living whereabouts makeshift and temporary, our lives followed the tortuous road of improvisation and experimentation. My memory of this time is like a futurist painting, a tangle of intersecting fragments of faces, objects, landscapes, buildings, and words that refuse to be reassembled into a comprehensible image. Against the backdrop of a Europe in turmoil, assaulted by the folly and fury of new ideologies nurtured in anger, the arts were frantically probing the new frontiers and the new alliances which our elders had envisaged and explored but barely exploited.

Although I missed Nora and Mannie, it was exciting to be in Milan, which despite the rhetoric of Fascism was one of the most energetic outposts of the European avant-garde. Everywhere I went I met people, young and old, who knew how to keep the embers of freedom burning. One could be sure to find an improvised gathering of artists and intellectuals every evening after nine at the Caffè Savini, the most fashionable of the many cafés in the Galleria Vittorio Emanuele, the high-domed, cross-shaped shopping arcade that still today is the center of the city. They were painters, sculptors, architects, poets, writers, all congregating for no other apparent reason than the pleasure of being among kindred souls and joining in conversations and discussions that only they could understand and be passionate about. Most of them lived in Milan, but there were always one or two who had just arrived from the most diverse places in Italy and from other countries. Some of us, and I should be counted among them, came almost every evening. The waiter knew us by name. While the conversations were mostly in Italian, there were always a few, huddled in a corner, who spoke German or French. In those days English was seldom heard.

Shortly after my arrival in Milan in 1934, I was befriended by Edoardo Persico, editor of *Casabella,* an architectural monthly of great prestige. Persico was a brilliant and fascinating personage, enormously gifted with both words and images. He not only edited *Casabella* single-handed but was able to maintain active contact with the architects of the free world, whose work he would publish and discuss despite the protests of the ruling party. It was he who gave me my first writing assignments, and little by little he became my friend, mentor, and moral reference.

Persico's anti-Fascist internationalism must have been known and carefully watched if not by the local authorities then by OVRA, the Fascist secret police. It was easy to find proof that with the excuse of dealing with worldwide news about architecture, the magazine abounded with obvious innuendos to remind its readers that a free world was the only world where the arts could flourish. When I handed Persico my first article for *Casabella,* he read it and after a long, painful silence said, "It's fine, but you should always end with an important upswing word like 'freedom' or 'peace' or 'humanity' or 'democracy.'" Persico believed in the power of words. After all he was an editor, a Neapolitan, and a Catholic.

Edoardo Persico died in 1936 of a heart attack; he was not yet forty years old. I remember standing next to his casket on the sidewalk that circles Milan's immense Municipal Cemetery. There were four or five of us. I don't remember what had happened or why we were waiting there. I didn't cry, but I felt tragically, desperately alone. I couldn't find words important enough to close this chapter of my life.

To say that so far as I was concerned my Milan years were my university is not just a daring metaphor. This personal institute of higher learning that had its headquarters around a small table at the Caffè Savini may not have had the spacious auditoriums of Harvard or UCLA, or the glamour, but the intellectual standards of the faculty were the highest to be found in Italy, with some of the most prestigious names in Italian literature, philosophy, and the arts—an intense and varied group of artists and intellectuals who could be expected to hold forth with passion on the latest, most controversial developments. The group—my faculty and friends—who could be expected to show up on most evenings at the Caffè Savini included the poets Leonardo Sinisgalli, Alfonso Gatto, Raffaele Carrieri, and even the Nobel Prize winner Salvatore Quasimodo; the painters Domenico Cantatore, Renato Birolli, Aligi Sassu, and when in town, Renato Guttuso; and the sculptors Marino Marini and Lucio Fontana, who became famous for tearing and punching holes in his canvases; as well as a host of art collectors, *appassionatos,* and historian-enthusiasts.

It was during one of the routine evening gatherings at the Savini that I met Walter Cohrssen, a Jewish fugitive from the Hitler regime. Freshly arrived from Berlin, he knew only enough Italian to order a cup of coffee, and he looked desperately lost in the storm of Italian words that swept through the terrace of the Savini. I was the only one among those present who spoke German, and it was not long before we found ourselves engaged in conversation. He expressed his surprise at how much freedom was tolerated by Italy's Fascist regime compared with Germany, where no one would dare to talk freely in a gathering of more than three or four people, certain that one of them would be a Nazi informer. He gave me a long, detailed explanation of the origins of his name and told me that he had recently graduated from the Berlin Academy of Music as a composer and conductor but had earned his living as an industrial photographer. His parents lived in the Rhineland and like so many German Jews were determined to remain in the Fatherland under the illusion that, as good, patriotic citizens, they would surely not be persecuted. Besides, he confided, his sister had a relationship with a minor *Gauleiter,* who would see to it that nothing happened to her family.

Walter was a few years older than I. He had a fine, spiritual face with large, light blue eyes, a shy, gentle smile, and the pedantic mannerisms of a schoolteacher. Later, on our way to the pensione where I was staying, Walter told me more about his difficult predicament as a penniless newcomer in Italy without knowledge of the language and practicing a profession that offered little more gratification than the pleasure of musical small talk. We parted with a promise to meet the next day, but when I was alone in my room, although I had the strong feeling of having found a friend, the prospect of meeting him again gave me a slight sense of anguish. I liked Walter and found him interesting, but there was an air of joylessness about him; he was like someone who is constantly afraid of being punished simply for being who he is.

Suddenly my mind cleared and I recalled that Walter had told me that he had done photographs for an architectural magazine in Berlin and that he had a camera with a perspective correction lens. Perhaps, I thought, we could talk Persico into having him take photographs for the magazine and for the architects I had met there. I knew that Persico trusted my judgment and taste, and although my knowledge of architecture was improvised and intuitive, I was confident that I could direct a good technician, which Walter probably was, to take pictures that, like appropriate adjectives, would define the characteristic elements of a building. Certain that I had solved the survival problem for both of us, I envisioned the design of our stationery and calling cards: Lionni and Cohrssen, architectural photography. I got up and made some sketches; I couldn't wait for our next day's meeting. This was the beginning of a strange, difficult, often infuriating partnership, and yet a devoted friendship, which, with several long intervals, was to last until Walter's death in 1978.

Walter's moods were unpredictable. Only when the subject of conversation was music could one expect from him the liveliness, enthusiasm, and commitment that artists usually bring to their discussions. He was eloquent then, and happy to fill in the facts of music history with spicy personal anecdotes stored in his prodigious memory. His comments on the work of composers were often illustrated by relevant phrases or even entire pages, which he would hum in perfect pitch or quote sketchily on the piano. When I recognized them, as sometimes happened, we would hum together, and in the case of opera we would choose roles and sing out loud. Those were moments of singular joy; they kept our difficult friendship, often on the verge of collapse, alive. In those inspired moments Walter exuded an unexpected warmth and charm. We shared the same passion for Beethoven and Schubert symphonies, trios, and quartets, and all of Mozart and Bach. But the first time I mentioned the Brahms Violin Concerto I so loved, Walter looked at me disapprovingly. "You like that trash?" When we listened to music and I wondered if what we were hearing was Brahms or Beethoven, Walter would say, "You see, if you are in doubt you can be sure it is Brahms." This gave me a new way of recognizing Brahms, but little by little, fascinated by Walter's further elaborations on Brahms's weaknesses, I too began to hunt for phrases that seemed to be lifted verbatim from Beethoven. "You are right," I would say, proud to have learned a professional secret, "it is sheer imitation, it has no backbone, it swerves around in thin air. This is flaccid music." Whenever possible I avoided listening to Brahms. The Brahms records I owned ended up in the garbage. I now belonged to the elite of music lovers.

This distinction would have lasted my entire life had it not been for an evening in the square of Cennina, a quaint little hilltop village in Tuscany, where a small group of graduate students of the Siena Music Conservatory were giving a chamber music recital. It was a glorious night in the summer of 1978. The silence was almost total, the stars shivered in a velvet black immensity, the young performers sat tensely waiting with their bows suspended in air. With a nod from the first violinist, the music took flight—pure, glorious, vibrantly alive—and as the space of the music slowly filled with astonishing interlaced variations that reminded me of Beethoven's last quartets, tears sprang to my eyes. Nora, next to me, was holding our only program. "What is it?" I whispered in her ear. "Brahms." Then and there it was as if I woke from a sleep of decades. When the last notes had been played and the audience rose for a standing ovation, I found myself shouting, "Bravo! Bravo!"

Le Tre Vacche was our private name for the café on the corner of Piazza Piola owned by three hefty spinster sisters. The main attraction was a French billiard table. It was there, I believe, that I met Saul Steinberg, who was then an architecture student at Milan University. Neither Saul nor I was particularly gifted at a game that requires daily practice, but we treasured our amateur standing because what we lacked in skill we made up for by taking wild chances. In fact, when for old times' sake after ten or fifteen years we would once more meet for a game of billiards, we would take up exactly where we had left off. Throughout our lives our scores have remained virtually unchanged.

Billiards were not the only attraction of the Tre Vacche. Opposite the café was the building that housed the offices of *Le Grandi Firme,*

Pittigrini's erotic scandal magazine, where Cesare Zavattini was assistant editor. Often, thoroughly disgusted with our lack of progress at our game, we would walk over and drag Za out to join us for a redeeming espresso.

While Saul and I were the same age, twenty-four, Zavattini was ten years older. But he seemed even older than that. He looked and moved like a tough Po Valley farmer, and he dressed like one. The frayed tweed suits he wore were two sizes too small for him and always in bad need of repair and pressing. He was stocky, and his head was large, but if I were to paint him from memory I would make it a smaller head, a slightly smaller version of his body, for that is the way I remember him.

He talked with the greasy accent of the dialect that is spoken in the countryside near Mantua, where he came from. He did not stutter, but at the beginning of each sentence or short paragraph, like a carpenter who makes three or four trial swipes in the air with his hammer before the actual blow on the nail, he would repeat the first syllable a few times with an anguished grimace on his face, as if the thinking process was physically painful. But then, once started, with a profusion of *non è vero* and *vero,* the originality of the ideas, the brilliance with which they were expressed, the fine humor, and the boundless inventiveness would leave his audience speechless.

Za was always in a great hectic rush, for editorial jobs paid very little, and his four children and their mother and relatives of both families, who on their Milan outings would sleep on cots in the corridor of the Zavattini apartment, all made for a lively and chaotic household requiring a steady income out of reach for most Italian intellectuals. So in addition to his editorial work, he wrote stories and books and film treatments and did odd jobs for several publishers.

Always excited, enthusiastic, and exhausted but never discouraged, he also kept a lover who lived in Monza, a crowded workers' suburb of Milan. He had only one hour for lunch, but no matter what the weather was, he would rush out of the building at noon sharp, grab a sandwich at the Tre Vacche, jump on his motorcycle, race to Monza while eating his sandwich, pay his respects, and be back at his desk an hour after he had left. No one who knew him well was surprised when he became, some years later, the great innovator of the Italian cinema as ideologist and above all as the mind behind Vittorio De Sica's films.

One day after Walter and I had announced our joint venture as industrial photographers, the architect Gian Carlo Palanti asked me to photograph an apartment building he had designed that was about to be completed. This was when I saw our apartment for the first time.

Number 23 Via Pacini, near the university, was the most aggressively modern building in Milan. The facade was a white concrete rectangle of twelve balconies, six rows of two, inserted deeply into a frame of blue tiles. I was excited when I first saw the building almost finished and free from the wooden scaffolding but still encrusted with smudges of plaster and concrete and still lacking glass in the windows. In the midst of its typical Milanese heavy-handed middle-class neighborhood there was something virginal and playful about it. A child-building brought home from school. I reserved one of the apartments on the fourth floor and started renting procedures, but Palanti told me it would be at least three months before a certificate of occupancy could be expected.

In the meantime, since we had all our belongings in my parents' apartment in Amsterdam, where life was pleasant and comfortable, Nora had decided to sit out the winter there with Mannie—the move back to Italy would be easier in the spring. And since the photography business was not flourishing, I went to Cavi to prepare for my first-year exams at

Number 23 Via Pacini, Milan

the Scuola Superiore di Commercio in June. I passed economics, economic geography, civil law, public law, and English. Although I still could not identify myself as a potential accountant or business manager, I must confess that it felt good for once to find myself in a normal situation. Was I on my way to becoming a "real" person?

Two years after our marriage we were summoned by Nora's uncle Rezia—a civic engineer and notary and a close friend of the Baldini family, whose estate he managed—to discuss Nora's part of her mother's inheritance. Now that all three sisters were married, he felt there was not much sense in considering the inheritance as one estate with an income to be divided at the end of each year in four equal parts for them and their brother. Although he would continue to advise and help us, he thought the time had come for us to assume full responsibility for our investments.

Neither Nora nor I had the slightest idea what to suggest. Ever since Nora had come of age she had received a monthly check from Zio Rezia—it was what had kept us going even during the periods when I was not earning a centesimo. Perhaps from a sense of guilt toward her mother, who had died when Nora was twelve, perhaps through fear or laziness, or even because the world of finances did not exactly enjoy our sympathy, we had simply ignored the sources of an income that arrived punctually each month, like a miracle.

But when we heard that Uncle Guido Baldini had decided to sell the hilly terrain adjacent to his villa's garden in Cavi, a splendid location that could easily be divided into lots of an acre or so, all with a full view of the sea, I suddenly felt an irresistible impulse to try my hand at designing a group of small houses. Because of the articles I had written for *Casabella* and my involvement and friendship with the Milan architects, I considered myself an active propagandist in the cause of the modern movement. And besides, hadn't Frank Lloyd Wright and Corbu practiced without a degree? Out of a dark corner of my memory Uncle Piet's drawing board appeared, with its four constellations of pinholes at the corners. I could smell and feel it as I drew the first rough sketches, and soon six rectangular boxes scattered among the pine trees made their appearance on every empty square inch of paper in the house. In a frenzy I got out all my back issues of *Casabella* and *Domus* and read the advertisements for roofing materials, floors, doors and windows, venetian blinds, bathroom appliances, and kitchen equipment. I took measurements of the terrain and made an approximate scale model of it out of crumpled newspaper and plaster of Paris, and I had meetings with Uncle Rezia, who was going to make working drawings to be approved by the town architect. I was playing again—full scale. By spring of the following year, the six small villas— three for Nora and three for Bruna, who had joined in the venture—were ready for occupancy. They were so severely "modern movement" that in the village they called them the chicken coops.

In the fall I took formal possession of the Milan apartment, and I moved in a few weeks later, when the furniture from Amsterdam arrived. As Walter was both homeless and penniless, I suggested that as long as Nora and Mannie remained in Cavi, he could stay with me. I was only too happy to have someone to help me, and we also had a place to develop films. As a photographer Walter turned out to be uncompromising, pedantic, and painstakingly slow. On the few jobs we were commissioned to do, I had to stand around for hours waiting for him to adjust his lenses and the lights, measure the distances, move the camera, read and check light meters. By the time he was ready to shoot, I had forgotten why we were taking that particular angle or detail, and the pictures we produced were technically perfect but dead.

L & C did not survive our first clashes, and our ménage only lasted a few months, until one day Walter's fiancée, Carla, arrived from Germany. Carla was of a North German Christian family, and had the German police known of her relationship with a Jew, the consequences would have been tragic for both of them. That was the reason, Walter explained, why he had never mentioned her to me, and why she may have seemed secretive in her behavior. Sometimes she would leave for a few days without telling us where she was going. Her presence, somewhat austere and motherly, put a whole new light on Walter and on our friendship. I admired Carla, but often she made me feel a little embarrassed, as if I were the difficult, demanding guest in my own house. When one day Walter and Carla moved to another temporary secret hideout, much as I hated losing the good sides of Walter's nature—his sense of humor, his intelligence, and above all his knowledge of music—the pleasure of entering into full possession of my apartment was deeply felt, and my gut reaction was the typical "never again." But when Nora's cousin Bruno, who had recently been released after having served his two-year jail sentence in Viterbo, asked me if he could stay with me until Nora came, I was delighted. To be with Bruno was quite a different proposition. We had become close friends over more years than seemed possible for two men as young as we were. The months that followed were some of the happiest I remember.

*The chicken
coops of Cavi*

• • •

It was through Persico that I met Dino Villani, the advertising director of Motta, the most important confectionery in Italy, whose panettone,
the traditional Milanese Christmas bread, was famous throughout the
world, partly through Motta's magnificent posters. And a few months
later Villani offered me what I would call my first real "real job." As his assistant, I had the opportunity to meet many of the designers and illustra-
tors who in the early postwar years would astonish the world with the
"Italian miracle," in which design played such an important role. One of
my first recollections of the job is working with Cassandre on the new
poster for Motta's Colomba Pasquale. I remember witnessing the artist's
arrival at the Motta plant in his Rolls-Royce preceded by a taxi. He explained to me that when he arrived at the outskirts of a city, he always
had a cab guide him to his destination.

At Motta, I was directly responsible for window displays of the
Motta stores and cafés and for its impressive pavilion at Milan's annual
fair. When I began working with Villani, the deadline for having the pavilion ready was nearing, and still no decision had been taken as to whether
a new one was going to be built or the old one refurbished with minor
changes. When this characteristically Italian crisis exploded, Cavaliere
Motta, the proprietor of the firm, asked me in person for ideas. I suggested
exploiting our problem by leaving the pavilion as it was—having a dozen
or so realistic, life-size mannequins made, wearing overalls, and setting
them up here and there throughout the pavilion in working poses—
sawing, hammering, and painting on stepladders of various lengths.
When the fair opened, the "unfinished" Motta pavilion was finished. It
was a huge success and the most photographed structure of the fair.
"Fine," I thought in a complacent moment, "but if it isn't graphic design and it isn't architecture, and it surely isn't Art with a capital *A,*
what is it?"

One early morning in May 1935, I was jolted out of my sleep by the arrival of Gianna, the youngest daughter of neighbors of Bruno's. "You have
to leave Milan immediately," she said. "Bruno has been arrested. They are
searching the apartment. There are policemen and OVRA agents all over
the place asking people questions, checking their papers, and taking photos of whoever enters the courtyard. They'll come for you next. You'd better beat it while you can." After Gianna left, I sat down at the kitchen
table to think.

I eliminated the scenario of a dramatic flight, which, whatever the accusation, would mean an unequivocal admission of guilt. The remaining options were: (1) return to bed as if nothing had happened and await developments; (2) phone Zio Fabio, Bruno's father, and with any banal pretext ask him to let me talk to Bruno; (3) wait a while and if nothing happened, get dressed, go out, and see if I could locate Birolli, an artist friend, and ask him for advice; (4) trust the power of my Dutch passport, walk over to Via Bronzetti, and naively ask the police and then Zio Fabio what had happened.

This last option seemed to be the most natural, and that is what I decided to do. I calmly dressed and walked toward Via Bronzetti. When I got to Number 37, I saw at once that Gianna's description had been accurate. A police car was parked on the sidewalk near the entrance of the building, and although I saw only one police officer, who was talking to an old woman near the entrance, there was a middle-aged civilian aiming a small camera in my direction.

The apartment bore visible signs of a police search. "I should clean up this mess," said Signora Gioconda, the white-haired housekeeper, in her thick Po Valley dialect, as tears came to her eyes, "but I feel like I'm paralyzed. I don't know where to begin." Zio Fabio, nervously fussing with his beard to conceal his rage, made a heroic effort to belittle the importance of the event. "Maybe it's just a routine check." I asked him if he had any idea where the police might have taken Bruno. "I imagine they took him to the same place they took him last time, to the OVRA headquarters in Piazza Belgioioso." That gave me an idea. I remembered the mysterious Signore Rotesi, who had stayed at the same pensione I had while waiting to take possession of our apartment. Signore Rotesi had turned out to be an officer of OVRA. I looked at my watch, embraced La Signora Gioconda and Zio Fabio, and a few moments later took a taxi to Piazza Belgioioso.

When I asked for Capitano Rotesi, I was told by a secretary that *il capitano* was extremely busy and could not be disturbed. By now I was so entangled in the affair that I had to know more. Switching to option three, I took a bus to Birolli's studio, only to find the door locked. A profound sense of sadness came over me. I felt lonely and impotent, and vaguely guilty at being a free man. Two days later, Zio Fabio called to tell me that Bruno had been transferred to the Milan prison of San Vittore. There he was condemned, together with a group of Torinese friends, among them Cesare Pavese, for "conspiracy." The sentence was three years' confinement at Bagnara Calabra, a small town in the south of Italy, but he was released in mid-July of 1936.

*Early dips into advertising: one of a series of small ads
for Motta panettone and a rough layout for a Campari
ad that never saw the light of day (thank heavens!)*

Bruno's arrest was not the only time during my Milan years that I witnessed Fascist persecution of artists and intellectuals. In 1936, on a stormy winter night, most of my Savini friends, including Birolli, Sassu, and Cantatore, were picked up, taken to the OVRA headquarters, interrogated, and the next day released after cross-examination. When Birolli told me what had happened, I was sorry I hadn't been among them. They were well rehearsed for this occasion and had their answers ready; they would refer only to the history of Art rather than to politics. I remember verbatim Birolli's version of his questioning by a young OVRA officer as he told it to me in a small café near Piazzale Baracca the very day he was released.

OVRA Officer: When you boys talk of revolution, what kind of a revolution are you referring to?
Birolli: That depends. I would say that most often we would refer to Paul Cézanne, whose revolutionary idea was that a painting of a moun-

tain, for instance, Mont-Sainte-Victoire, which was a subject dear to him, is something totally independent from real mountains, the ones we climb or make tunnels in. A pretext, I would say—a thrust at ideas that might become revolutionary reality like objects or things in a situation of temporary suspension. See what I mean? As revolutionary artists, we must, at the risk of becoming incomprehensible even to ourselves, be their liberators, free the image of things from the things themselves. That must puzzle people like you, for it is the very incomprehensibility that constitutes and defines the revolutionary phase we find ourselves in right now. Do you understand?

OVRA Officer: Yes, but what does that have to do with Marxism?

Birolli: Nothing! That's the whole point! One thing is a mountain and another a human being. Don't you see?

And on and on it went. Each one of the painters was being interrogated in a different corner of a large, empty room, and since Birolli had talked loudly from the beginning, the others fell in, and soon it was just like a discussion during a strike at the Academy of Fine Arts.

Between isms

• • •

In 1936, when I decided to leave Motta and open a small design studio, the news somehow reached the president of the National Foundation for the Prevention of Accidents. Signore De Michelis belonged to that small, mysterious cast of survivors whose specific qualifications or obscure connections enabled them to slide painlessly and unobserved into the new order, with privileges and dignity intact. Some had conserved enough power and influence to be able to help old friends find jobs and get permits to emigrate, and even to intervene on their behalf in cases of Fascist persecution. Previously minister of emigration, gentle and generous, De Michelis seemed to float serenely above the hassles of ordinary everyday living.

I had met him the year before, when I had proposed a series of posters on accident prevention in the home, but despite the fact that he had been the upstairs neighbor and close personal friend of the Maffis during their Roman years—a circumstance which in Italy, and especially in the capital, could carry considerable weight—nothing had come of it. My ideas were probably too modern for his taste, and I had not seen him since. And so when, a month after I had settled my design paraphernalia in two rooms of our new apartment on Via Santo Spirito, De Michelis's secretary called to say that His Excellency would like to see me, my first thoughts were that he might have changed his mind about the posters. It was with this happy illusion that I went to see him in his impressive offices in Via Manzoni. He received me with great warmth, asking about Nora and her family, but as soon as he began talking business, I realized that the posters were a dead issue and he had something entirely different in mind.

He told me that the Ministry of Education was planning an important international congress on education to be held in Rome in the spring. The plans centered around the construction of an impressive ultramodern complex which would include schools, office buildings, and a convention hall. Bulldozers were already disposing of one of the most densely populated slum areas of the capital to make way for it.

De Michelis explained that at this moment the foundation's main interest was a national campaign for the prevention of accidents in homes and schools. It was therefore imperative for the foundation to have a strong presence at the congress. My heart missed a few beats as I savored visions of pavilions, posters, films—the Works. "Now what we need," De Michelis continued, with an appropriate change of voice and rhythm, "is a thoughtful, well-researched, intelligent paper on the peril of accidents in the classroom. And so I thought immediately of you, *caro* Lionni. You could be really useful to us in these circumstances. You could make an important contribution to the foundation." A paper? Classrooms? I was astonished. All I could do was mumble a hardly audible *grazie*.

That very evening I saw Bruno, and since I didn't have the slightest idea how to handle this situation, I pleaded with him to help me. And a month later I was back at the foundation handing in our joint opus. "Why don't you read it to me?" said the *presidente,* leaning back in his armchair, resting his head on his crossed hands. I read. I read about slippery floors, sharp-cornered desks, poorly designed seats. About loose windows, swinging blackboards, exposed electrical wires. I showed statistics, and I read and read. De Michelis was ecstatic. *"Meraviglioso!"* he exclaimed. "I want you to represent the foundation at the congress and personally read the paper."

Toward the middle of April, I received a long letter from De Michelis notifying me that a whole day (May 13) had been reserved for the discussion of problems relating to "Safety and the Child" and that my paper was to be read in that context. Although the paper lay ready in a file and May 13 was still three weeks off, I panicked. I had never spoken in public before, let alone on a subject I had not the slightest interest in and knew nothing about. A wave of nausea came over me. In a calmer moment I thought, "All I have to do is to read a paper, a ten-minute affair. After that I will be a free man with two days in Rome."

On the twelfth I took the Lombardy Express, had a luxurious lunch in the dining car, and arrived in Rome in the late afternoon. After checking in at my hotel, I took a leisurely walk to the Piazza di Spagna and then through Via Babuino to the Piazza del Popolo. I hadn't been in Rome for some time, and what struck me as before was the uninhibited relationship between modest human beings and the most prestigious architectural and sculptural monuments of Western civilization, how people sat scattered here and there in small groups defying the elegant symmetry of the Spanish Steps, how children climbed onto the bases of sculptures two thousand years old, waded in the Bernini fountains, and played hide-and-seek behind the columns of the holiest of churches. What makes the beauty of Rome unique is not the ancient monuments and sumptuous palazzi but the supple interaction of body and space, the innocent alliance between mind and thing, the lightness of living. I had dinner at a small trattoria in Via Ripetta and was on my way to the Caffè Rosati nearby when for no apparent reason a new wave of panic hit me. Tomorrow morning! Fifteen hours from now!

I grabbed a cab, and ten minutes later I was in my hotel room nervously thumbing through my paper. When I realized the absurdity of what I was doing, I decided to call Nora, needing to hear her easy, joyous voice.

I woke the next morning miraculously relaxed and walked to Piazza Colonna, where I would catch the bus to the congress. Since there was almost half an hour wait, I sat down at the corner café and had my third cappuccino. Across the Corso the Galleria was slowly coming to life, while on the other side the Chamber of Deputies was still veiled in a deep slumber. Despite my earlier fears, I now felt alert and coldly aware of where I was and why. I boarded the bus with a noisy group of six-year-old Fascists, in their scaled-down uniforms, their hair too smooth, their cheeks too pink, and after a brief ride to the outskirts of the city, I found myself facing the Palazzo dei Congressi, a white box perhaps twenty feet high with one immense glass wall.

I was early, and the endless rows of seats were still empty. I discovered that on each seat there was a small stack of notices and folders, and on top, bound in a bright yellow cover, a copy of my paper. When I saw it, my knees buckled. Across the huge wall facing the audience there was a platform stage two or three feet high. The dais was a long, narrow table, covered with bright green cloth. There were fifteen chairs, and for each of the participants there was a bottle of San Pellegrino, a glass, and an ashtray. A small group of microphones, which at first I had taken for a bouquet of black tulips, was clustered in the center. Assuming that I was to read my paper from the dais, I approached a young woman who appeared to be an usher and asked if she knew where I was to be seated. "Wherever you want," she said, pointing to the sea of empty seats. I sat down in the end seat of the third row. It was then that I noticed that high up on the huge wall directly above the center of the dais there was a small balcony with a dozen microphones. A workman in blue overalls was testing each one with a "*pronto pronto uno due tre, pronto pronto uno due tre,*" that flew through the immense space like a flock of birds.

Finally the congress began. There were some shuffling noises and some coughs, then suddenly my name crashed through the air like thunder, and all eyes rose to the empty balcony. A long, deep silence followed, and once more my name was called. By now I had completely excluded myself from the reality of the scene. Struck by terror, my heart drumming, my mind blank, I tried to rise, but my body was frozen to the chair. When my name was called again, I heard it as if it came from outer space. I felt faint, and after a timeless void, strange words reached my consciousness, and I thought I recognized a motherly voice whispering close to my ear, "Are you feeling ill?" "I'm all right," I answered. "It must be something I ate." The real world had returned; I couldn't go through with it. To pose as an expert, representing an organization that reflected the easy corruption and amorality of the time, was suddenly more than I could stomach, and I quickly left the hall. Mine wasn't a heroic rebellion, just a sickening recognition of hubris. Still, I take refuge in the memory of the printed speech lying on the seat of every chair in the Palazzo dei Congressi that day.

I don't know what prompted me to rent that elegant mansard apartment in Via Santo Spirito right next to the Hotel Manzoni. Did I feel the need to commit myself to my newly discovered, still fragile identity as a graphic designer by extending it to include my private life? Or was it to be the stage for still another act of my never-ending one-man play? Or was it simply one more symbol of my fear of facing the realities of my dream of being a painter? Perhaps it is because of all these things that in my memory the image of the apartment is barely visible. Although it was completely furnished, I have a feeling we never lived there. The only image I can produce of myself at work in the small studio includes little more than the top of a drawing board and the window through which my eyes can wander over the rooftops of mid-Milan all the way to the towering Duomo. I cannot even remember the name of my assistant, the only one I have ever hired, a neat young man with light gray eyes and his straight hair brushed back. Was he real or part of the furniture?

Only one scene has survived clear and hard in my mind, and when it appears, the anguish of its presence weighs on my heart like a slimy chimera.

It is way beyond midnight. I am sitting at a small writing desk with nothing on it but some sheets of paper, a fountain pen, and a portable radio. A familiar voice has announced the end of the evening's Italian broadcasts, and although the last drumming notes of "Giovinezza," the Fascist hymn, have melted into the soft hum of a starless sky, I keep hearing them as the threatening background for the only words that—hard, slick, and black—still fill the screen of my memory.

HITLER'S TROOPS
INVADE
SUDETENLAND

Nora was in Cavi. Were it today I would have picked up the phone and called her, but what was churning in my mind was too important, too complex, too difficult to formulate, too painfully emotional to be trusted to an improvised conversation. I have searched in my old files, in Nora's diaries, in all the hiding places where the letter I wrote that night almost sixty years ago could possibly have landed. In vain. Nora's memory of it is fairly sharp. She was terribly upset when she read it and convinced that I was having a breakdown of sorts. She sent the letter on to my father in Holland, who was equally shocked. Only Papà Maffi agreed with my decision to leave Europe. When on the following weekend I walked into his study to discuss the letter, he grasped my shoulders in his outstretched hands, looked at me with a sad smile, and said, "I understand that you want to go to America. I think you are right. Here in Europe hell is going to break loose. Go! The sooner the better!"

If I believed in parapsychology I would probably have no difficulty accounting for the accuracy with which I had foreseen the dramatic events that were going to rock the world in the years to come. It certainly was not a feat of normal intelligence or logic. Was it fear? I can think of no other way to explain how I, who had never acknowledged the importance of reading newspapers, listening to the radio, or discussing current political events, had mustered the courage to decide the fate of my family on the shaky basis of a four-word headline. Steadfast in my resolve, I set out to reorganize my life. It was not an easy task, and had it not been for a sudden inspiration we might never have made it.

It happened one morning when, to celebrate old times, I was having coffee with Za, who, interrupted by telephone calls and unexpected visits, told me in bits and pieces what was going on in his life. His relationship with the actor-director Vittorio De Sica, whose films he had contracted to write, had reached a point where remaining in Milan no longer made sense. Rome was where the Italian film industry had planted its roots. "I don't know what to do with all the junk I have here in Milan. There isn't a healthy chair in the house to sit on, nor a drawer you can pull open or close. Moving that stuff to Rome would be like carrying your daily garbage to Piazza del Duomo. I need more room." I laughed and said, "I need *less* room," and suddenly I had an idea. "I'll tell you what," I said, half serious, "why don't you take the furniture from my apartment—clean, elegant, stylish—ship it to Rome, and throw that junk of yours in the city dump? It would make the perfect setting for your new role in the Rome film world." Za mumbled something incomprehensible and bit furiously on the butt of his Toscano. "You mean that?" I nodded. "How much would you want?" In a flash I saw Za's Rome apartment. People were slowly moving about carrying martinis, looking at the pictures, laughing at jokes. In a corner I could see De Sica, surrounded by four or five starlets.

Za was sporting the generalized smile of a Roman host. "Tell you what, if you can get the entire contents of our apartment out in a week, pots and pans included, with the exception of the easel, all I want is the symbolic sum of one thousand lire to celebrate our friendship." "You are serious?" "Totally."

Paolo

In the first days of December 1938, with the end of Nora's second pregnancy in sight, she and I decided that it would be wise to have the baby in Switzerland. The probability of war was, of course, a factor, but the main reason was that emigration to the United States was based on a quota system that greatly favored the smaller nations. For Italians the wait for a visa was close to six months, whereas a Dutch or a Swiss applicant could get one in a day. But there were other, more personal reasons.

It was a nerve-racking period for both of us. Nora, like so many Europeans before the advent of the communications era, had only the most approximate notions about life in America. Hollywood had promoted a vision of the United States in which the predominating elements were hatred, violence, and, because of the Depression, misery. For a young mother, this was not a pretty frame for the romantic visions of a carefree, happy future that her imagination had been painting during the years of her adolescence and early adulthood. Not to speak of the terror of an impending war, which, after all, was our main reason for leaving Europe. Worried as I was about my own departure, the long separation between us, and uncertainties about my earning capacity, I was probably unaware of her torments.

In this context, Switzerland seemed like an enchanted island of love, peace, and prosperity, which in retrospect it was. In Ambri, an alpine village in the valley below the Gotthard, lived Papà Maffi's youngest brother, Giotto, a gynecologist, with his wife and their three children, all a few years older than I. Zio Giotto, like Papà Maffi, had immigrated to Switzerland at the turn of the century for political reasons but, unlike his brother, had chosen to remain and eventually become a Swiss citizen.

The Ambri Maffis lived in a villa at the edge of town—an unpretentious but comfortable cube at the bottom of sloping meadows where grazing cows and goats dangled their bells and from time to time, touched by a sudden frenzy, would throw themselves into a wild gallop and just as suddenly stop and peacefully go on with their grazing as if nothing had happened. On previous visits, those meadows had been Mannie's personal paradise. Now, covered with three feet of snow, they had other attractions, as attested by the giant snowman he built with the collective assistance of the other males of the family.

In the nearby village of Faido, on the road toward the Italian border, was a small but well-equipped hospital where Zio Giotto had an office. It was there that he and I, leaving Mannie in the pampering hands of the rest of the family, took Nora when she began her labor pains—which stopped the moment we entered the hospital.

In a few minutes she was settled in a sun-flooded room, with beech-wood furniture, bright blue bedcovers, and gleaming technology, fussed over by a trio of giggling young red-cheeked nurses. It was all very Swiss, very reassuring, and very much a woman's world. I felt like an intruder, superfluous and ineffectual. Nora, thoroughly in control, suggested that Zio Giotto and I take a walk, and we didn't argue. Slowly we walked toward the village, deeply inhaling the inebriating air. From an occasional horse-drawn sled came loud greetings I didn't understand but which I answered with an Italian *"Buon Natale."* In the village we went for a cup of hot chocolate at the Kongli Stube. When the owner heard why I was there, the hot chocolate was immediately transformed into a festive outpouring of schnapps. And then I suddenly felt that what we were celebrating might actually be happening within minutes, and I would have rushed back to the hospital had it not been for Zio Giotto's reassuring words. So only after a longish good-bye did we start back, chatting about this and that.

When we entered the hospital the place looked deserted, but when we turned into the corridor where Nora's room was, we were greeted by a noisy reunion of nurses who had congregated in front of the door. "Congratulations, it's a beautiful baby boy!" I dashed into the room, and there was Nora, a little tired looking but all smiles. "Well," she said, "how was the coffee?" Then she pointed to the crib. And there he was. A little bundle of wrinkles. A child. The normal miracle, once again.

In a few days the little miracle had filled out his wrinkles, but he was still without a name. To argue about it had become a soothing game, but now, prompted by the town's registrar, we had to decide. Again and again we went through the list of surviving candidates until finally out of nowhere the name Paolo appeared. Simple, solid, radiant. Paolo. A person.

New York, 1939

In order to spend a few days with my parents in Amsterdam before my departure for the United States, I had chosen to sail from Rotterdam with the Holland America Line. In Amsterdam a surprise was waiting for me. Father had decided to accompany me to New York. The official explanation was that he thought he might be able to help me find a job through his Philadelphia connections. He had arranged everything. He had booked a cabin next to mine on the SS *Rotterdam* and made hotel reservations for the two of us at the Hotel Wellington on New York's West Side.

I confess that while I was moved by Father's decision, I was slightly disappointed. What had seemed audacious and wise about my emigration had suddenly sunk to the level of a family outing. Besides, my romantic nature envisaged some startling adventure on my solo voyage. But my personal feelings aside, I didn't think Father should leave Mother alone in Amsterdam when the international situation was so fragile that anything was apt to happen without forewarning. Wasn't I leaving Europe for that very reason? With Hitler's troops at the border, Holland, I thought, was in a particularly hazardous situation, and although the Dutch Nazi party seemed insignificant in numbers, one could not ignore the possibility of a coup. There had been sporadic episodes of swastikas on the doors of Jews. All things considered, wouldn't it be better if Mother came too? But Father wouldn't budge from his original plan. He was firmly convinced that Holland would remain neutral. "You don't know the Dutch!" he said.

And so on a misty morning in March 1939, while the SS *Rotterdam* slid out of her pier to the lonely laments of foghorns and the peppy sounds of "Happy Days Are Here Again," we waved good-bye to Mother. And from the first slow rolls in the open sea, Father lay sick in his cabin. Once more revealing the gentle side of his steady disposition, he did not lose his sense of humor, nor would he impose his misery on others. "Don't worry about me," he said with a caustic smile, "I have survived worse ups and downs than these." Father's even temper, his unrelenting quest for objectivity, and his quiet, firm nature had forged an impenetrable shield, behind which, in reserved loneliness, he occupied the fragile structures of a world he could no longer hear.

He hadn't always been that way. Up to the time of his induction into the army during the First World War, he was known as an extroverted, highly gregarious, daring young man. What exactly happened during those few months of military duty at the German border has remained an unsolved mystery. All I know is that although when he was inducted his hearing was normal, the cause for his sudden honorary discharge four months later was his deafness, which, I had often heard, was attributed to exposure to cannon shots. If it hadn't been for the development of ever smaller and more effective hearing aids, he would not have been able to hear at all.

During the first years of his marriage, Father apparently had several nervous breakdowns and suffered from severe migraines. But he also underwent profound character changes and miraculously was able to come to terms with his handicap and invent for himself a style of being that allowed him to complete a successful career and enjoy a serene and relatively happy life.

It was probably because of his deafness that Father came to rely so much on his subtle humor and the charm of his easy smile. He had refined to such a degree the art of hiding his impaired hearing that often people were convinced they had had a pleasant, interesting conversation with him when in reality he hadn't understood a single word of what had been said. He had developed an expression of wise understanding which in most instances was far more than the conversation deserved.

Despite the rough sea and the uncertainty of our situation, I had a good time all the way across the Atlantic. I enjoyed socializing, no matter how high or low the intellectual or social level might be. I didn't have to make the slightest effort to adjust my mood and manners; like a good Actors' Studio graduate, I was always immediately and deeply involved in my role of the moment. Dancing, drinking, and endless Ping-Pong games on the high deck required no effort, and I could be found at every organized fun-and-games gathering, whether it was a shuffleboard competition, a silly hat contest, or late-evening foolishness at the bar, where I would take off my jacket and improvise corny jazz on the piano.

During our first week in New York, I spent the mornings showing my portfolio to the art departments of the most important employment agencies, but I soon realized that there was little if any demand for the kind of design I was showing. The reason became clear to me when one morning I saw the annual exhibit of the New York Art Directors Club. In Milan I had followed those yearly advertising extravaganzas with the condescending irony that Italian designers liked to bestow on the work of their American colleagues. I was surprised to discover that if these Madison Avenue masters lacked some of our raw Mediterranean vitality, daring, and modernist savvy, the works on display—seen in their originally intended dimensions, and in their natural habitat—revealed a degree of professionalism, a concern with technical perfection, that in Italy was unknown.

The contrast, as it seemed to me, between this work and my own joyous experiments was shocking. "I shall never be able to make the transition," I thought—not knowing that one day it would be my very inability to conform that gave my work its originality. But it is not surprising that at this time in America my work could well have been interpreted as being irresponsible and "more of that modern stuff." Although most of the people I met were courteous, I began to fear that I would have to drastically rethink my already precarious situation.

Worried and disappointed as I was about my failures, I hadn't paid much attention to Father, who spent most of his mornings and part of his afternoons at the midtown Merrill Lynch headquarters writing down quotations of certain stocks as they appeared on the Big Board in *cyfertjes* (little numbers), as he affectionately called them. Back in his hotel room, he would transfer them into a large loose-leaf book especially designed for statistical analysis and interpretation of the stock market. When Father showed me his working papers, I could hardly believe what I saw. Each sheet of the book was filled with six columns of minuscule numbers and groups of small charts. "You have your art, I have mine," he said, smiling, as he let the pages slip slowly through his fingers. "But why do you do all of this?" I asked. "I'll explain it to you one of these days."

Father never did explain, but his motive was obvious. He believed that he had invented a system to "beat the game," as he called it. "Look," he said, pointing to the last little charts drooping like grass in a steady rain. "It looks pretty bad right now, but there are signs of a selective upswing." He then suggested that we go to Philadelphia for a few days and try our luck there. He called Mr. Anderson, his former boss at the Atlantic Refining Company, and a meeting was arranged. And to my surprise, he reserved a room at the most luxurious hotel in Philadelphia, the Bellevue Stratford.

Philadelphia

This time Father seemed to be in a different mood. He was excited about taking me, an adult now, to the place where he had made his spectacular career. We had a corner room as large as Oma Rose's apricot boudoir, and from the window you could see, towering over Wanamaker's department store, the tower with the statue of William Penn, the work of Alexander Calder's grandfather. And between the hotel and the Academy of Music, the realm of Leopold Stokowski and Bruno Walter, stood the clean, sober building of the Atlantic Refining Company.

We had arrived late Saturday afternoon, too late to do any of the things I had planned. I was dying to revisit, with adult eyes, the place where I had lived on Chestnut Street, and the Wissahickon, where a six-inch trout was twelve inches long, and I wanted to see what had happened to Penn Charter, my school on Eleventh Street, which the year after I went to Italy had moved to Queen Lane, an elegant Philadelphia suburb. What had happened to the adjacent Quaker meetinghouse? I was excited. And what was the name of my only friend? And what was the name of the street where he lived?

I woke up in my enormous bed at ten in the morning. Father's bed was empty. I found him in the lobby, asleep in a deep armchair. We had hot chocolate and a doughnut at Valley Green Inn. Nothing had changed. I walked to the bank of the stream, rolled up my sleeve, pushed my hand under a large stone, and recognized the slimy moss. No little turtle. We didn't go anywhere else. We had long naps and two leisurely meals at the hotel, but much as I tried to enjoy the last hours and memories and echoes of a distant past with Father, the scenarios for tomorrow's event took full possession of my mind. Before going to bed I opened my portfolio and looked once more at the samples. It was the first time that I dared think that they were really beautiful. The appointment with Mr. Anderson was for eleven the next morning. I was unreasonably euphoric. I couldn't wait. I had decided: come what may, I was going to remain in Philadelphia. It was my speed.

I had met Mr. Anderson some ten years before when, as executive vice president of the Atlantic Refining Company in charge of foreign operations, he visited Genoa. I remembered him as a handsome gentleman, very much a high-ranking American business executive, perfectly cast in his role. Relaxed and kind, spare with his words and a good listener, Mr. Anderson liked and trusted Father, who in many ways resembled him. And both he and his wife were enormously impressed by the fact that at the age of sixteen I spoke five languages fluently. This factoid had been the cause of one of Mother's great and memorable gaffes. It had happened when Father was summoned to Philadelphia for an important policy meeting and Mr. Anderson arranged a luncheon in his honor. Mother had also been invited. On similar occasions, tense about her husband's handicap, afraid that he might not hear, she would courageously (and not without pleasure) assume the role of prima donna and whenever possible monopolize the conversation.

When introducing Mother and Father to the other guests, Mr. Anderson mentioned that their son, age sixteen, had perfect command of five languages! At this point Mother felt the impelling need to amplify the magnitude of my accomplishment and interrupted Mr. Anderson with the following understatement: "And you know, what is funny is that he learned Dutch in Amsterdam, where the worst Dutch is spoken; French in Brussels, where the worst French is spoken; German in Switzerland, where the worst German is spoken; Italian in Genoa, where the worst Italian is spoken; and English in Philadelphia."

Mr. Anderson must have remembered the episode, because when Father and I entered his office on Monday morning he greeted me with, "And how is our polyglot?" When he heard why I was in Philadelphia, he immediately told us that the company had reorganized its advertising policy by giving the direct responsibility to the branch offices. What was left was public relations and occasional publicity events. It was clear that there was no job for me at Atlantic, but Mr. Anderson had another idea. "Please get me Harry Batten on the phone." "Harry is a good friend of mine," he explained later. "He is the owner and president of N. W. Ayer, one of the best and biggest advertising agencies in the country. They have been our agency for many years."

When we left, I had an appointment with Ayer's art director, Charles Coiner, for that very afternoon. It was the first time I'd set foot in the impressive headquarters of a large American advertising agency. Ayer's thirteen-floor building of Indiana limestone was built in the late twenties and timidly enriched by Art Nouveau. It stood on the west side of Washington Square, a peaceful park in the historic center of Philadelphia, a few steps from Independence Square and the Congress Hall. A veritable continent away from New York's Madison Avenue. The art department was on the ninth floor, and when I stepped out of the elevator, Coiner's secretary stood waiting to guide me to a spacious office flooded with sunlight. Charles Coiner came toward me with a big smile. I must have been trembling with anxiety as I stood face to face with the most famous and progressive art director in America, the man who had the power to decide on my fate then and there and who, in a way, did.

Charley Coiner was a handsome, very tall Californian. He laughed easily and from the heart, but he was also capable of fine irony. He was familiar with the work of every painter and illustrator in the States and abroad, and I was amazed at the soundness of his comments. When finally I showed him my work, he laughed. "I have to make a confession," he said. "When Harry Batten asked me to look at the work of the son of one of their executives, it gave me the willies. I've been through that many times before. This time I'm glad he did. This is good and interesting stuff. The problem is that I don't have an opening right now. I just hired someone two weeks ago." My heart sank. Once more nothing was going to happen. Then with a start Coiner said, "Wait! I have an idea. Can you keep yourself busy for a few days? I'll call you. Keep your fingers crossed."

Father went back to New York. I accompanied him to the station that morning, and we both cried as we stood in a long embrace and exchanged silly and useless bits of advice. Be careful. Write as soon as you know something. Get enough sleep. Embrace Nora and Mannie and Paolo for us when you write. Tell Mother I love her. I'll keep my fingers crossed for you. When I returned to the hotel, lonely and depressed, the desk clerk handed me a small envelope. In it was a message: "You can uncross your fingers. Congratulations. Call me. Chas Coiner."

N. W. Ayer

I met Leon Karp in Charley Coiner's office the day Charley gave me my job. I don't remember much else about that day. The emotions of my first week in Philadelphia were such that I just floated with the stream of events without being totally aware of what was happening. But I do remember Leon's reassuring smile as he led me to his office. Although it had not been stated officially, I had been hired to be his assistant.

Leon's office was one of a row of six identical cubicles, not much larger than our bathroom in Via Pacini, partitioned off by five-foot-high wooden panels. The only real offices on the floor were Charley's and those, much smaller, of the three "art buyers." Nothing in Leon's office was what I had expected for an important American art director's office. At the center stood a small, badly scarred wooden office desk and three chairs, and in a corner a small drawing table, a one-legged concoction I had never seen elsewhere. Leon looked amused. "I know how you feel, it must all look very strange to you. It reminds me of my first days in Paris at the Academie Roncard after I had graduated from the Philadelphia Academy. It took me days to understand how the easels were put together."

A young man walked in through the swinging door and threw a small sheet of paper on the desk. Leon grabbed it and read. "Oh hell," he said, "always in a rush. Sorry, but I have to take care of an urgent job for De Beers." "De Beers diamonds?" "Yes, that's one of our accounts." I laughed. "My grandfather had a seat at the London Diamond Exchange right next to the De Beerses." Leon turned toward me, slowly removing his reading glasses. And then, smiling mysteriously, he whispered, "You know, I was the only Jew in this whole goddam building. Now there will be two of us. You can say whatever you want, but that is progress." He then turned around to the drawing board, only slightly larger than the large pad of paper that was pinned to it, picked up a carpenter's pencil with a quarter-inch-wide lead, grabbed a T square, and then gave the most extraordinary drawing performance I had ever witnessed. In less than five minutes he had sketched the rough but perfectly comprehensible essence of an illustration for a full-page advertisement representing a young couple in a romantic tropical setting, suggested an elegantly lettered headline—"A diamond is forever"—and ruled in the few lines that represented a very short text. He then picked up the telephone, dialed, and said with a defiant nonchalance, "OK, boy, come and get it."

After the first two or three weeks a certain routine had begun to govern my workdays. I spent most of my time assisting Leon with practical aspects of the work, like ordering photocopies, sizing artwork for reproduction, and specifying type, thus starting to learn the tricks of the trade. It was the first time I had worked with someone else, day after day, and before long Leon and I had developed an intimacy I had never experienced before. We were both avid talkers, and there was hardly a human experience that one of us hadn't been exposed to. Every subject that casually came up, no matter how banal, could be expected to unleash a confluence of anecdotes, references, memories, confessions. Leon's light, diffused sense of humor and gentle disposition and my eagerness to learn and to sink my young, wounded roots into the rich and generous American soil provided the ideal conditions for a happy, easy relationship. Several times he invited me to dinner at his house. Instead of coming into the city by train, he would then drive in, and after work he would take roundabout roads to show me the beauty of the wooded countryside now bursting with the frenzy of spring.

The Karps lived in Norristown, at the outskirts of the city, in a large, eighteenth-century, white-painted house surrounded by huge trees. The driveway curved through an informal, densely planted garden, known for the size of its white peonies, and ended in a clearing at the back of the house, where there was a barn that had been transformed into garage and workshop. I was moved by the unmistakably American mood, the gentle, uninhibited disorder of the place. It brought back vague memories of the backyard of the shaded Valley Green Inn on the Wissahickon, where there was a perennial mountain of crates and boxes and a large, empty cage which, I was told, had once housed a black bear that danced.

The first time I went to the Karps' for dinner, Leon showed me his studio. It was a large attic with an immense skylight, shaded by the kind of horizontal curtain that I associated with ones I had seen when I was a child in Amsterdam and Brussels in the studios of photographers. Dozens of canvases of all sizes and proportions were leaning against the walls. There were two easels, a model platform, several old armchairs, and a sofa facing a freestanding round black stove. On one of the easels stood a large canvas evidently not quite finished but clearly a portrait of his son, David, in a mummer's costume, standing next to a table covered by a gray shawl. On it was an irregular pile of books against which leaned a larger book, wide open to two pages, one with a suggestion of a text and the other with a drawing of a young mummer, presumably David again. Partially hidden by the books was a large crystal vase with a bouquet of white peonies that spread their dark leaves over most of the upper third of the painting.

"Are you shocked?" Leon asked in an uneasy voice as I stood there staring at the portrait. "Shocked by what?" I noticed his embarrassment. "Well . . . you probably find this very old-fashioned." "Old-fashioned? Oh no, I wasn't thinking that at all. I'm surprised. I'm not used to *real* paintings anymore. This is real painting. I mean, it looks painted," I said, with the accent on *painted,* aware of not making much sense.

I turned to look at the other paintings that lined the walls. They were mostly still lifes, many of flowers; others were portraits, one or two of Grace, Leon's wife. All of them had the subject outlined against a plain gray or dark brown background. Like Manets. They had a curious air of heavy silence about them. Was it the thick, lumpy paint? Suddenly I noticed a smell—a smell of honey, I thought. I remembered the sweet smell of turps and linseed oil that hung in the air close to the copyists in the Ryksmuseum when I was a child. "That smell," I said. "Venice turps," said Leon, smiling, as we sat down on the sofa.

Leon Karp

I couldn't prevent a silent monologue from developing in my mind, for I was vaguely aware that something of major importance was happening to me. I suddenly felt with great clarity that the few paintings I had done and the many I had dreamt had more to do with "expressing an attitude toward the world" than with the desire or the impulse to paint, which I suddenly recognized had been my true motivation ever since I had watched the copyists at the Ryksmuseum clean their palettes. Leon's paintings said little or nothing about the world, but they were generous in offering the beauty of the act of painting which was responsible for their being. I now understood why the faces in Leon's portraits were expressionless. Although the painter's sentiments toward the people portrayed were real and sincere, they were there only by chance, and they were not allowed to disturb the stillness to which the colors danced.

The Power of a Woman

Barely two months after I had tiptoed onto the stage of the American advertising world, I got involved in the birth of a slogan that was destined to become part of the vernacular of the early forties. I was having a leisurely chat with Betty Kidd, one of Ayer's most influential copy supervisors. A comfortable, middle-aged woman with the complexion of a Russian doll, snow white hair, large blue eyes, and a memorable dimple, Betty was a bright, sophisticated woman of the world who had traveled extensively in Europe, had worked on Madison Avenue, and had had a hard time adjusting to Philadelphia's provincialism. She liked to talk with me about Milan and Paris, which she knew well and adored, and in fits of nostalgia she would invite me for a cup of tea in her office.

It was during one of these sessions that my eyes caught a crumpled piece of paper in a wastepaper basket within reaching distance of where I was sitting. The few words that emerged from the folds of the discarded memo intrigued me, and I tried to make sense of them. Curiosity finally got the better of me, and I nonchalantly picked up the note and smoothed it out on my knee. Before I could decipher the handwriting, Betty said, "Oh that! It was an idea for *Ladies' Home Journal,* but hopeless to illustrate." I read, NEVER UNDERESTIMATE THE POWER OF A WOMAN! folded the note, and put it in my pocket. When I returned to my office, I found a rush job awaiting me and promptly forgot the whole episode.

Two days later I found the note again, read it once more, and then sat down at my drawing board and doodled some silly two-scene cartoons about situations in which women succeeded and men failed. I sent them to Betty by messenger with a note that said something like, "Never underestimate the power of a cartoonist," and in less than an hour Betty was sitting in my office very excited about my scribbles.

She asked me to design a series of six ads, each with a different cartoon and no copy other than the resuscitated slogan and the magazine's logo. The following week, Betty showed the series to the Goulds, the *Journal*'s editors, and their advertising manager. The campaign was enthusiastically received, and over the next six years I must have produced close to a hundred cartoons that ran steadily as ads in *The New Yorker* and other leading magazines. The last one was drawn in the fall of 1942. It showed a disheveled Hitler, his arm raised in the Nazi salute, and below him a proud Statue of Liberty holding up her victorious torch. By that time I was so tired of the whole idea that I urged Charley to hire someone to continue the series. We persuaded a young illustrator, Roy McKie, to take the job. He began by carefully imitating my drawings, but little by little he developed a style of his own and became a successful cartoonist.

The "Never Underestimate the Power of a Woman" cartoons were an incredible stroke of luck. I was paid on a freelance basis, and when the

dramatic moment came that Nora and the children, after harrowing political and bureaucratic difficulties, were able to emigrate, I had a savings account with a balance large enough to pay the extravagant price of $3,000 for their passage on the *Conte di Savoia*—the last liner to brave the ocean before Italy's formal entry into the war—and to rent and furnish an apartment.

Not surprisingly, this unexpected success, plus a New York Art Directors Club medal for a newspaper-size drawing of a frog for a separate *Journal* ad designed by Leon, colored my feelings about this new, unsolicited caprice of my talents. And in the illusion of being at the edge of Art, I did hundreds of funny drawings of ostriches in absurd situations for my new colleagues and friends. Finally one day I went to the zoo, where I discovered with dismay that real ostriches had entirely different proportions from mine and that when they ran, their feet were turned in the opposite direction from the way I had been drawing them. I was never able to draw another funny ostrich. It was the end of my short career as a cartoonist, except for the fact that three of my ostrich drawings ended up, I don't remember how, in the permanent collection of the Philadelphia Museum.

Painting followed quite a different itinerary. During the long summers I painted steadily in the evenings after work and on weekends with Leon in his studio. I painted mostly still lifes, but together we also did some landscapes en plein air—more, I believe, out of a romantic sense of admiration for the Impressionists and nostalgia for France than in response to an authentic inner urge.

Unlike most of his academy companions, Leon had steadfastly refused to bend his manners and taste to current fashions. What he needed for his still lifes and portraits was the silence he found in the paintings of Manet and Goya. The plain gray background, invented to be neither space nor thing, had isolated and freed the subject of each painting from its traditional surroundings, to bring it forward, closer to the painting surface, endowed with a new, more forceful reality. I became more and more attracted to the Cubists, my claim that the space in painting gave me dizzy spells being no more than a polemic gag. But it did express my fascination with the cubist work of Picasso and Braque, where the paint stood naked before the eyes of the beholder.

Ed

A few weeks after my induction into the advertising business, a phlegmatic young man walked into my studio, sat down, and with a voice that sounded vaguely familiar, introduced himself. "I am Ed Zern. W-w-w-w-we talked on the phone yesterday."

I recognized the slight stutter at the beginning of his phrases and the long silences between them. "I w-w-was wondering," he continued, "w-w-what are you doing this weekend." "Why?" I asked, intrigued. "W-well, m-m-my wife and I were thinking that you could come and spend it with us in Arden. It's not much of a place, but it's cooler than this goddam town. And we have some common interests, I understand." The invitation was so unexpected that I unconsciously fell in with its cryptic style and found myself saying, "Sure. Why not?" Whereupon he got up from the chair, muttering something like a promise to discuss details tomorrow, smiled, and left. That was more or less the way I met Ed.

Friday evening after work, Ed and I left for Arden. While driving out of town, heading west, we exchanged stories of our youths, mine in Holland and Italy, his in Pennsylvania. But it was not clear what the common interests he had mentioned were supposed to be. The two-hour drive through the Pennsylvania farm country, however, was breathtaking. An enormously magnified version of the Dutch landscapes of my childhood memories slowly melted into the heightening red of the setting sun. Then the fields became wooded shadows, and finally, in near darkness, we pulled into a lane with lights flickering through the branches and stopped in front of a bungalow.

The door opened and Ed's wife, Evelyn, came out to greet us. Once in the small living room, we sized each other up. Evelyn was a small, shapely young woman, with a pretty, lively face framed in dark, wavy hair gathered in a bun, large, green, almond-shaped eyes and high cheekbones, all of which might presuppose a dark Oriental skin, whereas her most striking feature was a fair, luminous complexion which in the poorly lit room seemed to reveal an inner glow.

We were sitting on a wicker sofa, cheerfully chatting away, when I suddenly realized that Ed had not reappeared since he left to park the car in back of the bungalow. When I asked Evelyn where he could be, she answered, "Oh, don't worry about him. He's probably asleep." Noticing that I was somewhat taken aback, she explained that it was Ed's habit to lie down no matter where and sleep whenever he was tired, depressed, or had a headache. Then after consulting her wristwatch she announced that nearby there was a street party for Republican Spain at which she was expected, and she asked me to accompany her.

The party was in a lane a ten-minute walk from the Zern bungalow. The block was closed to traffic by red ribbons stretched between two trees. From a record player in the garden of one of the cottages came the muffled sound of the German version of a French war song, "*J'avais un camerade.*" I realized after a while that the music was from a single album of songs performed by men of the German Brigade, fighting in the Spanish Civil War. The same records were played over and over again, and during the long evening almost everyone hummed or sang the German lyrics of "*Madrid du wunderbare.*"

There were perhaps forty or fifty men and women, my age or older, and after Evelyn had introduced me I realized from their looks and names that many were recent immigrants like myself. In the middle of the lane, there were two long tables, one with Spanish and Soviet books and magazines and another with a coffee percolator, buckets with bottles of Spanish wine and beer, and a grill for hot dogs. On one of the garden lawns, under

Ed Zern

a powerful oak decorated with strings of Chinese paper lanterns, was a circle of a dozen wicker armchairs. There we sat to eat our hot dogs, but before long Evelyn got enmeshed in a violent political argument whose gist I have forgotten. But it unleashed a sharp dialectic ability that was surprising in this charming young woman who, until that very moment, had entertained me with her sweet, light, almost frivolous conversation.

When we returned to the bungalow after one in the morning, we found Ed, stripped to his underwear, sitting at the dining table reading Isak Dinesen's *Out of Africa* while gobbling up a bowl of cornflakes and cream. Evelyn showed me the tiny guest room, only slightly larger than its double bed. I must have fallen into a heavy slumber. It was eleven in the morning when I opened my eyes and saw Evelyn sitting on the chair facing me, with her head resting on her fists like Rodin's *Thinker,* ready to catch my waking glance with her green eyes. When she noted my embarrassment, she rose and announced brusquely that brunch was ready to be served.

Ed was still sitting at the table in the dining alcove, absorbed in his book. "Have you been sitting here ever since I last saw you?" I asked. "No, I was out in the brook for rainbows." For a moment I thought he was mad, but then he showed me two twelve-inch trout lying near the kitchen sink. "On a royal coachman!" he said, triumphant. I didn't ask what that meant, but from the tone of his voice I understood that it was something important that should not be made fun of.

In the months that followed, Ed and Evelyn introduced me to left-wing politics, American style, while Leon became my maestro. These friendships turned out to be lifelong, and even if during the tortuous path of events we often lost track of each other, somewhere in my behavior and in my work there are the permanent, tangible traces of their presence.

During the rest of the summer, Arden became my home away from home. When I couldn't spend the weekends painting or drawing with Leon, I would end up in the hammock that hung stretched between the two oaks in the backyard of the Zern bungalow, with Evelyn below me in the wicker rocking chair deeply immersed in the pages of *The New Yorker,* the *Daily Worker,* or one of the many exotic small magazines that lay scattered in the grass.

Often Ed was out visiting friends or on one of his fishing expeditions, leaving us alone. It was a bizarre arrangement, and I never quite understood the relationship between Ed and Evelyn—nor the real nature of mine with Evelyn. It was a period in my life when I found myself lost in a dark vacuum between two radiant worlds, a world of memories and a world of dreams and expectations. The ambiguity of Evelyn's diaphanous presence seemed to soothe my anguish without violating the sacrality of my loneliness. I missed the warm presence of Nora, the miracle of our long silences so full of easy love.

Reunion

With summer coming to an end, I had the feeling that the change of seasons would perhaps alter the dynamics of time and space and carry the images of the reunion with Nora and the children that crowded my mind into the sharp, happy light of reality. And sometimes I had strange notions about distances and directions. I would think, "Perhaps I should no longer go to Arden." Philadelphia was closer to the water that bathed the sand and the boulders of the beaches of Europe, and every mile inland could only lengthen the distance that separated Nora and me just enough to make a simple embrace a hopeless undertaking.

At work I was free from these nightmarish hallucinations. The continuous presence of friends, the discipline of office hours, and above all the never-ending, all-absorbing challenge of problem solving, which, after all, is what makes art and design such obsessive occupations, conspired to keep my days relatively free from major anguish.

Meanwhile, Europe was relentlessly rolling on toward the inevitability of war. And finally, the very day the news broke that the German Army had crossed the Polish border, I received a cable from Nora with the news that the U.S. consulate had granted her and the children visas, and if all went well they would be sailing on the twelfth of September. I was unable to determine when the cable had been sent.

The news threw me into a panic. I was suddenly faced with the reality of a scene I had witnessed in my fantasies each night before falling asleep since the day I sailed from Rotterdam. All communications with Europe were suspended. I had stored a thousand questions for Nora. For the second time in my life, I had to decide on my own where and how to live. And I had all of twenty days.

During a dramatic lunch with Ed and Leon, I planned the general strategy. Would it be feasible to find and rent an apartment, buy the necessary furniture and household paraphernalia, and have a comfortable home ready for Nora's arrival? Daniel Menkin, Evelyn's father, who sold insurance and real estate, offered to find an apartment; Grace could take care of the crib for Paolo and a bed for Mannie and whatever else was necessary for them; I, assisted by Leon, would buy the rest of the furniture; Evelyn, with her training as a political activist, would coordinate the whole operation.

As far as their arrival was concerned, Ed suggested we take his car to collect them at the pier and drive them home. He and I would go to New York the night before to be sure to get to the pier on time. He said he knew a small hotel on the West Side and would make reservations. Evelyn suggested that better than going directly from New York to the apartment would be to drive them to Arden, where we could stay comfort-ably at the Pig and Whistle for a few days while the apartment was being readied.

I honestly cannot boast of remembering all the details of these complex operations. As a matter of fact, I had better confess right now that the weeks following the arrival of Nora's first cable lie shrouded in my mind like a coma. I seem to remember only small, insignificant splinters of what I was told many years later by some of the participants. It was a drama that thousands of Jewish and political refugees like us had the incredible good fortune to experience. The one thing I do remember is the generosity and solidarity of our many new friends, who spared no effort to help us during our first difficult months in the country where we, like millions of children, women, and men before us and in far more tragic circumstances, came with the firm determination to reinvent a better world than the one we had been forced to flee.

When the moment came to shop for furniture, I searched my mind for our apartment in Via Santo Spirito, but all I could remember were two or three of the most important pieces: the long row of birchwood cabinets in the living room, the Swedish folding dining-room table, and the two tubular Breuer armchairs we had bought two months before our wedding, when we still had no idea where we were going to live.

Fortunately I had one stroke of luck; in Lit Brothers, an unpretentious but well-stocked department store on Market Street, the entire collection of "organic design" that had been the stylish protagonist of the Museum of Modern Art's first exhibition of modern furniture was on sale for prices that at first I couldn't believe. The salesperson assured me they were correct; in this conservative city there was practically no demand for anything so "modern." I bought enough Eames- and Saarinen-designed African mahogany cube units to furnish an entire house.

Luckily, when I returned to my senses, the Zerns were happy to acquire my surplus, and apparently several friends of theirs got the rest of Lit's stock. Today, after more than half a century, the units, still triumphantly modern, line the walls of my studio in Tuscany, and the armchairs, recently reupholstered for the first time, are the only handsome yet comfortable seats I can offer to visitors.

Daniel produced a pleasant, spacious, and reasonable apartment in a neighborhood that bordered on a wild, woody stretch of Fairmount Park. By the time Nora and the children were due to arrive, there was a lovely apartment, fully furnished and equipped, waiting for them. In addition, Leon had promised me his old Ford, and Charley had granted me a three-day vacation.

My anxiety had infected the entire art department. From Charley to the messenger boys, everyone followed the events of the rapidly spreading war with horror, gathering in Charley's office to listen to the latest news— a strange scene for a city that was as insular in its mentality as Texas. It is unlikely that my little drama would have elicited as much interest in New York, the traditional point of arrival for immigrants and refugees from Europe. During the late thirties, thousands of European Jews who had succeeded in saving themselves and their families from the Nazi persecutions had found a haven there, the greatest Jewish city of the world,

Paolo and Mannie with me

where with little difficulty they found languages they could understand and speak, manners and behavior they were accustomed to, and often employment in specialized fields they were familiar with. Of the Italian Jewish refugees who arrived in the United States in the late thirties, the great majority remained in New York, while to my knowledge only a handful came to Philadelphia. Unlike the millions of immigrants who had preceded them, the new crop of Italian refugees was mostly middle- and upper-class business people, intellectuals, scientists, and artists, a genus Americans had not been accustomed to.

On the nineteenth of September at four o'clock, Ed met me at the corner of Baker and Washington Square with Daniel's impeccably polished, dark blue Dodge sedan. I was exhausted and promptly fell asleep. When I awoke, we were in the busy center of Greenwich Village, in a parking lot decorated with strings of tinsel that swayed lightly in a cool evening breeze. I looked at my watch—it was close to eight. "A terrible jam at the Holland Tunnel," Ed explained. "I need a drink." Rye on the rocks was his before-dinner ritual.

Finding a bar was no problem. We were surrounded by them. I followed Ed as we ran across Sixth Avenue, dodging the heavy traffic, and entered a bar. There were half a dozen men sitting at the counter. Two were involved in a heated argument, the others seemed to be alone, hunched over their drinks or resting their heads on their elbows. Not a happy scene. "What'll it be?" asked Ed, grabbing my arm affectionately. "I'll have a Scotch and soda." In Italy I hardly ever drank strong liquor, but this was a special occasion, and I gulped it down with pleasure. "How about dinner?" I suggested. At that very moment the door opened and three black men walked in, nonchalantly threw a smile and a "hi!" to the bartender, and disappeared into a dark corner at the end of the counter. One of the men carried a saxophone case. "I'll be damned," whispered Ed excitedly. "That's Dizzy Gillespie."

Pretty soon the lights were turned on in the rear of the bar, revealing a small podium barely large enough for an upright piano, a bass, and a chair for Gillespie; groups of young people began coming in until the place was jammed and a line had formed outside. Ed, who was a jazz afi-

Mannie and Nora, circa 1960

cionado and had an extraordinary collection of jazz records, including all Gillespie's early recordings, was in a trance. The smile that appeared when he went to talk to the group didn't leave his face until we staggered out of the bar.

From there on my memory refuses to cooperate. I have been told that we had a sandwich and went to one or two other music bars, and that we didn't collapse into bed until deep in the night. What I vividly remember is waking up with a start, the bright sunlight streaming into a small, dingy hotel room, and realizing that what I thought was still yesterday was *today* and that the *Conte di Savoia* must *already* be lying moored at the Italian Line Pier.

Whenever Nora or I tell the rest of the story, we invariably get into an argument over precisely how long Nora had to wait after the customs officers and journalists had run up the gangplank and the first passengers began to disembark with no Lionni in sight. As if my remorse can be measured by minutes or hours. Although sometimes I have a moment of illusion that it never happened, I know better, of course.

Obviously life was going to be different, and not only because I had my first *real* job, which affected everything, regularizing the times for working, eating, sleeping, shopping. It was the first phase of our Americanization. As a matter of fact, many of the family habits we acquired then for which I blamed or praised our new homeland were not much different from those in Italy or any other country, for that matter. The rhythm of our lives and their style were determined more by the uncertainty of my own plans and ambitions than by the circumstances in which I found myself. No matter what I did or when I did it, before or after Nora's arrival, my life remained a continuous invention with unpredictable consequences. But with me working at a steady job with regular hours, it must have been easier for Nora to organize and maintain a reasonable family structure, for she was constitutionally prepared for such a way of living. Although to some of our Bohemian friends, our way of life may have seemed rigidly bourgeois, in the eyes of our other friends, it could hardly be called conventional. Neither my family nor Nora's could qualify as conventional, although both our families were loosely but comfortably organized.

The War

Hero (a dream)

I was ready, absurdly overdressed for the balmy air. Again, I touched the hardness of my revolver under the oily cloth of my coat and searched the sky for a known constellation, but tonight the stars, bright though they were, did not seem to fall into familiar patterns.

The water was black and smooth like silk, with quick wrinkles licking the side of the ship, a flicker of moonlight, and an occasional slow tchhh. *There were no other noises but the beating of my heart, which I was sure could be heard all the way to the coast.*

Once more I rehearsed my memory; the flat slate rock where we used to lie frying our skin, unseen by the bathers on the beach; the three-step rock to the right; then up the slope toward the first pine and straight for the path and the kitchen door. After that it was gravy. Even in the unlikely event that they had not received my message, they would instantly understand. My boots, still dripping, would tell more than I possibly could in such an emotional moment.

Against the sky's inner light, that special light of endless space, I recognized the silhouette of the hills. There, Marzo and his men would be waiting for me. I heard steps nearby, and out of the black Pietro appeared. "Are you OK?" he whispered. "Don't worry. It's the years when I was a kid all over again." I sounded very American, I thought. My God, how much of me had changed. "Come on," Pietro said. "Everything's ready. We checked the coast from Rapallo to La Spezia. You wouldn't know there's a war on." We tiptoed along the rail and then down to the lower deck, where three sailors were waiting . . .

I had dreamed, told, fantasized that scenario so many times, it had become a solid part of my memory. And now that an invasion of Sicily seemed to be in the cards, it began to press on my conscience. I had escaped the draft three times for reasons of age or paternity. That was destiny. But now my fate was in my own hands. Not to act would be unforgivable cowardice. I was going to volunteer.

I had talked to Nora about it, but although we had even discussed tactical details, the project remained abstract speculation—absurd, considering the easy reality of our lives. It was not until I talked to Clarence Jordan, an Ayer vice president who was our contact with the Pentagon for the army recruiting campaign on which I too had worked, that we were suddenly faced with the hard reality of the situation. It struck harder when Clarence told me a few weeks later that he had spoken to the chief of the Mediterranean Division of the OSS, who said I should arrange an appointment for an interview with his secretary as soon as possible.

A confusing mixture of fear, excitement, and near hallucinations took possession of every minute of the long days that preceded my meeting with a colonel I'll call Robert Xavier, an unexpectedly charming, intelligent, articulate officer, young for the importance of his post, whose mannerisms were more typical of a magazine editor than a career army colonel.

We talked for almost two hours in a subterranean enclosure that could better be described as a large garage than a room, for the floor was gray concrete and the only pieces of furniture were a tabletop the size of a Ping-Pong table on sawhorses and five tubular chairs with maroon plastic seats. "I apologize for the austere space," the colonel said, smiling. "Here at the War Department everything is temporary. We redecorate according to the latest news from the front," and then, more seriously, as an opening for the interview, he added, "And now the spotlight will be on the Mediterranean."

Had I not known the reason for our conversation I would have been tempted to say, "Well now, let's get down to brass tacks." But the conversation with all its easygoing informality was "it." Still, when the colonel asked me what I thought my qualifications were, and I mentioned my relations with the underground, and specifically with important members of the Communist party, some of its splinter organizations, and veterans of the Brigata Garibaldi that had fought in the Spanish war, he suddenly assumed a more professional tone, questioning me about various personalities and groups and my views of the political importance of the Italian intellectuals who, disregarding minor ideological differences, could be counted on to side with the Allies. I was explicit about my feelings that fomenting and expecting a general popular revolt against the regime was a waste of time and energy.

Colonel Xavier interviewed me for several hours and then announced in direct, simple terms, without rhetorical flourishes, that he was interested in having me "on his team." I would have to have FBI clearance and three months' basic training; then I would be given a captain's rank and transferred to Africa to prepare and wait for further developments. He handed me a batch of forms to be filled out, and that was it.

The return home was not easy. When I told Nora, she had a long crying spell. I was close to giving the whole thing up when suddenly she lifted her head, looked me straight in the eyes, and said with a strong, determined voice I had never heard before, "OK. Where do we start?"

Days, weeks, a whole month went by without a word from the War Department. I had sent back the forms Xavier had given me with a personal thank-you letter. Nothing. I had made arrangements with the bank for various payments and informed them of my probable departure in the very near future. N. W. Ayer, in a great gesture of patriotism and generosity, had promised to take care of the expenses for the boys' education. I was virtually packed and ready.

The fear fantasies, the little guilt crises, the doubts had given way to a hitherto unknown feeling of strength and manliness. I, who during my school years had always exploited the slightest affliction to avoid physical activities, felt sudden urges to run, to jump, to wrestle, and even, remembering the days on the Cavi beach with Mario, to box. Meanwhile, speculation about an invasion of Western Europe by the Allied forces began to fill the columns of the newspapers and weekly magazines. I read them all with avid identification. By the time the second month had run out, I had stormed all the beaches of France and Italy.

And then one day Nora, pale and visibly shaken, handed me a yellow envelope from the War Department. Unfortunately, it was lost sometime after we moved to the house on McCallum Street. But I remember the one sentence that summed up its content: "The United States Government wishes to express its gratitude for the service you have so generously offered, but since at present and for the near future there is no need for personnel with your specific qualifications, et cetera, et cetera, et cetera."

No emotions could have been more mixed than ours. Nora embraced me as if I had just returned unscathed from the front. The boys were clearly disappointed. How were they going to explain to their buddies that their heroic father had undergone an inexplicable metamorphosis? I went through a series of phases from disbelief to deep disappointment, reexamination, and then a secret elation at having escaped God knew what mortal dangers; to be here safe with my family and have the satisfaction of knowing that although I lacked proof that I could have been a hero, I had it in black on white that I was not a coward. Several weeks went by before I began to ask myself what had really happened. But it wasn't until after the war ended that I found out.

Walter Cohrssen, who had left Milan shortly after I did and was teaching music history at Seton Hall, had been inducted into the U.S. Army with the rank of corporal. He hadn't been sent abroad but remained stationed near New York City and had access to certain files, among which he discovered mine. It reported not only my association with so-called left-wing organizations that later, in the McCarthy era, were designated as un-American, but also my connections, direct and indirect, with important members of the Italian Communist party in Italy. Had my past been apolitical or even Fascist, I would not have been turned down.

Mother and Father were still in Amsterdam. Even after the Nazis and the Dutch collaborationists had gained control over the Dutch government in May 1940, Father was still optimistic. But when one morning, he found a Star of David painted on his door, he didn't delay a moment. "Get ready immediately," he told Mother. "We leave in ten minutes." And in ten minutes they closed the door behind them and climbed into a taxi. "Ymuiden," said Father to the driver, gambling big. Ymuiden was a small harbor, but it was the closest to Amsterdam. When they were halfway there Mother realized that the only thing she had taken was a large bottle of Quelques Fleurs that someone had given her. And with a pang of guilt she remembered that she had forgotten to turn off the radio. They laughed.

When they were close to Ymuiden, the driver asked, "Where in Ymuiden?" "The harbor," said Father without hesitation. At the entrance to the harbor there was a long line of official government cars, carrying German military officers, waiting to be let in. "Go with that line," said Father. After several minutes the line began to move. At the gate, Father just waved his passport and mumbled something incomprehensible, and they were admitted.

The harbor was crowded with boats of all kinds and sizes waiting for permits to depart. People were milling around trying to book passage to London, but apparently every decent sitting surface had been sold. It was Father's last chance. They walked from one boat to another repeating the one word over and over again: "Dover?" Finally, Father noticed a man in a fisherman's outfit. He went up to him and asked, "Do you remember me?" The man looked Father in the eyes and said, "I don't think so." "You are going to Dover, aren't you?" Father insisted. The man seemed to waver a moment and then began whispering with the young, dark-haired woman standing beside him. "Would you take us to Dover? I am a Jew, and this is my wife." "OK," said the man, "if you don't make a nuisance of yourself." That was it. A Jewish fisherman—the only one in the whole wide world.

They landed at the commissioner's office of Dover harbor. "They bombed us from the air!" Mother contributed. Since they had no regular documents, they were taken to a refugee center, where they were given bananas to eat.

In my memory I see them sitting with us at dinner in our McCallum Street house in Philadelphia. Nora is in the kitchen. Our dog, Chica, lies under the table at my feet, softly snoring. The silence is that of all my memories, but this silence has a particular sense of nastiness about it, of poorly repressed anger. "Mother," I finally ask, crashing the sound barrier, "what is going on?" Her answer is hard: "Ask your father." But Father is curved over his dish, slurping soup. "I can't get a word out of him," says Mother. "That is some nightmare you are coming out of," I say. "Give him time." A month or so later they moved to New York, where they stayed in a Fifty-seventh Street hotel. Miraculously, Father got a job as treasurer of an Anglo-Dutch petroleum combine. He got over his depression and was his old self again, though he was now stone deaf. He always managed somehow.

Behind all the happy recollections of my first sunny years in Philadelphia, full of the pleasures of new thinking and doing, still hangs, impenetrable, the heavy screen that was to separate forever the fictional war I had invented from the ghastly details of the reality. I saw it rise that day at the War Department, when suddenly it revealed with a vivid precision details now vanished forever, sucked back into the envelope of the War Department's form letter that coldly announced that the war would not be mine after all. And so it remained forever this monstrous abstraction, an immobilized nightmare, lying between me and the world.

Oh yes, I read the papers, I listened to all the broadcasts, I even designed publications for the U.S. Army recruiting campaign; I wrapped care packages, and then, as all the specific pains and rages melted into one vast chorus of indignation, I too discussed, as everyone did, tactics, maneuvers, encirclements, and deadly traps. But whereas then I could conjure up all the sufferings and deaths with the haunting precision of the imagination, now the imagery comes to the screen of my mind vague, out of focus, discolored, and strangely fragmented, as if the entrails of my television set were suffering from an incurable disease. I say this without the slightest guilt but with the recognition of an irreparable loss caused very simply by my failure to have lived and comprehended from within the ugly, smelly reality of war.

Art Director

During those years, the daily details of my life are registered in my mind with the innocent amazement and amusement with which I accepted—or rather recognized—the developments of my career. I felt more and more, as one fortunate event followed another, that my moves were being planned, without my knowledge, by a board of directors on the top floor of some outer-space office building. I just did the work as it came along.

In "my time," the capital of the American advertising world was, as it still is today, New York. It housed the headquarters of all the major agencies except Ayer, which stubbornly clung to the place of its birth, the City of Brotherly Love, only a few yards from Independence Hall. Although it was not much farther from Madison Avenue than many of the small towns in New England from where the New York advertising executives commuted, Philadelphia was perceived as another world. And so in many ways was Ayer.

Ayer then ranked third among the largest agencies in America, and probably the world. It covered the widest spectrum of accounts, from caskets to diamonds, from automobiles to perfumes, from AT&T to the U.S. Army. And it could boast more gold medals at the annual New York Art Directors Club show than any other agency in America. And yet, despite its importance, the mood of the Ayer art department was that of a small design office. It was easy, friendly, and informal, and the interaction between colleagues was generous and in many cases even affectionate. In fact, our closest friends were fellow art directors and their wives. But if all of this, plus the vicinity of the romantic Wissahickon Valley, good public schools for the boys, and one of the finest orchestras in the world, had made our lives almost idyllic, the overpowering vitality of New York never ceased to flicker on the horizon.

*Man Ray, standing far left;
Ferdinand Léger, next to
him; I'm squatting on the
right*

After my legendary stroke of luck when I rescued a line of copy from a wastepaper basket, I had been assigned the art direction for the Container Corporation of America account, which Charley himself had initiated with the courageous use of Art with a capital *A*.

Walter Paepcke, the president of Container, as we called it, was an impressive German-American, a handsome and intelligent aristocrat with interests that ranged from manufacturing and finances to an ardent infatuation with poetry and philosophy. The two names that he had appropriated and that represented him were Goethe and Container, but later he had added Aspen, Colorado, determined to make the small silver-mining village into a world center for cultural exchange. The moment we met we recognized our common European provenance and were drawn to each other in a bond of mutual trust and understanding that in future meetings—first because of the advertising for Container and later because of my involvement with the Aspen International Design Conference—developed into an authentic friendship. This was soon extended to include Walter's charming and beautiful wife, Elizabeth—Pussy to her friends—who had graduated from the Chicago Art Institute, and as artist in residence had great influence on her husband, whom, in tender moments, she would address in a sexy whisper as *Schnuckelschweinschen.*

As art director for Container's advertising, I extended Charley's idea of using "fine" artists to illustrate the advertisements by involving stronger, riskier, more adventuresome artists with the project—people like Léger, Hélion, Man Ray, and de Kooning.

During the war, most of Container's production was for the U.S. Army, and the goal of its extravagant presence in the advertising pages of magazines like *Fortune* was mainly to keep the company and its products alive in the minds of its peacetime customers. The objective of the campaign was simply to develop a sophisticated style that was visible, inimitable, and powerful enough to establish the name Container as the exclusive synonym for shipping cartons. The "International" series we developed, and for which I engaged the best-known artists from the countries that were part of the democratic alliance, soon became what was possibly the most advanced outpost of modern institutional advertising.

But while Container advertising had firmly consolidated my newly earned reputation, a bizarre event occurred that could have drastically changed the course of my life. It began one day when Charley summoned me to his office to tell me that we were in trouble with our largest account, the Ford Motor Company. He had decided to ask each of us art directors to contribute ideas for the advertising of Ford, Plymouth, and Lincoln with or without the collaboration of the copy department. We had a week's time, during which I designed three daringly "modern" color pages for each car, the kind that the president of the most important employment agency in New York had singled out in the portfolio I showed him when I had just arrived in the United States with the comment, "You will never get a job in America with this European kind of stuff!"

A trunk full of proposals was shipped to Detroit for a meeting with young Edsel Ford, Henry's son, who had only recently been made responsible for all of Ford's advertising. Young Edsel enthusiastically chose my proposal and demanded that I be put in charge of the art direction of all Ford advertising. And so, less than three years after Charley had told me to uncross my fingers, I found myself as the new head of the so-called Ford Unit, handling one of the most prestigious accounts in the United States at what was probably the lowest salary being earned by an assistant art director. Luckily, this situation lasted only a few months, until a modest raise finally put me, with typical Philadelphia stinginess, at the end of the art directors' lineup.

Unfortunately, I never had the chance to realize the automobile ads I had proposed. It took me six months to finish the campaign that had been initiated by Wally Elton, who had art-directed the Ford accounts for many years. Wally was a real pro, and that is precisely how his ads for the Ford group looked. They had that characteristic and inimitable American look of definitive correctness, of being exactly the way they were supposed to be. In fact, they were faultless. But to my eyes, still restless and filled with doubt and wonder, they lacked the one ingredient European designers were always aiming for—the subtle imperfection that testifies to the presence of the shaping hand.

But by now I was well aware of the fact that there were reasons for that polite, sane, middle-class look. Compared with European budgets, the amount of money invested in American advertising was enormous. While French businessmen could easily afford the cheap luxury of flamboyant risks like a poster by Cassandre or Colin Henrion, Americans had to be certain to get a reasonable return for their money. The testing of copy and illustration was a logical answer to this need, and Ayer was among the first agencies to test important campaigns before they were released. I don't know how serious and independent that process was at the time. I felt strongly that since you can only test what exists, testing must by nature be conservative and manipulative—conditions that surely do not encourage experimentation. The result was that Ford ads, which like most auto ads were the direct or indirect result of testing, while representing the best in the American tradition of quality advertising, looked tired and déjà vu.

To be suddenly confronted with the task of seeing Wally's sketches through to the finish represented for me a real trauma, and while I was flattered and happy to have been chosen to run the Ford Unit, the job of finishing what others had originated was depressing and time and nerve consuming. From the slick, traditional watercolor illustrations through the typography and insipid hand lettering of the headline to the product itself—I hated it all. I hated the smug professional look, all perfectly balanced, with the correct type style and color scheme, and I hated the "human interest" being a chauffeured Lincoln parked in front of the canopy of a Southern mansion waiting for a couple in tails and evening gown. When, six months after I had been entrusted with the Ford account, we lost it to J. Walter Thompson for what were called "political reasons," I was delighted. The workload had been heavy and artistically unrewarding. And in the end I had nothing to show for it other than a campaign that someone else had designed.

Since the Ford account had represented one-third of the company's revenue, its loss meant a major crisis; in fact, many employees were fired. Ironically, among them was Wally, who as art director for the account had been earning what in Philadelphia was considered a New York salary. I, still a novice with the company, instead of a raise or a bonus had been handed a phony gold medal with the encouraging inscription, "Keeping everlastingly as it brings success." But Wally had the last laugh when he was hired by J. Walter Thompson for far more money than he had been making at Ayer to art-direct the Ford account once more. Paradoxically, while many of my colleagues were getting their last paychecks, I finally got my first substantial raise.

Although I felt the general shock as much as my cubicle neighbors, I must confess that I was not unhappy with the strange twist of events. The pressure in the Ford Unit to finish a new batch of ads almost every night in time for the Red Arrow to Detroit was almost unbearable. I would come home from the office exhausted, unable to read or work on my private projects or even play with Mannie and Paolo. Now the job would return to a more civilized rhythm, and spare time could once more be enjoyed in the company of Nora and the children, as well as with friends. And finally one evening I dared open the door of my attic studio to find on my easel the half-finished cubist painting of a string quartet abandoned for almost a year. I was now ready to rethink painting, if for no other reason than once more I felt the compelling need to reinvent myself.

Most major advertising efforts go through a tormented period of gestation, in which proposals for next year's campaign are formulated, elaborated, discussed, and presented to the client for approval. This is the time when the workings of the creative processes, normally so mysterious and difficult to define, can finally be measured by the complaints of stomach pains and the consumption of dry martinis, antacids, and sleeping pills. The length of these periods varies according to the complexities of the message, the intricacies of the client's mind, the ability of the agency's representative, the ingenuity of the copywriter, and the physical and mental stamina of the art director. They are nerve-racking weeks, when ideas and opinions are being juggled, discussed, and cruelly dissected until at the right moment a copywriter, an art director, or someone's spouse or child comes up with a slogan that everyone salutes with the magic word "terrific," illustrations and copy are outlined, and the long, boring process of metamorphosis from sketch to shiny proof can begin.

To have been art director for Container, Ford, General Electric, *Ladies' Home Journal* carried enormous prestige, but for me, who still considered myself a painter, it also meant access to whomever I was interested in meeting. When I list some of the names of the people I befriended or simply came to know during those few years, I have to smile at the size of the canary that, unnoticed, had flown into my mouth the day Charley hired me. Willem de Kooning, Andy Warhol, Piet Mondriaan, Naum Gabo, Walter Gropius, Louis Kahn, Man Ray, Herbert Bayer, Zero Mostel, and Josef Albers among them.

Black Mountain

One warm spring day of 1945, Josef Albers entered my cubicle at N. W. Ayer. To meet a Bauhaus master on my terrain was a new thrill. And when he told me the reason for his visit, I could barely hide my excitement. Albers asked me if I could come and teach for one month at Black Mountain College. "Teach whatever you want." Though I said that I would have to talk with Nora about it, in my mind I was already there, sitting around a large table with seven or eight students. I felt that now I was a real Bauhaus person. And that was just the way it was in August, the day after we had driven from Philadelphia to the foothills of North Carolina. We were met by Josef and Anni Albers, who showed us our bungalow and warned us of rattlesnakes and diamondbacks. Then we had our first meal at the cafeteria with them, Leo Amino, an American-born Japanese sculptor, and Jacob Lawrence, the best-known black painter in America, and his charming wife. Albers explained how the summer school was supposed to function, and I told them what I wanted to do with the students: explore the possibilities of building with photographs and parts of photographs a visual grammar and syntax parallel to the verbal ones. Could that be done? I didn't know. But to me it was Bauhaus: purely experimental. A question from the edge of my knowledge.

It was a strange but fascinating experience. We lived in a world of wood. Our cottage was a raw wooden box with a pitched roof that stood half hidden in the trees at the edge of the campus. After a few days, our bodies, our clothes, and everything else smelled of wood. The boys and I loved that macho scent, but Nora hated it. It gave her a headache, she said. Paolo, in a fit of giggles, claimed that it made him feel like a cigar.

Not far from the cottage, down the lane, was the beginning of a path that led to a secluded corner of the lake. Nora and the boys spent most of their time there reading, swimming, playing. Partly hidden in the woods, it lay motionless and silent except for unexpected water noises, *glcks* and *ploks* that rippled the air. Only we and Leo Amino seemed to enjoy the romantic beauty of the place.

Mannie, by now a reasonable American, had brought his rods and reels and caught two perches and a small bass on his first day at Black Mountain. I would usually come up to the lake in the late afternoon, lie on the raft, and swim and splash around with Nora and the boys. We loved our little secluded beach. In a few days it had become home, and the cottage our pied-à-terre in town.

The campus was a curious mixture of bungalows, primitive cottages, and two long, sophisticated, white concrete buildings that hugged the slopes of the Blue Ridge Mountains. At the center there was a cafeteria, which was lively at breakfast and dinner, but during the first week of our stay the campus seemed strangely and inexplicably abandoned. Most of the time the roads were deserted, the windows closed, and except for the muffled sound of a distant radio or an occasional truck, the silence was so complete that every once in a while we would catch ourselves whispering.

I had been assigned a studio next to Albers's. It was the first time I had worked in a space that was not my own, and the large canvas I painted during that month never gave me the feeling that it was my own creature. I painted it as if it had been commissioned. Afraid of public failure, I had programmed it carefully before leaving Philadelphia, bringing with me a scale sketch and even the title: "In my Father's house there are many mansions." Conceived as an enormous doll's house, its rooms were boxes crowded with gesturing figures and fragments of furniture. There were angels and devils and men and women in sumptuous togas dancing. And suns and moons and stars and flying comets. Katherine Kuh wrote in her review of my Norlyst exhibition, in which this painting was shown, that there was nothing wrong with the show, and that was precisely its weakness. She was right. The paintings did not originate from an irresistible urge within. They lacked courage. It was my first serious show, and I was afraid of failure. The paintings were somewhat like the paintings in a stage set—they were made to look like paintings. Luckily I was unaware of the trouble I was in. I had learned to perform, but I still lacked insight.

One morning I was locking the door of my studio while next to me Albers was closing his. We were both headed for the cafeteria. On our way Albers stopped, looked at me, and said, "You have a good time painting, don't you?" I laughed. "If I didn't I wouldn't do it. Would you?" "This morning I hate it. It's hard work." I was shocked. Albers clearly meant what he said.

Although he had a desperate need to be loved and admired, Albers was a difficult man to like. His voice and German accent did not help—neither did the angularity of his features and the stiffness of his movements and bearing. His many-sided personality was confusing. Yet he was as strict and hard edged with himself as he was with others, and though he was outrageously pedantic, he could be gentle, funny, and forgiving. All this was very German. Equally German was his dedication to art and teaching. I believe that he lived his life weighing colors and making squares because he was afraid of painting.

My infatuation with the Bauhaus had begun when I was ten or eleven years old and first heard the word. It was strong and simple and hard, like building blocks, and it entered my vocabulary as a word to remember and use. Years later, a romantic rebel in search of a cause, I learned that in the year 1919, in the German town of Weimar, a young architect by the name of Walter Gropius had proclaimed: "Let us then create a new guild of craftsmen without the class distinctions that raise an arrogant barrier between craftsman and Artist! Together let us desire, conceive, and create the new structure of the future, which will embrace architecture and sculpture and painting in one unity and which will one day rise toward heaven from the hands of a million workers like the crystal symbol of a new faith."

That was all I needed. Bauhaus was instantly promoted to the level of revolutionary ideology, ranking with constructivism, futurism, cubism, dadaism, surrealism, and all the other isms whose task was to rethink and reshape all that was thinkable and shapable.

Then, as I aged and slowly matured, so did Bauhaus, the word. And by the time I was actively involved with architecture, painting, and sculpture, it had already been solidly incorporated into my personal vocabulary, assimilated not only as a word but as a name that defined both an ideology and me. I was Bauhaus the way I was an agnostic, a liberal, a Jew. What I thought and felt about things was Bauhaus. What I did was Bauhaus. My style? Bauhaus.

And I learned about the great Bauhaus invention, the Foundation Course, entirely devoted to questions. Self-taught, I knew how to invent answers but knew next to nothing about questions. Design a table set. What is a table? I learned to ask basic questions. What is a painting? Are paintings things? Is a painting the sum of its parts? Is a painting of a painting a painting? What is the color of color? What are shapes? Are there things without shape?

At Black Mountain
Left to right: Leo Amino, Jacob Lawrence, me, Ted Dreier, Nora, Beaumont Newhall,
Gwendolyn Lawrence, Lee Gropius, Jean Varda (in tree), Nancy Newhall, Walter Gropius,
Molly Gregory, Josef Albers, Anni Albers

Now I consider myself a Bauhaus graduate. Although I never even saw the Bauhaus, I always think and speak about it with nostalgia and a sense of belonging. And when occasionally I meet an ancient Bauhaus master, I embrace him or her with brotherly affection, admiration, and the assumption of tacit understanding.

I had seven students, five of whom were girls. This was normal, Albers said, for an ill-promoted summer course. Trusting a sudden intuitive whim, I had decided to work with the class on a phenomenology of space, a project I have since lectured on from time to time and which had its origins in my Black Mountain experiments. It would have been an exciting experience, but unfortunately it was clear from the very first seminar that I had grossly overestimated the intellectual level and experience of the students. I decided to shift to a simpler and more accessible subject. Luckily I was able to locate Suzanne Langer's *Philosophy in a New Key* in the library, and with that as a guiding background for the students, I tried to open their minds and eyes to the meaning and manipulation of space and images. But I was still unable to arouse their enthusiasm. There was a strange negative mood on the campus, a pervading pessimism and lack of vitality. The students themselves were aware of it and ventured theories, but no one had a plausible explanation. The most reasonable hypothesis was that the end of the war had left a void of purpose. The future, which for the young generation had been in the hands of fate, had now suddenly landed back in theirs.

Luckily, after we had been at Black Mountain almost a week, the news spread that Varda, a San Francisco artist whom Albers had invited to run the painting class and who had mysteriously vanished from the earth, had finally arrived in his overloaded Model A convertible painted magenta and orange, tooting what looked like a rubber enema, and waving like a presidential candidate. Although we knew little about Varda, the moment we heard he had come, we all felt joyously relieved, as if our destiny had been revealed.

I find myself at a baffled loss to describe Varda. The very stillness of words would be enough to disqualify them from evoking the inexhaustible mobility of his mind. He had been described to us as Bohemian, a romantic, a saint, a pied piper, and a "great uninhibitor." I came to see him as a Master Zorba, who reinvented life as he went along, guilt free and in a perpetual state of wonder and pleasure.

Now that Varda was here, the summer school could truly begin. No sooner had he gathered his students than he announced that preparations for a big Greek party less than three weeks hence should be started immediately, that costumes, props, and decorating the hall were going to be the substance of his course. In no time, the dark, moody campus had been transformed into a craft-crazy village where in every corner someone could be found hammering, sawing, painting, or sewing. What a group of some of the cleverest intellectuals, most challenging philosophers, and exciting artists in America had failed to achieve, Varda obtained with a wink. Hours after his arrival at Black Mountain the mood had drastically changed.

Although Black Mountain College as we knew it has long since disappeared, whenever I meet someone who has been there, I know that we share feelings and knowledge that were unique to Albers's teaching philosophy and to Bauhaus.

Norlyst

It was through Ed Zern that I met Elenor Lust, who ran the Norlyst Gallery, a New York art gallery that showed mostly surrealist-oriented works of established masters and younger painters like myself. Ed had brought her with a friend to my studio one weekend when they were visiting the Zerns at their Arden bungalow. The friend turned out to be Jimmy Ernst, her companion of several years, son of the famous founder of surrealist painting, Max Ernst.

I had known and loved Max Ernst's paintings ever since my two Brussels years, when during my weekly visits to Aunt Mies, I had become so familiar with the works of the most important modern artists that even at that young age I could recognize reproductions in books and magazines without reading their names in the captions. While waiting for lunch to be served, Uncle René would play a game with me that we called Name the Artist; it was simple and fast. Uncle René would point to one of the canvases that filled his walls, and I was supposed to name the artist. For each correct answer I would get ten centimes. It wasn't much of a game, but in those years, when very few people had even heard the names of Picasso, Matisse, or Miró, I was already well acquainted not only with their works but with those of Picabia, De Chirico, Braque, Chagall, and Ernst, who was one of my favorites. Most of Uncle René's paintings were engraved so sharply in my memory that still today, seventy years later, I think I could paint fairly exact copies without seeing the originals.

Once I had freed myself from the seduction of Leon Karp's devotion to the great tradition "in modern dress," his Manet-inspired realism, I had moved naturally in the direction of pictorial storytelling, of which the first masters I had met were Klee, De Chirico, and especially Ernst, the most outspokenly literary of the three. The paintings that I showed my visitors were clear evidence of my devotion to their work. To meet Max Ernst's son and to have him interested in my paintings was no less a thrill than if he had been his father, especially since his open and enthusiastic manner invited an immediate relationship.

Elenor Lust was a vivacious and charming woman, several years Jimmy's senior. They had met at the Art Students League, where her most famous exploit had been her answer to the league's refusal to admit her large briard to classes: she registered the dog as a student. By 1943, a few years after she had opened the gallery with Jimmy's help and influence, she was showing mostly young painters with surrealist tendencies, and the place had become an after-work hangout for many of the most important artists in New York. To my great excitement, I received a letter from Elenor a week after her visit, offering me a one-man show. My first in America.

As I set out now to describe the paintings that were exhibited in that show, I am reminded of an episode that took place in the late seventies in the Bonvicini Foundry near Verona, where I was preparing a large wax sculpture to be cast in bronze. Quinto Ghermandi, a sculptor-friend from Bologna who was working not far from where I was standing, had stopped what he was doing and was staring at me over the rims of his glasses. "You always tell stories, don't you?" he said.

What did Quinto mean? When I asked him, he mumbled something unintelligible. Of course. To him, whose work is abstract, I thought somewhat resentfully, everything else is probably a story. But as I kept thinking about the puzzling remark, I had to admit that there was some truth in it. Later I realized that he had meant it as a compliment, and it was a profound and important comment on all my work. He hadn't meant it literally, of course; it is impossible to tell a story, an event that develops over time, in a single, static image. What is possible is to endow it with figurative references to the passing of time. The piece I was working on represented a specimen of my Parallel Botany, a project I had been working on since the early seventies and which had been the theme of several of my shows, both in Italy and in New York, as well as of my work at the 1972

Venice Biennale. The idea had originated with my need to free myself from
my ten-year obsession with the endless series of small imaginary portraits
that had been inspired by the Fayum portraits at the Metropolitan Museum. I had found an unused canvas, narrow and tall, and on the spur of
the moment had begun painting a tree. It had a smooth trunk and dense
foliage, and although it looked real, it wasn't any particular genus. Like
the sitters for my little portraits, whose urban habitat existed only in my
mind, the model for this painting existed only in a botany I had invented.

When Quinto was watching me work, I was busy marking the smooth
skin of the plant with small imperfections here and there—scars, carbun-
cles, wounds that implied a struggle for survival while enriching it as an
object. It was substance; now I was giving it its particular time span.

After the war, when I showed Giorgio Morandi's pictures in America,
the general reaction was a sarcastic and dismissive "Bottles." In that
same year I showed the works of Ben Shahn in Italy. The disparaging reaction there was "Illustration." The two comments are perfect examples of
what Quinto meant: Shahn was fundamentally a storyteller—his paintings always refer the beholder to an event. Nothing could be further from
Morandi's intentions. He pursues the static completeness of the objects as
the only valid option for a painter.

There is no substantial difference by which we can attribute a
higher aesthetic value to one choice or the other. Our preference is a question of a personal, irrepressible urge. Of style. Yes. Quinto was right:
"telling stories" was the essence of my style.

The paintings in the Norlyst show were an involuntary homage to
my mentors, the surrealist storytellers among whom I include Ben
Shahn, who, when he saw the show said, "Finally! I must confess I never
liked those portraits, still lifes, and landscapes you were doing before.
They weren't you."

JWT

On an unusually chaotic Friday morning in February of 1946, I was sitting curved over my drawing board in my eighth-floor cubicle, struggling
with a new slogan for General Electric to be discussed at a meeting that

very day while at my back two messengers were arguing vociferously about whose turn was next, when the telephone rang. Feeling under pressure, I decided to let it ring, but when it didn't stop I picked up the receiver. I thought I recognized the voice of one of the young copywriters, an inveterate jokester whose specialty was making crank telephone calls. So when an unfamiliar voice said, "Leo Lionni, this is Arthur Blomquist of J. Walter Thompson speaking. Leo, I would—""Jerry," I yelled, "if you have to pull that gag, choose a better moment. I'm terribly busy," and I hung up and returned to my drawing board. "That was Jerry with his latest," I said to the messenger boy who was first in line and who couldn't have been less interested. "He calls you," I went on, "and says he's Jesus or the president or something and wants to talk to you a——" The telephone rang again. "Hello," I shouted, and I heard that voice again: "Leo, this is Arthur Blomquist. Do you have just a few minutes to arrange a meeting to discuss—" This time I didn't even answer. I simply hung up.

But when the third call came, and I picked up the phone again, it was a woman's voice on the line. "Mr. Lionni, please forgive me. I am Mr. Blomquist's secretary. Mr. Blomquist has been trying to reach you, but there seemed to be some problem with the connection. Could you speak to him now?" "Of course," I answered, suddenly aware of having made a terrible gaffe. "Leo, oh! I finally have you on the line! I've been trying to reach you for the last half hour, but I always get some idiot yelling on the other end. Since it's fairly important, I had to insist. Forgive me. The president has asked me to see if you would be interested in getting away from the Philadelphia humidity. Leo, would you have a chance to come to New York in the near future?" "It doesn't look like it. I'm up to my neck in deadlines." "Well then, suppose we meet in Philadelphia for a leisurely dinner one of these days—could you make that pretty soon, tomorrow possibly?"

It was with immense difficulty that I managed not to call Nora that afternoon and tell her about my next day's dinner meeting with the most important agency art director in the business. The sudden vision of moving to New York was a thrill I could barely handle. When I finally broke the news to her, she sat down on one of the kitchen chairs and looked at me with an expression I had never before seen on her face. It was as if life ran slowly out of her, leaving the lines that defined her handsome face flawlessly drawn, like the precise rendering of a plaster cast enveloped in the white silence of the paper—an Ingres. "You're not excited," I finally said, sotto voce. She smiled sadly. "Oh, I don't know—the prospect of more change scares me." She had said it so clearly that I felt relieved; so reasonably that I was sure it would be easy to get her to agree with whatever my decision was going to be. "Besides," she went on, "you don't really know what it's all about, do you?" I didn't answer. I didn't dare tell her how clearly I had seen myself sitting in my Madison Avenue office, in my Brooks Brothers gray-flannel suit and blue-striped shirt. I had trouble finding the right tie. She suddenly jumped up and embraced me, laughing. "You're excited, aren't you?" I grinned stupidly. I was dazzled once more by that incredible gift of hers, the slow, effortless, direct leap to the very last instant of simplification. I would paint her like that.

When I met Arthur Blomquist the next night, it was immediately clear to both of us that we had been through enough business meals to know that the main topic of conversation is not supposed to be served until after the dessert. "We know why we are here—let's get it over with so that we can enjoy the food and talk," he said, pushing back his chair and stretching his legs. "Would you like to move to New York?" He pulled a cigar out of his vest pocket and lit it in deep concentration, as if he had stepped into a new time zone. "Would you be interested?" He sucked hard on his cigar. His face disappeared in a cloud of smoke, and before I knew it I had said, "Yes." I can't remember saying it, but the sound of it still hangs in my ears. He had taken me totally off guard. No preamble to cushion the shock, no paving the way. The essence. He didn't mention the job. He didn't mention money. He had summed it all up. Would I like to move to New York? Yes. And now?

Thank God, he talked. "Well, we have been looking very seriously at your work, and we could use someone like you, with your verve, your imagination, and your Italian touch." Once more his face disappeared in a cloud of bluish smoke. When it reappeared I had composed a reasonable answer, in sync with his flattering remarks, but suddenly I had a shiver of revolt, an intuition perhaps, and I said something truly aggressive like "Let's forget the polite game. Tell me what the deal is." Blomquist straightened out, leaned toward me, looked deep into my eyes, and said, "I like you." He said it directly, without feeling. A simple observation. And then he went on. "OK. That suits me fine. We want you for the Ford Unit—I don't have to tell you, you know all about it. Ford would be your only account, but we'd like you to take a critical look at the whole of J. Walter's art and copy operation. I mean for all the accounts. Sort of a critic in residence."

That was far more than I had anticipated. I was stunned and did not hide it. "Well," I said, scratching my chin, "although I have serious reservations about the Ford account, I must admit that it sounds enticing." I

don't think Arthur even heard me, for he had launched into a long description of J. Walter's operation. And he talked money. I was astonished—it was more than double what I was making. And that was about
the extent of our so-called negotiation, to be rediscussed in detail when I
visited New York.

When I returned home late that evening, Nora was sound asleep. I
tiptoed to the bed, and when I kissed her she sat up and immediately
asked, "What happened?" "You won't believe this . . . he offered me the
Ford account." "Well, that's that," she said with her Swiss rationality. "It
isn't that simple," and then I told her the whole story. "And the upshot?"
she asked. "No upshot," I said. "I practically had to carry him to his room
at the Bellevue. He'll probably call me tomorrow morning."

And then, as I was undressing, the realities of the evening slowly
penetrated. "Hey, you know, I don't think I have to deal directly with the
Ford account. . . . I could just supervise it from a comfortable distance.
Do you know that I'll be making twice as much as I do now, not to speak
of a bonus? Twice as much. You know how much that is? We could live in
the suburbs." Nora grabbed me by the arm. "What do you mean *could?*
You wouldn't want the kids to grow up in New York City, would you?"
"You've got a point. I'll buy a Ferrari for the city and a Lamborghini for
Connecticut." "And I'll get myself two fur coats—a mink for weekdays
and a sable for Sunday." And so it went, until an hour later we were both
asleep.

Arthur called at eleven. "Leo, could you come up one day next week
to look the joint over and meet some of the boys and the president? It's
only fair that before making a decision you should get a smell of the
place." "Spend a day at the shop? How about next Wednesday?"

Our minds were made up. My unequivocal yes to Blomquist had
been smoldering under various disguises for quite some time. Every trip
to New York had strengthened my conviction that ultimately there would
be no other choice, and now J. Walter's concrete offer made it all relatively
easy. The work didn't worry me—I had learned that many professions are
much less arbitrary and more open-ended than one would assume. By
now I could boast a pretty good record of improvisation. We already had
quite a few friends and acquaintances in the heart of Manhattan as well
as in the New York suburbs. Some lived in elegant brownstones in the Village, others in Connecticut farmhouses as far as the Massachusetts border. We knew our options, and they all seemed exciting. No matter what
our preference was going to be, we would have the money to pay for it.
Wasn't that what the American dream was all about?

Paolo

Until now our lives had almost automatically guided us to where we were. Mannie had landed with very little effort in Central High, an excellent high school with a college rating. Paolo, with his bizarre combination of talents and troubles, was not yet of an age where one school or another was going to make an important difference; a change might even be beneficial to him—he needed to be challenged, his teachers said. Nora had developed a life of her own in Philadelphia in which the Academy of Music had considerable weight, but the Big Apple probably offered the best and densest choice of music in the world. She adored our house, but she agreed that Philadelphia was hopelessly provincial; many women had "a little black dress" just for New York! There were our friends, but they would visit us no matter where we went, we would have a special party for them once a year, and we would spend weekends in Bucks County to see all of them. We did not realize, of course, that in a few days our vision of a future in New York had taken on the style of those damned Ford ads. All the details, thanks to Wally's campaign, seemed to be within our reach. And then there was Europe. As an executive I would have to visit our European clients. Now that the war was over, we could spend Christmas in Paris or Venice. Venice in the snow was spectacular. At any rate, the alternatives were worth a good argument. And in the early hours of the morning Nora and I argued about where we would have a permanent pied-à-terre. Aix-en-Provence? Sils Maria? One thing was certain: Philadelphia had become unlivable and New York was at least a thousand miles closer to Europe. It was in this elated spirit that I made the trip to my new destiny.

It was my first glimpse of a large New York ad agency. I know that I was impressed, but my memory is sketchy. I know that I had a brief chat with the president and with the head of Copy, but no images of faces appear in my mind. I met some of the art directors, and then Arthur opened a very large door and there it was—the enormous square room with cubicles all around. Fifteen? Twenty? There were no windows; some cubicles were empty. In others, young men and women sat at their typewriters, furiously typing away. And in one cubicle two men and a woman seated on the edge of a desk and a small table were talking and gesticulating, blowing clouds of smoke, and then suddenly I made an amazing discovery: the cubicles had swinging wrought-iron doors, four feet or so high, Art Nouveau branches swirling around each other like snakes in love and here and there an occasional ivy leaf. The kind of wrought-iron gates that are used to separate the boutiques in elegant men's stores. Was it the Great Reptile Hall of the Amsterdam Zoo? I saw it sharply—had I wanted I could have read the glittering brass nameplates of the snakes: *Crotalus adamanteus, Vipera berus, Natrix sipedon, Micrurus fulvius, Agkistrodon mokeson, Lampropeltis getulus.* It was magic. I almost mentioned it to Arthur, but just in time I remembered where I really was and why I was there. I turned my eyes toward him.

"Let's go and see the president," he said. I pressed my thumbs hard against my eyes and with great difficulty managed to shake myself loose from the thorny branches that had grown around me. I knew in my mind that I wasn't going to take the job. I went through all the motions and played my role to the very end, until late that afternoon I took leave of Arthur and boarded the Philadelphia Express. From the window I saw him walking slowly down the platform, like a professor who had delivered his very last lecture, and no one had applauded.

My return trip to Philadelphia seemed endless as the unexpected turn of events kept churning in my mind. For most Europeans who like us had fled the old continent, the end of the war was not just a cause for celebration, it was an event that had shaken the fragile foundations of our reinvented lives. Now all had changed once more, and many among us found ourselves assailed by ancient nostalgias and new desires. I knew that it was not only because of some wrought-iron doors that I had rejected the move to New York I had thought I so intensely desired. Now, in distant hindsight, I realize that my last-minute reversal was part of a much more complex pattern that had at its center a gnawing need for continuous, unobstructed mobility. Again, as so often in my life, I had defended myself from the threat of a predictable future.

The moment I spotted Nora and Paolo on the platform of North Philadelphia Station I shouted a triumphal "It's off!" Nora ran toward me yelling an unexpectedly American "whoopee!" and joyfully embraced me.

Of course it wasn't all that simple. Our wish to move to New York had not been absurd and had not lost its validity. The particular circumstances of place and time had obviously been wrong, but they were useful in defining the eventual right conditions. For the time being, my rejection of the J. Walter Thompson adventure had freed us to face possibilities that we wouldn't have dared consider only a few days earlier. And before we knew it we were discussing details of a year in Europe. Having definitely if indirectly rejected an important career in advertising, I was now free to move where my heart would take me without guilt or regrets.

Home

We shed no tears when the Genoa-bound SS *Subiesky,* a remodeled Polish warship, slowly pulled out of its moorings in New York harbor while a tinny four-piece band played an off-tune "Happy Days Are Here Again." The *Subiesky*'s decor and so-called facilities surely did not reveal proverbial Italian craftsmanship. The remodeling into an ocean liner had been done hastily and was evident in every corner of the ship. The new paint had already begun to peel, all the metal parts that are traditionally a ship's pride were dull and dirty. While the only Poles on the boat were members of the crew, the signs, safety regulations, and the day's events were in Polish. God knows what we missed. On the Fourth of July, the U.S. citizens—and we were among them, having pledged our allegiance in 1945—were invited in broken English (or was it Polish?) to join Kaptan Giungevisky in an informal ceremony on the top deck. When a little group had assembled and the American flag was raised, the *kaptan* delivered his short speech, beginning with the memorable words: "Ladies and gentlemen, thank you for being so numerous and promptly."

We had enough trunks, suitcases, and crates onboard for a permanent change of continent. In addition to a very large crate containing a generous sampling of everything Italian that we knew or assumed to be scarce, selected by Nora and prepared by Manganaro, then one of the best authentic Italian grocery stores in New York, we had two smaller crates, and then there was our old Plymouth. It was the last week of June, vacation time; the passengers were joyous, the air was clear and soft, and we were going home—although it didn't seem we had a home to go to. In his last letter six months earlier, Nicola, Bruna's husband, mentioned that one of Nora's Cavi houses had been bombed and was virtually destroyed, but we had no idea what the reality of the situation was. Besides, we had already arranged to stay at "the" house with Papà Maffi.

The arrival in Genoa was as emotional as we had expected. The family was there to greet us: Adda, her very tall husband, Popi Besana, a textile engineer, and their three children, who had come, one-two-three, in the first three years of their marriage; and Bruna, with her lawyer-husband, Nicola, and their three children. Only Mario and Papà Maffi were missing. Mario had spent the war years as a British prisoner in India and gained international notoriety for his two abortive attempts to escape, bearded and dressed like a Sikh. He was now working on an experimental snake farm in the jungles of Brazil. And Papà was awaiting our arrival in Cavi. A few tears of happiness were shed, and everybody was impressed with the size of the boys and admiringly patted our well-filled American stomachs. In Italy, they said, they hadn't seen bellies like those in five years. They stood around us, examining our anatomies as if we were racehorses.

I couldn't take my eyes off the city of Genoa, which with its great circular gesture embraced us. Seen from the harbor, it was as spectacular as it had remained in my memory. But as we stood there like actors on the stage of that enormous, steep amphitheater, I got a closer look and noticed that here and there were heaps of rubble and craters, and straight ahead, near the station, the Hotel Miramare's windows were boarded up, the fancy white facade gutted.

We had a rich lunch at l'Olivo, in my time one of the best fish restaurants in town. It was our first direct encounter with the new Italian reality after the ravages of war. When we walked in I recognized one of the old waiters, but he confessed that he didn't remember me. The place was completely redecorated and had lost its air of the wonderful no-nonsense Genovese eating place in exchange for a glossy, garish international-style restaurant. The wall with the buffet where the dishes were stacked was now an ambitious, complicated mosaic of a heap of fish of all kinds on a table, a veritable miracle catch, with five huge and detailed lobsters and, God knows why, a cauliflower in the foreground. The colors were the familiar ones of the Genovese painters I used to know, Saccorotti and Rambaldi, but there was a profusion of arbitrarily placed gold tesserae that gave it a vulgar twinkle.

When we came back to the pier, we found all our luggage—the trunks, suitcases, and the three crates—standing against the wall of the customs office, and looking up I saw the Plymouth in chains, poised for its descent onto the pier. Soon a customs man appeared with a copy of the contents lists for the crates. The officer gave the large crate a serious look, read the label, tilted his cap to scratch his head, and said to the two longshoremen who were standing by the equivalent of "OK, boys, open her up!" One of the men climbed on top of the crate with a crowbar and managed to remove enough slats to reach inside and triumphantly reveal the first package, containing twelve rolls of the finest, softest toilet paper available. We figured that in a country where even in peacetime neatly cut pages of the *Gazzetta dello Sport* hung from a hook near the toilet, the superior extra-soft brand would be a welcome if somewhat daring gift. Our intuition was confirmed by spontaneous applause from family and bystanders, but the applause died out when the man on the crate pulled out a second package and a third. "There is nothing but toilet paper!" "Twelve packages of twelve," said the customs officer reading from the list in a sober tone of voice. "What else do you see, Gianni?" "Here is a bag of flour, and below—" "OK," said Customs, "close her up. Do you have anything valuable to declare?" "No," I said, "just some small presents for the family—you know, we haven't seen them since 1939."

I shall never forget our first meal in Cavi. Annetta had been at it since very early in the morning. On the white marble kitchen table, perfectly aligned as if they were to be reviewed by Escoffier himself, lay what looked like a hundred ravioli meticulously identical, with their tiny pleated skirts all around. Annetta looked at me as I stood there mesmerized by such maniacal perfection, and not knowing what to say she just covered her mouth with her hand and laughed and laughed. "Oh, Signore Leo," she said, and exploded once more in laughter. "I am happy too," I said, and then she turned around and dried her tears in her apron. It was a festive dinner, and Annetta was generously applauded.

The question of where we were going to stay had been easily resolved. Our rooms were ready, and the possibility of staying in one of the "chicken coops" would be discussed on our return from Amsterdam, where we would go for a week or so after we had caught our breath. We had a whole year ahead of us. We were home.

part three

1948–1961

Fortune

Our generation can claim to have had one privilege that future genera-
tions are not likely to enjoy: the boat trip to Europe and back. Eight days
of complete detachment from both continents—eight days to take stock of
failures, achievements, and expectations. It had taken me no more than a
sporty walk around the decks to decide that there was no one onboard as
interesting as I myself. So I left Nora and the kids at the pool, dragged a
deck chair to a hidden corner of the top deck, and lay down to think.

It had been an extraordinary year. Except for two months making
mosaics in Ravenna, I had painted a lot, sometimes with fury and sometimes with tranquil dedication. In the "coop" next to the one that had been
Nora's, bombed clean by an American plane, I had installed my studio.
There, in the loneliness of what remained of the pine forest, I painted still
lifes, landscapes, and the wild rocks of Sant'Anna. I painted the spooky
accordionist from the Chiavari market with his glossy black top hat and
a red silk scarf around his neck; three chickens scratching the city soil;
and the lion of a bad dream advancing slowly toward his meal—me.
These images, still fresh with their actual light and smell, paled as they
settled in my memory, and as we floated farther from Genoa harbor and
closer to Madison Avenue, other memories forced their presence into my
mind.

The hard evidence of the year in Italy, the things I had found and
made—the ceramics, the pebbles, the paintings, the photographs, mosaics, and drawings—had been stored in the Maffi house in Cavi. Given
my uncertainty about the future, I had decided to return to Philadelphia
with all options open. It must have been a deliberate act. How could I
have know that in another ten years I would make the great decision of
my life?

For the present, I no longer dreaded my return as an art director. I didn't even mind the words "commercial artist," which yesterday would have plunged me deep into gloom. I accepted the stereotypes. Looking at the advertising world from the European vantage point, I could view American graphics with a certain nostalgia, glorifying the status of graphic artists, exalting their professional attitude, and praising their sensitivity and originality.

But after our return from Europe, it took only a few months for me to begin to feel restless. After this long spell of freedom, I knew that I would never be the same again. My easel was still encrusted with the colors of the Mediterranean autumn. I wanted to write, to draw, to walk, to float slowly along the Cavi coast. I wanted to return to Ravenna and cut tesserae from the glass paste of Byzantium and the glass pies of the Venice furnaces, and cut the tiniest ones—I was good at that. On my little homemade anvil I could cut green bottle glass into one-millimeter-square tesserae without losing a drop of blood.

I began to hate myself for being an advertising man; I felt ashamed to have designed so many successful campaigns. I was in full rebellion. I didn't want another job, I wanted my own studio, in New York.

Early on a Tuesday morning in February of 1948, I boarded the train for New York. I had only the vaguest idea of what to expect. I had made five appointments—with *Fortune,* Procter & Gamble, MoMA, CBS, and the American Cancer Society. Bill Golden, the art director at CBS, a close friend of Ben Shahn, would surely have some project for me. And I trusted John Fistere, *Fortune*'s promotion manager, whose ads I had art-directed at N. W. Ayer since 1941, when he said they would have plenty of work for me. And then there was the curator of graphic design at the Museum of Modern Art, Mildred Constantine, a distant cousin of Leon Karp, who knew and liked my work.

Exhausted and elated, I returned to Philadelphia that evening on the six-thirty express with enough assignments to keep me busy for a few months. It had turned out to be a day full of surprises. Bill Golden had the text for a booklet lying on his desk as if it had been waiting there for me. His instructions were typical Bill: "See what you can do with this." While I was in his office, Ben and later Jerry Snyder, who was the art director for *Scientific American,* showed up. What was supposed to have been a business meeting turned into a coffee klatch, where politics and art were discussed and new Jewish jokes were launched on their cross-country careers, while silently, efficiently, and unobtrusively Bill took care of the business of promoting the greatest radio and television net-

The Family of Man

The greatest photographic exhibition of all time—503 pictures from 68 countries—

created by Edward Steichen for the Museum of Modern Art

Prologue by Carl Sandburg

Cover for *The Family of Man* catalog, 1955

ABOVE LEFT: Cover for *Fortune*, February 1960

ABOVE RIGHT: Cover for *Fortune*, January 1955

BELOW LEFT: Book jacket, 1953

BELOW RIGHT: Ad for wool manufacturer Rossi, Milan, 1935

OPPOSITE: Competition poster for American Institute of Graphic Arts, 1959

Going for a walk with a line

a step into the world of modern art

BY DOUGLAS AND ELIZABETH MACAGY

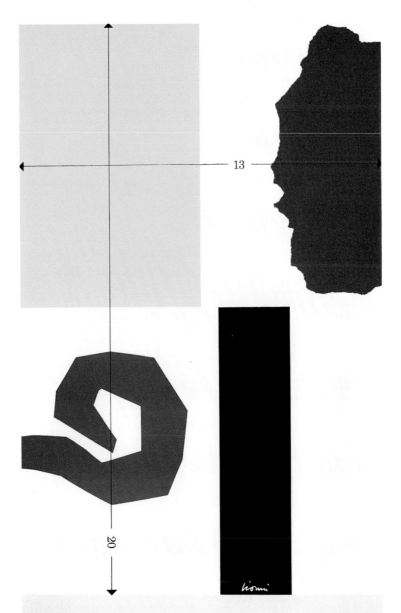

13

20

Poster Competition: National Graphic Arts Expositions, Inc.

Seventh Educational Graphic Arts Exposition, to be held at the New York Coliseum,

September 6–12, 1959, New York City First Prize,$1,000; Second Prize,$750

Judging and awards to be conducted under the auspices of The American Institute of Graphic Arts 5 East 40th Street, New York 16, N.Y.

PURPOSE: The purpose of the Poster Competition is to obtain a poster for the Seventh Educational Graphic Arts Exposition to be held at the N. Y. Coliseum, New York City, September 6 through 12, 1959. This Exposition organized by The International Association of Printing House Craftsmen, Inc, the Printing Industry of America, Inc., and other leading organizations of the graphic arts, will represent manufacturers of printing machinery and supplies which are designed to improve production efficiency and the quality of the printed product.

DATES: Design entries should be mailed by midnight, Friday, January 30, 1959. The jury will meet during the week of February 16-20, 1959, following which announcement of the prize winners will be made. Selected designs may be exhibited at a place and on a date to be announced.
CONDITIONS OF CONTEST: 1. There is no limit to the number of design entries which may be submitted by one designer.
2. Entries must be submitted by working professionals, not students or amateurs.
3. Each design must include the emblems of The International Association of Printing House Craftsmen, Inc., and the Printing Industry of America, Inc., as well as the words "Seventh Educational Graphic Arts Exposition, Printing and Allied Industries—Coliseum—New York, New York—September 6-12, 1959.
4. Not more than four basic colors may be employed in the designs. That is, it must be possible to reproduce the poster (and from it a small sticker) in not more than four printing impressions.
5. Designs must be submitted in a size suitable for reproduction in the size 13" x 20". Submissions

should be matted with three inches for each dimension.
6. The selections will be made on the basis of suitability of the design to the nature of the exposition, pictorial value, and the originality of conception.
7. The two prize-winning designs and copyrights thereon become the property of the National Graphic Arts Expositions, Inc.
8. Designs are submitted at the owner's risk. Neither The American Institute of Graphic Arts nor the National Graphic Arts Expositions, Inc., will be responsible for loss through fire, theft, or any other cause while designs are in their custody or in transit.
9. The winning designs will receive publicity in the daily press and in the trade press, as far as can be arranged by the two sponsoring organizations.
10. Submission of a design for this competition shall in itself constitute acceptance of all the conditions herein set forth.

IDENTIFICATION AND DELIVERY: All entries must be accompanied by entry blanks (two are enclosed). Additional entry forms may be obtained upon request.

Design entries should be mailed or expressed to the Chairman, Poster Competition Committee, The American Institute of Graphic Arts, 5 East 40th Street, New York 16, New York. The name and address of the sender should appear only on

the upper right hand corner of the back of the design. No signature should appear on the face of the design.

All designs not awarded prizes may be called for, or will be returned collect by U. S. mail or express upon request at the close of the competition judging.

THE AMERICAN INSTITUTE OF GRAPHIC ARTS: The American Institute of Graphic Arts was founded in 1914 to stimulate and encourage those engaged in the graphic arts, and generally to do all things to raise the standards and aid in the extension and development of the graphic arts. AIGA not only recognizes successful achievement, but also nourishes the desire to learn and to achieve success, and encourages this desire with the full power of its resources.

OFFICERS: Edna Beilenson, President; Alvin Eisenman, Vice President; William P. Gleason, Vice President; George M. McCorkle, Vice President; Joseph Blumenthal, Vice President; Honore H. Nahm, Vice President; Bruce Gentry, Secretary; Leonard Shatzkin, Treasurer.

POSTER COMPETITION CHAIRMAN: Robert Cato.

JURY: Joseph Blumenthal, The Spiral Press; Mildred Constantine, Associate Curator of Graphics, The Museum of Modern Art; Leo Lionni, Art Director, Fortune; Paul Rand, Free-Lance Designer; James Johnson Sweeney, Director, Solomon R. Guggenheim Museum.

DESIGN: Leo Lionni.

Ad for Container Corporation of America's Great Ideas of Western Man series, 1948

COLUMBIA MASTERWORKS ML 4990

Peggy Glanville-Hicks: sonata for piano and percussion
New York Percussion Group and Carlo Bussotti, piano, conducted by Carlo Surinach

Peggy Glanville-Hicks: concertino da camera for piano, flute, clarinet and bassoon
New York Woodwind Ensemble and Carlo Bussotti, piano

Nikolai Lopatnikoff: variations and epilogue for 'cello and piano
Nikolai Graudan, 'Cello; Joanna Graudan, piano

ABOVE: Record album cover, 1964

BELOW LEFT: Poster for UNESCO, 1955

BELOW RIGHT: Book cover for paperback edition of *Michael Bakunin*, Vintage, 1951

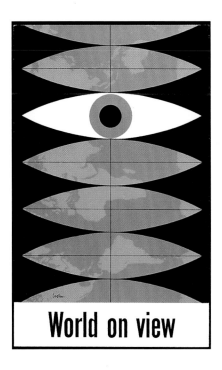

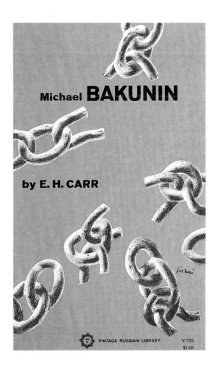

The Olivetti
"Lettera 22"
Portable Typewriter

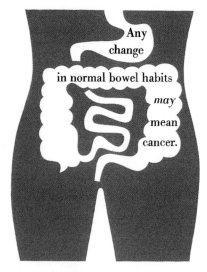

Any change
in normal bowel habits *may* mean cancer.

Cancer is curable
if treated early.

Great Ideas of Western Man... *one of a series*

Plato on Wisdom in Government

Until philosophers are kings,

or the kings and princes of this world have the spirit and power of philosophy,

and political greatness and wisdom meet in one,

and those commoner natures who pursue either to the exclusion of the other

are compelled to stand aside,

cities will never have rest from their evils.   (The Republic, 4th century B.C.)

Artist: Leo Lionni   Container Corporation of America

ABOVE LEFT: Promotion
piece for Olivetti, 1954

ABOVE RIGHT: Poster for
American Cancer Society, 1950

LEFT: Ad for Container
Corporation of America's
Great Ideas of Western Man
series, 1948

Print

ITALIAN ISSUE X:2

Cover for *Print* magazine, 1956

LEFT: U.S. Pavilion, Brussels World Fair, 1958

BELOW: Olivetti showroom, Chicago (with architect Giorgio Cavaglieri), 1956

RIGHT: Banner for the Palio,
Siena, 1994

BELOW: Mosaic mural
for housing development,
Washington, D.C., 1959

Photographs   ABOVE: Forms of the fifties, San Giovanni Valdarno, Italy
BELOW: Parallel botanies, Mexico

ABOVE: A sacred horse in a Shinto shrine, Japan
BELOW: Seven characters in search of a city, Mexico

Ahmadabab, India, 1956

work in the world. It might well have been during this séance that Bill doodled the eye that would transform every TV set in America with its CBS Cyclops.

My lunch with the promotion director of the American Cancer Society was pleasant but strictly business. A shy, young intellectual, he asked me if I would be willing to undertake the graphics of all the American Cancer Society propaganda material. He talked at length about the difficulty of informing cigarette smokers of the risks they were taking, as revealed by the latest dramatic statistics. The problem was whether or not to frighten the public—since doing so might well have the opposite effect from what one would expect: "What's the use? We're doomed anyway, so we may as well enjoy ourselves; have a cigarette." Having stopped smoking three years earlier, I could speak from experience. The end of the lunch was sealed with a drink to our collaboration, which would begin as soon as possible.

And then at three I was to have the most important meeting of the day. The week before, I had called John Fistere to make an appointment. When I told him that I wanted to open my own studio in New York and hoped that he would give me freelance what I had been doing for *Fortune* at Ayer's for the past five years, there had been a long silence on the other end of the phone. Finally John said, "Why, of course, but wouldn't you rather have the job of art director of the magazine?" It had caught me totally unprepared. What did I know about art-directing a magazine? Not one thing. Besides, I told John, "I just quit a job—I don't want another one." "Well," John insisted, "why don't you talk with Del Paine, the editor, and see? I'll set up an appointment for you."

At three I stepped out of the elevator on the twenty-first floor of the Empire State Building. A young woman at the lobby desk called Mr. Paine's secretary and then walked me to his office. Through half-open doors I saw men bent over their desks, women working at their typewriters, gazing out of windows as if in deep thought. They were fast flashes, but to me, familiar as I was with the rushed life in the cubicles of Ayer, here there was a surprisingly easy silence, like that of a university library. The rugs and the books and the nonchalant disorder of the offices, and the fact that many of the men wore suspenders instead of belts, suggested that this was not a normal commercial enterprise.

After welcoming me very cordially, the first thing Del Paine said was that he was certain we could work out a deal so that I could start as quickly as possible. I hadn't expected such sudden developments. I hadn't had the opportunity to show my portfolio or give even one of the little speeches I had carefully rehearsed. Evidently, John had done the selling, and now all that was left was our signatures on the dotted line. Del was a typical aristocratic New England intellectual: elegant, despite a very baggy Brooks Brothers tweed jacket with leather elbow patches and a corny Abercrombie and Fitch necktie with little pheasants woven in; handsome, despite irregular, almost caricatural features; and eloquent, despite what I first thought was a speech defect but soon discovered to be Timese mumbling. In that exotic language the first word in a sentence is almost inaudible and the last one drowned in a cloud of smoke. And enormously charming.

In less than fifteen minutes he had put me so much at my ease that I didn't hesitate to present him with the list of unacceptable conditions I had devised so as to be able to stick to my original determination to open my own studio. First of all, I did not want to be a *Time* employee because it would exclude the possibility of having my own studio. Second, I would only work three days a week (except in case of emergencies). Third, someone would be appointed to attend meetings (a notorious waste of time) and report to me. Fourth, collaboration in whatever form would begin no sooner than ten days after the opening of the trout season in Pennsylvania.

Up to the fourth condition Del listened to my performance with a gentle if slightly sarcastic smile, but when I mentioned the trout season he raised his eyebrows and looked at me over the rim of his glasses as if I had suddenly gone insane. "Did you say trout season?" "Yes, sir." "Where would you be going, may I ask?" "The Beaverkill." At that he grabbed the phone as if calling an ambulance, and a few minutes later a tall, handsome woman walked in, shook hands, and sat down. "This is Debbie Calkins," said Del. "She has been acting art director since Burtin left a few months ago. She knows more about art than . . . what's the name of that fellow, Deb? The one at the museum in Boston." Debbie laughed and winked at me. "You mean Berenson?" "Right! And less about magazines!"

I was impressed. We then fell into a pleasant conversation about the state of the art world, about Italy, about Philadelphia, and suddenly Del stood up, glanced through a long memo that was lying on his desk, and while Debbie and I left the room for her small office, he mumbled a quick, absentminded good-bye.

"Well, what happened today?" asked Nora as we walked to her car and the train rolled softly out of the Philadelphia Station. "I don't know. I think I'm art director of *Fortune*." "Art director? As a job?" "I believe so." "What do you mean, I believe so?" "That's exactly what I mean."

Greenwich

• • •

My first year with *Fortune* went smoothly, and I got what I had asked for. Taken together, the staff had enough specific know-how and technical knowledge to design the magazine without an art director, and I didn't have to make a frantic effort to understand and learn the specifics of the job—I could just let them trickle in and use my common sense. I instinctively felt that the important part of my job was to develop an atmosphere that was open to change. And change was in the cards—in fact, it happened when we moved from the Empire State Building to the Time & Life Tower in Rockefeller Center. Change always seems to invite more change. It was during the move that I hired Walter Allner, a Bauhaus orphan, to be my special assistant and help with the design of a new, softer, less aesthetically polemic, more readable *Fortune*.

Meanwhile, besides my responsibilities at the magazine, work for my personal studio, which I had rented with the Italian painter Di Cocco, began to pile up. I had promised to help Olivetti with their American advertising and was preparing an exhibition of my graphic work and a catalog for the Museum of Modern Art. When it became clear that it was absurd to continue the daily commute to Philadelphia, Nora and I intensified our efforts to find a house in Connecticut. One day an agent who must have sized us up as two psychomaniacs showed us what had survived of a white clapboard Southern carriage house that at the turn of the century some madman had transported, piece by piece, from Kentucky and placed on a rise in an abandoned two-acre garden. The agent added that it was close to the center of Greenwich and near good schools. We were glad he told us where we were, because we had no idea where he had driven us that day and were ashamed to ask. A month later we were legally registered Greenwich residents frantically restoring and redesigning a Southern carriage house with the help of the New York architect Giorgio Cavaglieri. And six months after that we moved into a real house with a two-story studio and the largest, highest living room we'd ever had.

Recently Mannie, after seeing Monet's house in Giverny, said that it reminded him of our house in Greenwich, both of them long, narrow, and severe. Even the sequence of rooms was like Giverny in Monet's time. I remember the Greenwich house mainly because of the unexpected assertiveness of the great white triangular sides. Seen from a distance, it could have been a circus tent.

Politics and Design

I probably owe it to my first encounters with the political realities of Fascism and Nazism that early in my adult life I reached the conviction that all human acts have social and political consequences. If this was not an easy principle to accept and live by, its natural corollary, responsibility, was even more demanding. My inner dialectics, in fact, seldom settled on dogmatic or utopian conclusions. I was more inclined to face situations as they presented themselves; to deal with real pains and pleasures was a naturally felt priority. Nevertheless, in my private, social, and professional life, principles have played an important part. The guilt I feel at having betrayed or ignored them more often than I like to confess is proof both of their validity and of my faith in their basic truth.

In America the first time my principles were put to the test was at Ayer's, when I was once given copy for an advertisement, the first of a series, warning the reader against the evils of socialism. The ad was sponsored by a group of electric companies and was scheduled to run nationally in general-interest magazines like *Time* and *The Saturday Evening Post.* Shocked, I took the copy home to consult with Nora, who generally was even less tolerant of compromise than I. She agreed that I had no moral choice other than a reasoned refusal to work on that account.

The next morning, sure that I was going to get fired, and anticipating the pains of martyrdom, I handed Charley the copy, but the speech I had so carefully edited and rehearsed during a sleepless night slipped out of my mind. Rather than run the risk of improvising something foolish, I said nothing. Charley read the copy, threw it in his incoming basket, looked at me with his characteristic ironic smile, and said, "Boy, that's some lousy piece of copy." The next (and only) thing I knew, a few days later, was that the account had been handed to someone else. I never figured out how that tall, charming, California cowboyish vice president of an important American corporation could have known what had been going on in my enigmatic European mind, but he had solved the problem without disturbing the status quo.

It was during the first months after my arrival in America that my exposure to political action had been the most intense. After the Italian anti-Fascist experience, in which secrecy was a sine qua non, to be able to express and discuss my beliefs openly without fear of dramatic consequences was almost unbelievable at first.

My early friendship with Ed and Evelyn Zern, and the general mood of Arden, though somewhat too bohemian, romantic, and dilettantish for my taste, was a perfect foundation course for my introduction to American radical politics. It didn't take long before I was actively involved, first with the Independent Artists, Scientists, and Professions for the reelection of Roosevelt, and later with the Progressive Citizens of America, its more radical outgrowth, sponsored by Secretary of Agriculture Henry Wallace, after Roosevelt had been elected. As Philadelphia vice president of both organizations, but free from any party affiliations, I was in an ideal position to learn in a practical way the ins and outs of political action in the United States, which at my level consisted mainly of raising

The Greenwich house, inside and outside

money for political causes, not to speak of witnessing the complex maneuvers for power.

From the very beginning, the theme of my articles and talks to various groups had been directly or indirectly centered on the social responsibilities of designers. I was always careful to include among those whose work affects our visible and moral environment—painters, sculptors, architects—both industrial and graphic designers, for as yet they had not been thought of nor had they thought of themselves as affecting the look of the world around them.

When in 1955 I took over the editorship of *Print,* a magazine that had started as a trade publication for people interested in printing, the format was that of many intellectual monthlies. The style I had chosen to allow, within the limits of readability and good taste—wild, provocative excursions with avant-garde design—visibly changed its format, and the choice of subjects under my editorship attracted the attention of those designers whose work was at the creative forefront of the profession. My principal motivation was to have a chance to give graphic designers an awareness of their status as responsible intellectuals. When, as often happens, I see old issues of *Print* in some architectural office, I am always thrilled to be reminded that it played its part in bringing the design specialist into a common arena. The magazine became, in fact, the mouthpiece for those who believed with me that graphic design is an integral and important part of the arts. I took advantage of the fact that the magazine got very little advertising support in order to give it a somewhat precious, elegant format. With no budget to speak of, I wrote many of the pieces and laid out most of the issues myself. Among all the jobs I have done in my life, I remember "my" *Print* as one of the most satisfying, and I still look at those issues with pride and pleasure.

Whenever possible and appropriate in my talks about the arts, I would bring in politics, declaring myself openly to be a man of the left. It soon became part of a deliberate policy to break down barriers and invite open discussion. As an overpoliticized European, I was amazed by how prejudiced and ignorant Americans could be in their judgments of political ideologies, but I soon discovered that this was a by-product of the Protestant attitude toward privacy, bound to promote secrecy and ignorance. I felt it was important to speak out fearlessly.

The first time I was to have lunch alone with Henry Luce, I went trained and polished like a horse at the Kentucky Derby. *Fortune's* managing editor, Bill Firth, briefed me on Luce's deafness, his absentmindedness, his abruptness, his naiveté, his religious background, and of course, his politics. The first question Luce asked me after he had ordered his martini was an abrupt "What are your politics?" Taken aback by his directness and the odd timing of the question, I answered with an awkward "I guess I am something of an anarchist." He didn't seem surprised and called the waiter. "Waiter, make it a double martini." This was my first verbal exchange with the greatest publisher in the world and the epitome of conservatism. Equally surprising was the episode years later when his secretary called me to his office, where without uttering a word Luce handed me a letter from Senator McCarthy, I believe (or was it a copy of *Red Channels*, the McCarthyite publication?) demanding that I, a "notorious fellow traveler," be fired. He then handed me a copy of his answer, which stated in very simple, direct words that my politics were my own private business.

Once Nora and I were invited to a formal dinner at the Luces'. There were four tables of eight, and Nora had the honor of being seated next to "Harry." (At Time Inc. the categories of workers were distinguished by the way they referred to Henry Luce: those who called him Mr. Luce, those who called him Luce, and those fortunate few who called him Harry.) In her amusing report on the evening while we were driving back to Greenwich, Nora told me that the end of the enormous dining room where she was seated was dominated by a monumental crystal chandelier. For want of anything else to say, and to break the embarrassing silence, she turned to her illustrious neighbor and said, "What a beautiful chandelier you have." Harry gave the chandelier a surprised look and mumbled, "Hm, never saw it before."

I liked Harry. I liked his always being somewhere else. I liked his way of summing up. I liked his shockingly simple questions. In policy discussions he always played courageously from the net. I liked his pronouncements—"People like people"—or the editorial variant, "People are interested in people." But much as I liked Harry, I disliked and in a way feared Clare. Cold, ambitious, arrogant—she was all of those. A Time Inc. executive once said of her, "Clare makes me feel as if I had soup all over my vest." I have seldom heard a better description. Once Clare said to me, "I am too busy to keep up with all that's going on in the art world. I would appreciate it so much if you would have dinner with us sometime so that we can talk about art. I have been doing some painting, and I wish we could get Harry interested. It would do him good."

Those dinners at the Luces' were, of course, interesting as a phenomenon, but the conversations that were supposed to illuminate the Luces' minds on the nature of art in the twentieth century never rose beyond the depressing banalities of amateurism.

Aspen

The idea of a national conference on design had been in the air for a while. Several graphic and industrial designers had discussed its feasibility privately, and in one form or another proposals had been aired in public. But it wasn't until Walter Paepcke's advertising director, Egbert Jacobson, took it on as an official Container Corporation–sponsored project that the idea finally took flight. Egbert was an exceptionally quiet, unobtrusive man. Although I had art-directed Container advertising for five years, I hardly knew him. That our relationship never went beyond mutual sympathy was probably due to Walter Paepcke's massive presence in the company.

I don't remember how the project actually took shape, but I remember vividly the first general meeting in Frank Stanton's office. Frank, then president of CBS, and I shared a close friendship with his art director, Bill Golden, one of the most gifted and respected graphic designers on the New York scene. There was an unusual assortment of twenty or so people at the meeting, all dedicated to the same basic ideology: to promote interest in good design by bringing together the people who could make it happen—designers, architects, manufacturers, and merchandisers. Present at this meeting were some important figures from the New York art and design scene: Wallace Harrison, Philip Johnson, René d'Harnoncourt, Mildred Constantine, George Nelson, Buckminster Fuller. During the discussion, cleverly manipulated by Egbert, I noticed that the conference had almost imperceptibly become an Aspen Conference. I didn't know then of Paepcke's ambitious plans to develop Aspen as a high-level conference center, and I was naive enough to question a location so difficult to reach and so far from the traditional brain centers of the country. When today, almost fifty years after that first meeting, I look back on the history of the conference and on what it has meant to me personally, including my affection for the spectacular beauty and mood of the now world-famous resort, I am happy that my doubts were ignored and that Egbert's behind-the-scenes diplomacy had so ably manipulated the birth of the project.

The first conference—Design as a Function of Management—took place in Aspen in June 1951. National and limited though it was in scope, resonance, and number of participants, it laid the foundation for what was to become the most important annual event in the world of design. Above all, it helped sharpen the focus of future conferences as it became clear that our real opportunity lay in a yearly international conference on all debatable aspects not only of design itself but of all matters that are or should be of interest to the design community.

I brought the whole Olivetti management group with me to that first meeting—at the time they were internationally recognized as the pioneers of a new industrial and graphic design. We arrived a few days early to have time to install a display of their design program, and I shall never forget the flight in a small plane from Kansas City to Denver through a storm so violent and spectacular that we arrived at Denver with the plane's windshield smashed.

The intellectual level of the people I met, the themes and quality of the discussions, and the personal relationships developed during the Aspen meetings gave me concrete evidence that my conception of the designer, which I had developed throughout my early years at the drawing board, was correct. I was now more certain than ever that the functions and responsibilities of the graphic designer lay in an area much closer to that of the architect than to the hard, pragmatic world of advertising. Direct contact with people like Christopher Alexander, Buckminster Fuller, George Nelson, Edgar Kaufmann, Josef Albers, Louis Kahn, gave tangible body to my growing conviction that what was at stake was less the power of design to influence sales than our mission to help shape a reasonable and civilized environment for all human beings.

This, of course, implied a substantial rethinking of our involvement as designers. It meant becoming an integral part of a community dedicated to a common ideology that would cover not only all formal and symbolic aspects of the visual environment but their inseparable political content as well. Dealing with design as a function of management represented only a small part of our responsibilities. The real, much broader, issue was how to deal with the needs of human beings and with the things they use and make to satisfy those needs.

It was probably because of my passionate promotion of these views that I was asked to chair the First International Design Conference in Aspen. Innocent as I was, I was very excited at having the opportunity to give form to the many ideas that were still vague and approximate in my mind. Although I had the backing of Container Corporation and did not have to worry about the physical problems in Aspen, such as housing guests and organizing and preparing the facilities there, the mere putting together of a program, and selecting speakers and dealing with them on an international scale, turned out to be a far greater undertaking than I had expected. I learned soon enough that what on paper seemed reasonable could well turn out to be unworkable. The idea, for instance, that one must have a program first and then choose the right speakers seems obvious, yet from the very beginning it was clear that the speakers I contacted would affect the structure and content of the conference as I had originally designed it.

On Friday morning, two days before the opening of the conference, confused, exhausted, and tense at the prospect of having to face, for the first time in my life, many of the most important of my peers, I climbed into the plane to Denver. My attaché case was bulging with my Aspen files, and the package I carried held the five hundred conference programs that had been waiting for me at the United Airlines gate. Luckily, I had a window seat next to one of the plane's emergency doors, which gave me extra legroom. This was the place and time I had reserved for putting together the notes for my introductory speech. Before takeoff I put my attaché case on my knees, pulled out the folder with the notes, and after a few minutes collapsed into a deep slumber.

When, hours later, the stewardess tapped me on the shoulder to inform me that we were approaching Denver, I woke up rested, clearheaded, and strangely euphoric. The No Smoking signs were on. The captain announced that we would land in ten minutes. "This is good," I thought. I had another three hours' wait for Mannie's plane from Boston, ample time to write what I hadn't written on the plane. I would go to the terminal's bar and write my speech there. Since I had decided that students should be invited to this and future conferences, I was happy to invite Mannie, who was now in his third year at MIT, studying architecture.

The airport bar was pretentiously chic, dark, and gloomy, but the low, black-leather armchairs were luxuriously comfortable. I pulled the Aspen file out of my attaché case and ordered a Dubonnet. The name Dubonnet always reminded me of the funny series of three posters by Cassandre that in the early thirties had invaded the walls of Paris: *Du beau—du bon—Dubonnet.*

Especially in Paris I liked the sense of aloneness and anonymity that overtook me even in the most crowded bars, cafés, and public spaces. I could sit for hours at the Deux Magots or the Flore, daydreaming, people watching, and when the inspiration struck, writing. At the Deux Magots I had written many pages of an unfinished, vaguely autobiographical novel, and once at the Flore I had even scribbled some fairly decent poetry with such maniacal concentration that I was unaware that Picasso had downed two beers and a *croque-monsieur* at the table next to me. A bar at the Denver airport wasn't Paris, but it was as good a place as any to collect my thoughts.

I wondered how I would be introduced on Sunday evening, when from the stage of the old opera house I would be expected to address and charm four hundred designers, art directors, architects, businessmen, and design students. Would I be standing there as a painter? a designer? an art director? a businessman? a master of ceremonies? I was about to begin formulating the first sentence of my speech when I felt a heavy grip on my heart and the sensation that my mind was suddenly paralyzed, incapable of proposing a single word. As a matter of fact, the very notion of the conference had slipped out of my field of thought. Never before had I experienced that frightening revelation of the mind perceiving its own void. It was as if my soul had shifted gears, making thoughts and feelings run in a new, unknown mode, mercilessly close to the core of my being and frighteningly far from the surrounding realities. How long did it last? A second? an hour? Then, suddenly, there was the edge of a table, an empty glass, brass tacks in the black leather, a tiny curl of string, the yellow pad, the pen, my hand, and when I turned, a sea of heads, the waiter, coats, hats—all sharply lit as by an inside fever. And then I knew who and where I was and ordered another Dubonnet.

I didn't know that this had been only a rehearsal; that each time I was to speak in public, the preceding day or two minutes before stepping up to the lectern or during the first sentence of my speech, the real world would suddenly drop out of sight, leaving a frightening void, only to return more gentle and steadier to the mind's mirror in a brilliant, happy new light. (Was this what had happened those many years ago when I had failed to read my paper on safety in the classroom at the Palazzo dei Congressi?) Oh, to hell with an opening speech! I concluded as I shut my attaché case. "I shall talk extemporaneously." I paid my check and got ready to meet Mannie.

The day before the opening, the Hotel Jerome, a silver-town classic as falsely real as a spaghetti western, was bubbling like a party headquarters on election day. It was a beautiful spring evening, and the garden was teeming with men and women who noisily embraced and waved and yoo-hooed, raised their glasses and exchanged calling cards. Apparently relaxed, I was going through all the correct social motions. But the truth of the situation stood out bright and clear in the sharp mountain air. I did not have a written speech. Worse: the ideas that had flourished during the previous sleepless night had faded with the early-morning light, and in an exalted moment of folly I had thrown my notes away. Now, hours before a possible disaster, while greeting old friends and new acquaintances on my way to the bar, I was frantically groping for runaway ideas and lost words.

The bar was jammed and chaotic, but in a corner near the window I found a comfortably seated group that most of the conference attendees seemed to be avoiding out of respect for the celebrity of its members. There were old friends who deserved athletic hugs: Bucky Fuller, sentimental as ever, who shed a tear when he hugged me; Enrico Peressuti, an Italian architect whom I had not seen since the end of the war; Xanti Schawinsky, one of the companions of our monthly walking trips to Milan's hilly hinterland during the thirties. The only one I had never met but regularly read in the *London Architectural Review* was Nikolaus Pevsner, the English architectural historian whose Penguin Pocketbook, *History of Modern Architecture,* was surely in every conference pocket waiting for an autograph. Charles and Ray Eames, bubbling with their childlike vitality, and the Bauhaus refugee Gyorgy Kepes, with his wife, Juliet, were there too.

I settled in a quiet corner of the bar next to Max Bill, the guiding soul of the new Bauhaus at Ulm. Wally Harrison, the creator of Rockefeller Center, and René d'Harnoncourt, president of the Museum of Modern Art, sat at a neighboring table. There was much talking and cross-talking, comparing clients and universities and journals, and everyone seemed to be enjoying the relaxed, festive mood of the evening.

I took leave early and went to my room to shower, rest, and meditate. Mannie, exhausted from jet lag and all the excitement, lay on his bed sound asleep. Much as I needed his company, I let him sleep. "Are you feeling ill?" I asked him when he awoke. "No," he said. "I'm just tired, I've never thought so hard!"

I arrived backstage at the old opera house half an hour before the opening session was to begin. Feeling surprisingly relaxed, I greeted people as they came in, talked with some, walked a few blocks, inhaling the mountain air, and sat backstage while Walter Paepcke welcomed the guests. Finally, when the moment came and Walter introduced me, I walked with uncertain steps to the lectern, had my instant of oratory void, and with a barely audible voice, said, "Hi!" For reasons that even now are not yet entirely clear to me, the audience burst out first in general laughter and then in generous applause. I couldn't help laughing myself, and when silence returned I spoke. My mind was sharp and clear. I devoted a few minutes to the prehistory of the conference, talked briefly about the two national design conferences that preceded it, and finally went into some depth about the structure of the present one, stressing the importance of having speakers from several European countries. And when I introduced Bucky, I was in control.

Del Pezzo

When *Fortune* moved from the Empire State Building to the Time & Life Building at Rockefeller Center, I thought that one of the advantages would be the great concentration of good restaurants within a short walking distance. But after only a few weeks of wild gastronomic experimentation, my choices had already narrowed down to two or three eating places. The Del Pezzo Restaurant on Forty-seventh Street, at the beginning of Diamond Row, between Fifth and Sixth avenues, ranked number one.

Del Pezzo was on the parlor floor and the one above of an old town house that had been remodeled in the early twenties to accommodate a store on street level and independent access to the restaurant. I well remember the subtle perversity of the steep staircase, as step by step it led you closer and closer to the source of the murmur of voices, the tinkling of glasses and plates, and the enticing smell of smoke and food, when that very morning you had solemnly sworn that today you would stop smoking and have nothing but a BLT on toast at a nearby delicatessen.

In those early postwar years, when Italian food, films, and fashion had not yet reached their later popularity, when cappuccino and zabaglione sounded like the leading characters in an Italian opera, and Maserati, Mastroianni, and Missoni some Italian cycling champions, the Del Pezzo napkins, the linoleum floor, the tableware, and the faces of the waiters already showed the corrosive signs of a long history of hard work. And so did many of the Italian customers who called the waiters by their first names and often engaged each other in loud table-to-table discussions. Cozy and unpretentious, Del Pezzo was a real Italian restaurant, where you could eat well and feel comfortably at home. Only one block from Rockefeller Center, the navel of New York, it had achieved the miracle of making NewYorkers who ate there look and feel like foreign tourists.

RIGHT: *Mannie and Mies, 1950*
BELOW: *Paolo, Nora, and I in Genoa*

Throughout the years I worked at *Fortune,* most of my important lunches and dinners took place at Del Pezzo. When alone, I could be sure of sharing a table with people I knew, often artists, writers, or designers who were freshly arrived from Italy on their first American adventure. It was at Del Pezzo that I met Alberto Moravia, Italy's postwar literary star; the Venetian novelist P. M. Pasinetti, who taught Italian literature at a women's college in California; Fabio Coen, who in 1959 had the guts to publish my first children's book, *Little Blue and Little Yellow;* Alfredo Segre, great storyteller and adventurer; Dario Soria, the creator of Angel Records; Corrado Cagli, the Roman surrealist; Sasha Schneider and his actress-wife, Geraldine Page; Constantino Nivola, who introduced me to Le Corbusier; Nico Tucci, who wrote touching stories about Italy in *The New Yorker* and knew everybody; and a host of others.

If some of Del Pezzo's habitués looked and behaved enough like Bohemians to give the place its Latin Quarter air, the most colorful little assemblage of Del Pezzoites was occasionally to be seen around the large table in the far corner of the center room. There, when in town, Alexander Calder and his wife, Louisa, would entertain their friends. The explosions of loud laughter and multilingual exclamations that now and then crashed through the restaurant's noise level usually came from Sandy's table.

Sandy's bulky and jovial presence exuded a playful gaiety. It was as if everyone in the restaurant was his guest. His bright red shirt, his luminous white hair, the disarming innocence of his large blue eyes, and above all that Calder smile, slightly distorted by an ill-concealed self-irony, never failed to lift the mood of a business lunch, however deadly.

Whenever I came into the restaurant alone and Sandy happened to be there, he would rise from his seat and invite me to join him. We knew each other from my Philadelphia days, when on a few occasions I had used his mobiles to illustrate some ads for one of the agency's more sophisticated clients. Although I considered Calder a genius, and he often went out of his way to invite me to his table, I had steadfastly resisted all temptation to enter into intimacy with a type of artist whose bizarre and flamboyant Bohemian behavior I had long ago rejected. Or so I thought.

The truth was that secretly I still yearned for the lifestyle which ever since the romantic years of my youth had been my most seductive and obsessive dream. But then the war had come, and responsibilities, and also unexpected opportunities. And they had led me into a career which under different circumstances I probably would have rejected. Now a successful art director (I hated the expression!), not only was I enjoying a standard of living way beyond my expectations but I had discovered that as a designer I could enjoy pleasures of craftsmanship and creativity that were not as dissimilar to those of Art with a capital *A* as I had feared.

There were moments in my professional life when I was suddenly reminded of the distant days when, in my little mansard room in Amsterdam, I was a celebrated artist, an important scientist, or even, when I rearranged the pebbles and weeds in my terrarium for the small creatures whose destiny was now under my control, the almighty God himself. Now, with all the earnestness of a child, I was playing another game.

Then one day, physically and mentally exhausted from a two-hour meeting with Luce, anticipating a relaxing, solitary meal, I slowly climbed the Del Pezzo stairs and was about to ask Papà Del Pezzo for a table for one when a quick glance told me that the Calders were at their usual corner table, miraculously alone. I couldn't resist giving the scene another, more accurate look, and sure enough, it was Sandy. He was wearing the usual red shirt and blue jeans with the heavy leather belt and silver buckle—I knew them by heart. Louisa was in an orange-yellow dress and a necklace—probably Indian—of beads the size of pigeon eggs. No sooner had our eyes met than Sandy waved and shouted, so that the whole roomful could witness, "Hey! Won't you join us?"

All my values, so carefully considered, sorted, and balanced, crashed into a hopeless confusion. In a split second I felt that the issue was not so much deciding whether or not to accept Calder's invitation but having to face once more, perhaps once and for all, the definitive choice I had so artfully avoided ever since, in Genoa, I had bought that German easel. Suddenly I saw myself as I was sure Sandy was seeing me: a cowardly, middle-class business slave, a mediocre Sunday painter with occasional dreams of grandeur.

I hated my gray-flannel suit, my black Madison Avenue tie, my careful haircut. Once more torn between the two self-images, the romantic Bohemian and the successful designer, I mumbled some incomprehensible excuse and forced my face into a pathetic smile. Then, like an embarrassed child, I turned around, and with a superhuman effort to look like someone who had suddenly remembered an appointment across town, I ran down the stairs with a heavy load of guilt and shame and left the restaurant. Hopelessly confused and profoundly unhappy, I walked back to the office, closed the door, and for the first time since we moved to New York, lost myself in a desperate spell of weeping.

When I returned home that evening, Nora told me that Elodie Osborn had called to invite us for dinner the following Saturday. The

Calders were going to be there. I was dumbfounded, but I didn't have the courage to tell her about my abortive lunch. I was hungry.

The Osborns and the Calders

Seeing Bob Osborn, whom I consider one of the great American artists of our time, was always a rare and exciting occasion, especially in his own house. The house, designed by Edward Larrabee Barnes, perfectly expressed the character of its owners and beautifully articulated the kind of life that Bob and Elodie lived. Solidly attached to the side of one of the most spectacularly beautiful valleys in Connecticut, it was full of little gifts of space, none of which was superfluous or really necessary.

"Look at the profile against the fresh snow!" whispered Bob. We were admiring the Calder stabile that stood on the terrace outside Bob and Elodie's bedroom. "Sometimes I lie in bed staring at that thing, wondering how that heavy bear of a man can handle steel with such impeccable precision, lightness, and grace." Then the bell rang. Elodie shouted from the kitchen, "Bob, the Calders!"

The name reverberated somewhere deep within me. Ever since we'd left Greenwich I had tried not to think of this encounter. Now I jumped up and followed Bob as he ran to the door. There was Louisa, her head covered with a bright yellow shawl, stamping the snow off her boots, Sandy waiting behind her. When she saw me she let out one of those ambiguous laughs that cover a range of such diverse feelings as pleasure, scorn, contempt, and embarrassment. "Oh hello! Are *you* here too?" It was typical Louisa. I had no choice but to smile. "Hello, Mrs. Calder."

"You call Louisa Missus?" grumbled Sandy with *his* version of Louisa's laugh, a jovial smile that slowly vanished into his habitual expression of noncommittal absence. "She's no Missus." I felt greatly relieved. Neither of them had mentioned Del Pezzo. I noticed the exact hue of Sandy's eyes, a pale ultramarine that made them bluer than I had remembered. Against the darkness outside, his hair seemed rather whiter and because of the cold wind his complexion redder.

Two more couples were expected: the Grays and the Styrons. Cleve Gray, a painter, was one of those younger Abstract Expressionists who

Sandy Calder

had inherited from their masters the mannerisms of self-assurance, verbal dexterity, and intransigence which seem to accompany all revolutionary breaks with tradition but without having experienced the "shock of
the new," the raptures of discovery, the anguish, and the fear of failure.
Cleve's wife, Francine du Plessix, was the stepdaughter of Alex Liberman,
the art czar of Condé Nast Publications. She was a writer—smart, civilized, aggressive, and fashionable—a New York woman of the fifties,
flourishing in the first stirrings of the feminist movement and the communications boom. The Styrons were late. "They usually are," said Elodie
when she summoned us to the table. At that very moment Bill and Rose
appeared. The dinner was exquisite. We had partridge Bob had shot in the
valley and smoked trout he had caught in the brook, all prepared and presented with impeccable style. Yet I remember the event as a noisy, awkward, somewhat nightmarish affair, for which I was greatly to blame.

 After my ridiculous performance at Del Pezzo, the very thought of
this encounter with the Calders had kept my nerves on edge. Had this
been my only problem, I could easily have handled it, but I was going
through a *crise de conscience* that was to affect not only my work as a
painter but all my various activities as an artist.

 I had begun as severe a self-analysis as I could bear, and after considerable turmoil and long discussions with Ben Shahn about the age-old

problem of the social responsibilities of the artist, I felt strongly that now was the moment in the history of our culture when the presence of Man in all his naked aloneness should be seriously and responsibly remembered and celebrated.

It was in this mood that soon after the trout had been served I lashed out, undoubtedly with exaggerated vehemence, at some innocuous remark of Cleve's. Unfortunately, this unchained a general discussion in which everything from Communism to alienation, impressionism to abstraction, painting to television, love to death became grist for controversy. Louisa was the one who spoke least, except for some short, sarcastic declarations that revealed, beneath her apparent shyness, the strong impulse of her feelings and basic convictions and her scorn for all that to her was unintelligible. She made it clear at the beginning that she would be only too happy to be excused from having to show interest in arguments that bored her. Nora, intimidated by the self-confident tone of the other women, especially Francine, and hating violent arguments, managed to have some normal conversation with Louisa.

Sandy, who like Louisa loathed theoretical confrontations, had little to say, and notwithstanding all the noisy goings-on, dozed off with a partridge wing in his fingers, luckily missing my diatribe against abstraction, from which, at any rate, I had diplomatically and ideologically excluded him. Bill, introverted and morose, would only intervene when Bob, Cleve, or I generalized about writers or writing and did so in the amiable, condescending manner of an expert.

I liked Rose Styron, who with the professionalism of a labor leader but with her own kind of courage and intelligence tried to identify the political meanings and implications of the arguments, so that from the foggy area of passion they could be led into the orderly rules of dialectic.

Bob, who always brought the topics in which he got involved to the unpopular realm of basic human feelings, sometimes expressed his ideas with such simple, poetic vehemence that although you might disagree with and often not even understand clearly what he was saying, you would want to jump out of your chair to kiss him. His comments were never "smart," but they had the weight of another order of logic, one that came directly from the guts and the heart. Bob had his own brand of Zen. His seemingly naive observations, at times slightly off the topic under discussion, would make our own words, as we remembered them, sound pompous, arrogant, and banal.

The discussion had been violent, swaying chaotically from one end of the table to the other, with many unexpected surges of ill-repressed anger. But in retrospect it turned out to be a fascinating exercise in self-presentation, and we had learned more about each other than if we had been on a world cruise. By the time we lifted our glasses to toast Bob and Elodie, and then Sandy and Louisa, and then all of us, everyone seemed relieved. In a mock ceremony of reborn brotherhood, Cleve and I clowned our way through a long embrace. And with smiles we slowly descended to the living room, ready for coffee.

Together we made the rounds of the walls and chatted about the pictures. There was the Klee for which Elodie, when she still worked at the Museum of Modern Art, had sacrificed all her savings, only to discover some years later that the image was slowly disappearing. The original sketch for a *Fortune* cover that Ben Shahn had done for me seemed unrecognizable in a new frame. We agreed in a conspiratorial whisper that the wall painting Sandy had made for the inauguration of the house, much against the protests of the architect, was really not one of his best. We admired instead the graceful mobile that fluttered lightly above our heads. We looked at Bob's large drawings that lined the corridor—the frightening skeletons, the tender Chaplins, the scheming tycoons—and warmly agreed that they were magnificent. I rejoined the group with a sense of elation at having discovered once more that sharing an understanding and a love of art is a strong, dependable bond.

In this surge of well-being I was about to hug Elodie when I suddenly remembered that I had brought some Italian dance records. Nora and I loved to dance to the old-fashioned little *valses,* mazurkas, and tangos that in Italy and France had survived the raucous onslaught of rock and roll. I quickly ran outside and came back with my briefcase, and soon the gay, flapping sound of a mazurka filled the room. Several guests jumped to their feet and began dancing, while Elodie and Louisa rolled up the rug and pulled it out of the way. I was standing there savoring the effect of the music when before I knew it I was grabbed in a firm embrace, lifted into the air, delicately lowered to the ground, and found myself dancing in Sandy's arms. I felt his warm body against mine, as the light, rhythmic pressures on my back guided me through intricate twirls and undulating walks. Deprived of my will, I had no choice but to abandon myself to the whims of my partner, a sensation I had never before experienced. "You are a good dancer," I said with true admiration. Sandy let out one of his grunts, guided me into a fast twirl, and said, "You're a good dancer too." It was the beginning of a great, though in many ways a strange, friendship.

In the fall of 1990, when I had my retrospective at the Museum of Modern Art in Bologna, there was a press conference on the morning of the opening. A young woman, the Italian correspondent for *Die Zeit,* said, "I understand that you were a close friend of Alexander Calder. It would

be interesting for our readers if you could give them some significant fragment of a conversation between you and Calder. Could you do that?" I
nodded. And I dictated my answer slowly: "I said to him, 'You are a good
dancer,' and he answered, 'You're a good dancer too.'"

India

"It comes from a deeper wound." A sentence remembered from a dream; it
had been an emphatic answer when someone asked me to explain my love
of India. I had said it slowly and in a solemn tone of voice, articulating
each syllable as if I were reading it from a sacred Sanskrit text and the
slightest hesitation, omission, or mispronunciation might have changed
its meaning entirely. The short sentence marks the conclusion of a quest
that began in 1957 with a three-month voyage from the floating gardens
of Kashmir to the temples of Trivandrum. This was a few years before the
tourist invasion, when cows were still lying on the trolley tracks in the
center of Calcutta and the foreigners in Katmandu could be counted on
the fingers of one hand.

That first, lonely voyage was my Indian childhood. I saw India as a
perpetual spectacle still disconnected from its dramatic meanings, a circus where birth, life, love, and death were the versatile protagonists, a
theater where people and things had not yet been assigned their specific
roles, a dusty arena where nothing happened because each living thing
was also all the others.

During my travels through India I met with the governor of Kashmir
and played poker with the naked, bearded, boneless gurus of the great
Juggernaut temple in Ahmedabad. In Calcutta I sat on Satyajit Ray's bed
talking with him about *Pather Panchali* and Madison Avenue; near Le
Corbusier's Chandigarh I joined the population of a village to watch fifty
cows with hands printed all over their wrinkled bodies stab hundreds of
innocent piglets to death with the thrust of their sharp horns; and on a tea
plantation in the high hills near Bangalore, I saw a young woman reach
into the large basket on her back, grab a silver tea container from under
the tea leaves, and throw it into the bushes because my shadow had
passed over the basket. I had a brief conversation with Nehru; and in the
hills of Jamshedpur, at the foot of one of the world's highest dams, I talked

at great length with a brazen American engineer who had found the way to let water flow on the arid plains of Mother India.

When I was a child in Holland, India was a five-letter sigh, very unlike Africa and America, happy hopscotch words that promised great spaces and distant horizons. India was the Indonesian shadow-play puppet that hung on the wall behind Mother's piano and the black, ocher, and blue piece of batik on the coffee table. It was a Dutch boy's dream of jungles and tigers and a native running amok, wildly wielding his blood-stained kris.

But above all, India was "the lush archipelago" that floated in the Indian Ocean "like a necklace of emeralds." Long before I could understand the beauty and pathos of that line, my father, guided by his socialist conscience, had made me memorize it. It came from the heartbreaking letter that the great Dutch poet Multatuli wrote to the queen, imploring freedom for the colonies. I never forgot it.

In the years of my adolescence and early adulthood, that India slowly sank into my memory, filed under the correct heading "Indonesia," while the true India entered my consciousness much later in life. When it finally did, it crashed in with the power of a hurricane. It all happened in less than an hour at the great India exhibition at the Museum of Modern Art in 1956.

I was overwhelmed not only by the beauty but by the inventiveness, the charm, and the stylistic coherence of the objects. They seemed to bask in an all-enveloping light that bathed each fold, each surface, each color— a light heavy and sweet like honey that I would later recognize as the light of India. I wasn't conscious of having decided then and there that I would go to India, but I was steering events that way.

It was not the first time that I forced myself to respect a promise by committing myself so strongly to a decision that it would be shameful to pull back. In the following months not only did I tell my relatives, friends, colleagues, and bosses that I was going to India but I gave dates. I was going in the fall, and I had an alibi: I was going to work on a photo portfolio for *Fortune*.

I went armed with my old Nikon and an Exakta with a fabulous Angenieux 90-millimeter lens, which, I always claimed, gave an image that was closer to the way we perceive depth than the short lenses (28 and 35mm) which most professional photographers prefer. The choice of the Exakta was also motivated by my lack of experience in shooting people nearby. I needed time to compose my pictures and was too shy to point a camera directly at their faces. With the reflex I could make believe that I was focusing on some other subject and sneak up on the actual victim without his or her knowledge. This expedition was to be my first semiprofessional try at large-scale documentation, and although I was excited by the possibilities, I was understandably nervous about the eventual results. But I was lucky. I hadn't taken into account the greatest accomplice I could possibly have found—India. Wherever one directed one's eyes there was a picture.

When I set foot on the ground of Bombay airport the night of October 17, I was of course unaware of the fact that it marked the beginning of a strange and beautiful love affair with a country and a people which would profoundly affect my life with unforgettable experiences, and fill my heart with the gifts of important friendships. All of this with my full knowledge of a people tragically enslaved by a perverse and destructive religion and fatally condemned to a future of great and painful upheavals. It took me years and many voyages to finally solve the mystery of India's irresistible fascination. What is different about India is that in India *everything* is different.

The Watershed

In the spring of 1959 I made a momentous decision. On my next birthday I was going to quit my *Fortune* job, resign as consultant to Olivetti, turn down all new assignments, sell the Greenwich house, move to Italy, and give myself totally to the arts.

This decision to put an end to a period of our lives that had been blessed with everything a man or a woman could desire—success, money, love, excitement, reputation, health, and happiness—had not been a sudden romantic *capriccio,* as some of my friends suggested. I had always had the capacity to walk away from situations without the slightest trace of the fear or regret that one would normally associate with such an act. Perhaps this was because I never gave myself entirely to what I considered the *grand jeu,* which I played with passion but which I nevertheless knew was a game. Or perhaps it was because of my curiosity, which kept my eyes forever focused on what was before me. On what came next. Only when I formally resigned from *Fortune* and realized that I was at the crest of a watershed did I turn to look back at what I had achieved since the day Leon Karp taught me how to sharpen a 6B carpenter pencil.

I had reached a point where my name looked natural and comfortable next to those of the older design gurus like Alvin Lustig, Paul Rand, Herbert Bayer, Buckminster Fuller, George Nelson, Charles Eames, and a few others, by now all personal friends. Although my portfolio did not burst from the bulk of hundreds of proofs, it did contain the documentation of a variety of memorable projects that ranged from the "Never underestimate the power of a woman" series to the "Great ideas of Western man"; from the Olivetti stores to the "Unfinished Business" pavilion at the Brussels Fair, not to mention the one hundred and twenty issues of *Fortune* I had overseen. I had designed the book *The Family of Man,* created the new *Print* magazine, and designed *Sports Illustrated.*

Throughout those busy years, trying to remain faithful to my youthful vow to become not a specialist but an artist in the widest sense of the word, I had not only become a pro as a graphic designer but managed to paint and work at the crafts of engraving, ceramics, and mosaics. And even in the field of music, as a devoted amateur I had been studying the flamenco guitar in Andalusia, and in India I had learned to pluck the nineteen wailing strings of the sitar. An exhibition of my work was on a national museum tour. I had "kept my hands in the pasta," as the Italians say. I had been making and doing.

Our personal lives had been equally exciting. Our Greenwich house, with its enormous interior space, was ideal for parties. We had some memorable ones for Indian friends, and our Sunday garden brunches with pasta with real pesto for the temporary bachelors of the Olivetti crew had their echo in Italy. Once Bucky offered to give a lecture on the geodesic idea for "fifty of our best friends." At precisely 9:00 p.m. his opening sentence was "I have condensed a nine-hour lecture to three hours," and exactly three hours later he looked at his wristwatch and concluded, "Well, that's it," and Nora was ready with the midnight snack. And at a smaller party, Bill Golden, the legendary art director of CBS, and Cipe Pineles, his wife, the no less legendary art director of *Mademoiselle,* had brought along their four-year-old, Tommy. I wondered if Tommy, who had been raised with one of the largest record collections in the world, had ever seen or heard an authentic musical instrument, so I went to the studio, got my accordion, sat down on the floor with it, and told Tommy to sit facing me. I played, and Tommy, wide-eyed, following every motion of my fingers and the opening and closing of every fold of the instrument, sat there mesmerized. And when I stopped he looked at me and whispered, "Will you now play the other side?"

Mannie was then living in New York with his wife, Naomi, and their children, Annie and Pippo. He had graduated from MIT in architecture and was now working for Skidmore, Owings & Merrill. Paolo was in Venice studying at the Academia and grappling with his version of Sturm und Drang. And Nora and I had traveled around the world at a time when there was as yet no road to India from Katmandu and an airstrip had been finished only a week before we flew in.

At Time Inc., my resignation caused a spell of gossip, comment, and speculation. I was certainly not the first to make such a decision, but few had ever seriously followed it up. Del Paine, who had hired me in 1949 and had risen through promotion after promotion to the thirty-eighth floor, appeared in my office one morning, mumbling something like "Did I hear correctly that you are leaving us?" "Yes, Del," I said. "You mean to say that you are not happy here?" "I am very happy here." "Then why are you leaving?" "Because I don't want to be that happy." It was a *boutade.* But it was also the truth.

Both *Fortune* and Ayer were great places to work. And for someone like me, who had managed to elude the rat-race, they represented unique environments where ideas fluttered around in swarms; where the need for half an hour of good, solid conversation on any topic from art to economics, from literature to world politics, from architecture to the true nature of God could be met in a matter of minutes; where mistakes were honestly called differences of opinion; and where Luce's art adviser took a three months' leave of absence to work for the presidential campaign of Adlai Stevenson.

I had enjoyed my years at *Fortune,* and the three managing editors with whom I worked at the magazine, Del Paine, Hedley Donovan, and Duncan Taylor, had become good personal friends. It had been a life full of fun. Yet it felt—and still feels, even as I write this—as if all my achievements had missed their target, as if it all had happened in a life that was not entirely mine. Although I was always passionately involved in what I tried to do or make, I never felt that I was an integral part of the landscape. The pleasure of succeeding was dampened by a kind of sobriety that was not my nature. Perhaps deep down in my subconscious I sensed that never again would I feel the joy that made me jump up and run to Mother yelling, "Look what I made!"

Could it be that despite the honestly felt emotion when on that distant first of April, Father and I had sailed past the Statue of Liberty and I had set my foot on American soil; despite the tears of pride I had shed when five years later I received my naturalization papers; despite my devotion to a radicalism that was profoundly American in its content and style; and despite the uncounted occasions when in private and public debates I defended *my* country, America, against stereotypes that infuriated me . . . could it be that I had never cut my European roots?

Deep inside me I perceived a nostalgia for my childhood dreams of a world of a different, more comprehensible scale, a yearning for a small enclosure with transparent walls where each small thing was visible and sharp edged in the evening sun. I was longing for the lonely pebble in my hand, the wagging tail, the silent smile, the single stroke of blue.

My only real client had been Olivetti, and my ties with that company had a long history of personal friendships. The founder of Olivetti, Camillo, had been a friend of Papà Maffi in the early days of the Socialist party. In the thirties, in Milan, the intellectual bodyguard around Adriano, who had inherited the company from his father, were all devotees of the Caffè Savini in the Galleria. That is where I met most of them and became close friends with some—the poet Leonardo Sinisgalli, who invented Olivetti's dramatically avant-garde magazine, and the writer and critic Giorgio Soavi, who later wrote a novel about a man of Dutch descent who emigrated from Italy to America, made a career as art director, and who in a moment of crisis and rebellion gave up everything to return to Italy and settle in Tuscany to paint and sculpt strange plants. There was Zweteremich, who ran the advertising department, and finally Adriano's youngest brother, Dino, president of Olivetti of America, who lived not far from us in Connecticut with his American wife, Posy, and shared his occasional secret import of white truffles with us.

If, as many of my friends believed, all I really wanted was more time to paint, couldn't I have easily lightened my workload? Both *Fortune* and Olivetti would have accepted any reasonable proposal for a part-time arrangement. But in no time an offer would come my way that I could not possibly refuse, and I liked my "commercial" work enough that I would always be tempted by new opportunities; I would end up worse off than I was. My struggle with the ghost in the Brooks Brothers shirt would start all over again.

As I observed the crazy itinerary of my life from the crest of the Watershed, I was overcome by a strange sense of calm. It was as if all speeds had suddenly slowed down, and the humblest objects in the arc of my perception had become little throbbing worlds. In this moment of near hallucination I felt that I had acquired the capacity of orienting and manipulating not only my thinking but my imagining as well. I could see in every object or event a hidden meaning and a metaphoric potential. I remembered that during the first months at Ayer, when I was to observe and learn rather than produce original ideas, I would fill some of my time

Turning my back on the Brooks Brothers suit

with giving form to an idée fixe that had begun to haunt me and that in a peculiar way had been triggered by the title of a popular song of that period: "Every Little Movement Has a Meaning of Its Own."

I had been toying with positions in space for some time. Recently, I found among stacks of old sketches some pages filled with small rectangles approximately two by three inches and remembered that I would tack them to my drawing board, close my eyes, and hit them all over with a pointed pencil. I would then open my eyes, examine each little rectangle, beginning with all those that contained one dot, then those with two, three, or even more, and let them suggest by leaps of the imagination situations involving one, two, three, or more human beings in a room or city square. I would then imagine the feeling that each position in space would provoke. A dot in the center might bring to mind a feeling of authority or formal exposure. A dot near a corner, embarrassment, fear, or informality. In experiment after experiment I developed a series of reactions that I believed most people would identify with. I used this theory in lectures on design, and later it became an important subject of discussion in courses on the phenomenology of space at New York's Cooper Union.

My recollections of this and similar episodes revealed one character trait I had never been conscious of before—a developing passion for insight—and I grew aware of the danger that theoretical stylization would stifle the intuitive impulses that are the blood of any form of artistic activity. I never failed to stress this with my students, and to point out that the important message of the theory was not to prescribe a series of examples but simply to be aware of the fact that every position in space has a meaning of its own. In practical and moral terms, you must feel responsible for every line you draw, for every decision you make.

Making a Book:
Little Blue and Little Yellow

Then a little miracle happened. It was the day I was to take my two grandchildren, Pippo and Annie, to Greenwich so that Nora and Naomi could do some shopping and come home on a later train. Pippo was five years old at the time, and Annie was all of three. They were an adorable pair, bright, lively, and totally uninhibited. It was the very first time I was alone with them, but they were intimidated enough by the surroundings and the uniqueness of the occasion to be on their best behavior.

To get them into a cab was no great problem, and neither was it difficult to guide them through the hurrying crowd at Grand Central Station. We were early and the car was almost empty, and in no time the two little angels had been transformed into two devilish little acrobats jumping from seat to seat. When the conductor appeared, I took advantage of their momentary immobility to grab them and catapult them into the seat facing mine. Since more and more passengers were beginning to board the train, I realized that unless I did some fast creative thinking this was going to be one hell of a trip.

I automatically opened my briefcase, took out an advance copy of *Life,* showed the children the cover, and tried to say something funny about the ads as I turned the pages, until a page with a design in blue, yellow, and green gave me an idea. "Wait," I said, "I'll tell you a story." I ripped the page out of the magazine and tore it into small pieces. The children followed the proceedings with intense expectancy. I took a piece of blue paper and carefully tore it into small disks. Then I did the same with pieces of yellow and green paper. I put my briefcase on my knees to make a table and in a deep voice said, "This is Little Blue, and this is Little Yellow," as I placed the round pieces of colored paper onto the leather stage. Then I improvised a story about the two colors, Little Blue and Little Yellow, who were bosom friends and went on a long hike together. One day they played hide-and-go-seek in a forest and lost sight of each other. Desperate, they searched everywhere—in vain. Then suddenly, behind the fattest tree of the forest, they found each other and embraced happily, and when they embraced they became Little Green. The children were transfixed, and I noticed that the passengers who were sitting within hearing distance had put down their papers and were listening too. So for their benefit I had Little Green go to the Stock Exchange, where he lost all his money. He broke out in yellow tears and blue tears, and when he was all tears he was Little Blue and Little Yellow again and their stock rose twelve points. The children applauded, and some of the passengers joined in.

When we got home I took the children to the studio and showed them how to transform an idea into a real little book. I found a blank dummy I had made some years before for a *Fortune* promotion piece that never saw the light of day, chose some pieces of colored paper, turned on

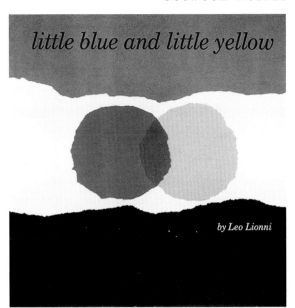

The beginning of a new career—my first book for children

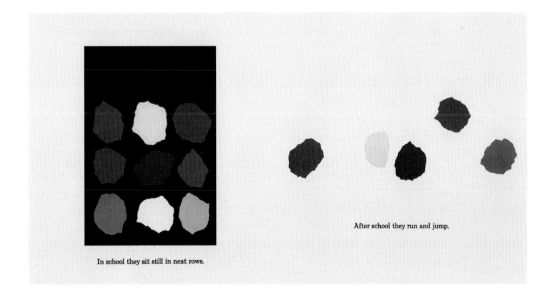

In school they sit still in neat rows.

After school they run and jump.

the radio, and sat down at my desk. I experimented with the dimensions of the color blobs, making them large enough to deserve the role of protagonists and small enough to have ample space to move in. Then I counted the pages and tore an equivalent number of blue and yellow, and half the number of green, paper disks. I tore them rather than cut them with scissors because I felt that a sharp cut would make too mechanical a shape for a living thing, whereas the torn edge gave a certain vitality. An unexpected difficulty arose when I realized how easy it was to "read" the round shapes as human faces, a rougher tear became hair and the smallest protuberance a nose. Finally I more or less retold the story I had improvised on the train, but this time I reasoned it out and designed it not only to narrate the action but to give it the right rhythms and conduct it in an uninterrupted flow from beginning to happy end. I played with the positions of Little Blue and Little Yellow on the page to suggest what they were doing or how they felt: when they were sad they would be at the bottom of the page, when elated high up. When I introduced them I placed them in the center of the page, and when they were looking for each other they were placed in or close to the corners, as if they were anxious to move to the next page in their search. While I was placing them and gluing them down with rubber cement, it occurred to me that I was repeating in story form the little games I used to play during my first weeks at Ayer when I experimented with positions in space to evoke moods and even to express meanings. Even at their young age the children "read" the story with ease, and they were impressed by their own capacity, never before tested. When Nora and Naomi arrived home from their shopping spree, the children ran to them shouting, "We made a book! We made a book!"

That was Thursday. On Friday Fabio and Silvana Coen came for dinner. Fabio had just become the children's book editor of a new publishing firm, MacDowell Obolensky. He had emigrated from Italy to the United States in the spring of 1940, after two years' exile in Paris and London. Following a bout as stage manager with a theater group in Virginia, he was drafted into the U.S. Army, fought his way into Italy with the American troops, and was released from the army in 1944. Like most of us, he spent the postwar years in a state of restlessness and experimentation while more and more he felt attracted to the world of books. During his voyages back and forth between Italy and New York, he befriended many important authors and publishers of both continents, and to set himself up as a literary agent or editor with a large publishing house would have been an easy and logical choice. But other prospects still tempted him.

When I first met Fabio, he ran a shop where one could find recent Italian books as well as some refined samples of Italian arts and crafts. It was only a tiny space, hardly big enough to house two gesticulating Italians, but chock-full of interesting things; the mood reminded me of my beloved Shakespeare & Co. in Paris. I was immediately taken by Fabio, an intense, generous young man strongly attracted to the arts but upon whom the Muses had failed to bestow the gift of natural creativity. Undaunted, he had chosen two tools that were to shape his life: enthusiasm and the word. Fabio represented that category of men and women who can change the course of history without ever getting their hands dirty. In our century of drastic transformation, these sideline experts have often assumed a status that artists themselves could barely reach. France was the country most generously endowed with critics, journalists, collectors, publishers—merchants specializing in steering the ship of Art into profitable harbors.

That Friday evening, when I told Fabio about my trip with the children and showed him the dummy I had made after our return home, his reaction surprised me. He took it in his hands and looked at it a long, long time in deep concentration. Then he said, "I'll publish it." I didn't take him seriously at first because I couldn't imagine any publisher would have the courage to publish what looked like a defiant object designed to *épater le bourgeois.* This was not the first time that I had created an abstract book: I had recently designed a large, showy promotion book for *Fortune* called *Design for the Printed Page,* a collection of abstract designs to show advertisers how exciting the creative use of the *Fortune* format could be. From text to layout and illustrations, it was my invention. I had published entire sections of *Print* that could be considered abstract. But this was a different thing altogether. This was going to be a real book sold in real bookstores. And it was going to be openly and officially mine. But it would take more than one evening with Fabio before I could fully understand how much the simple little tale of two blobs of color would affect my soul, my mind, and my way of life.

Fabio and I met in his office a few days later to discuss a contract and talk about the changes that would be necessary to clarify certain passages, to smooth the flow of the story line, and to prepare the artwork for reproduction. None of these problems was new to me—my experience with magazines had made me an expert in every imaginable production problem—and in a matter of days the illustrations and the text were on their way to a printer in Elizabeth, New Jersey.

I felt as if my only child had left for boarding school. Notwithstanding my busy schedule, I should have accompanied it to Elizabeth, where I could have made a photocopy to show my friends and to leaf through in moments of loneliness. Now, despite a regular contract, a few letters in a folder labeled "L.B.," and a check for my advance, which I was not going to cash for a while, I had nothing to show that I was an author.

Eternal weeks crept by. Luckily, our preparations for the move to Italy required our full attention. The Greenwich house had been rented for a year, a scale model and all the photographs and captions for the Unfinished Business Pavilion had been sent to Brussels, the flight and hotel reservations for a six-months' world trip were confirmed, the trunks with books, drawings, and folders had been shipped to Cavi, and the movers would begin wrapping the bulk of my art library and the paintings and drawings within the next ten days. All problems at hand could be expressed in numbers and dates, all except *Little Blue*. Fabio had been noncommittal and vague about a production schedule. Would I see the book printed and bound before leaving for Hawaii?

Then on a Friday afternoon a few weeks before our departure, when a hundred last-minute problems had crowded the book out of my mind, its presence crashed into my consciousness with such violence that all worries other than surviving until Monday melted away. Fabio had called to say that *Little Blue and Little Yellow* would be in one of Brentano's windows on Monday morning.

For ten years I had been a faithful habitué of the Madison Ave. Special, our name for the train that every weekday morning dumped carloads of advertising and publishing executives into Grand Central Station a luxurious half hour after regular employees had settled at their typewriters with their cups of coffee. Not that Monday morning, when I braved dawn to be at Forty-seventh Street and Fifth Avenue among the first New Yorkers to see *L.B.* displayed at Brentano's. I wouldn't have missed that very private ceremony had they offered me a signed copy of the *Recherche*.

At Brentano's there was no sign of life. Seen through the twisted bronze branches of the doors, the half-lit store looked about as cozily welcoming as a Horn and Hardart Automat after closing hours. All except one of the windows were empty—ready, I thought, for a spring display of the new hatch of children's books. While I was waiting I took some childish pride in being an author about to witness the appearance of his first book, perhaps the only person to know every single word of at least one of the items on display on Fifth Avenue, in New York, no, in the whole wide world!

As I began belaboring this pretentious idea, I saw a man inside the store walking slowly toward the door. He opened the three locks. I went in, trying to be just anybody, and walked straight to the children's books department. It was dead, exactly as I had seen it through the windows. I looked for someone to help me, but no one seemed bookish enough to qualify. Finally a saleslady arrived with a bundle of papers, plunged into a chair near the cash register, and closed her eyes. I didn't dare interrupt her, but suddenly right next to where I was standing there was a pile of *Little Blue and Little Yellow*! I don't know what gave me the strength to resist the temptation to pick one up, but I had vowed to remain anonymous throughout this performance. My little book was now out in the open, and this was serious stuff, with no time for ego games. I moved on a few yards and waited. During this maneuver a young woman who looked like a mother of a six-year-old child was moving from book to book with a fastidiously serious expression pronouncing judgment on each one. When she picked up *L.B.*, I looked away. I couldn't take it. When I finally gathered the nerve to observe the outcome of her investigation, she was smiling as she went over to the salesperson, who was sound asleep in her chair. "Ma'am," she said loudly, "would you . . ." It was a moment of great expectation and confusion. The saleslady sprang out of her chair and out of God knows what terrifying dream, knocking the book out of the customer's hand. I automatically picked it up and was about to hand it to the young woman, when I heard myself say, "Forgive me, I am the author of the book you are about to buy. If you don't mind, I would like to sign it for you because it is the first copy to be sold." There were many ohs and ahs, and my heart was turning somersaults in my chest, but I left the store feeling as if I had just won the Pulitzer Prize.

part four

1961–1985

Father and Mother

As old age began to plague my parents, it slowly dawned on us that soon they would no longer be able to manage their apartment on Fifty-fifth Street, the few things they owned, and above all themselves. This situation came to a head shortly after we had decided to put our Greenwich house up for sale and move to San Bernardo. This was not a minor undertaking, for our house was filled to the brim with "things," as we called them, as if they did not deserve higher status. The collection that we had gathered in villages and markets the world over was put together in a time when only a few aficionados, like Charles Eames and Alexander Girard, were treating humble objects as legitimate expressions of the world of design.

Father hated and never understood the collectomania that he accused us of. He wanted nothing for himself beyond the newspaper, a billiard cue, and the few essentials of daily life. How could we be so different? But in trying to help us solve the complicated logistics of our move, he had discovered a way to realize a dream of his own: a mid-Manhattan hotel apartment with a king-size bed and room service. So while the Greenwich house was being packed, Mother and Father moved into a splendid, uncluttered hotel suite on Fifty-seventh Street, and we took possession of their vacated apartment.

Such was the arrangement when very early one morning I was awakened by the telephone. Mother's desperate voice begged me to come over immediately. "Father's not himself," she said in a shaky whisper. As quickly as I could I got to the hotel. Father was sitting, awkwardly balanced on the edge of the bed, looking straight ahead, ignoring my presence. "Hello, Pop," I said to lighten the tension. Mother was shaking with fear. "I thought he was going to kill me," she said as I held her in my arms.

She told me that Father had woken her up in the middle of the night, yelling abusive threats and epithets. When Dr. Stern, our family doctor, finally arrived, he attributed Father's behavior to hardening of the arteries and had him taken to New York Hospital. As his condition deteriorated and he refused to speak English, we decided that the best thing to do was to take him home, to Holland. So it happened that I flew Mother and Father to Amsterdam. Father was settled in a clinic in nearby Amersfoort and Mother in her beloved American Hotel.

Months had passed with Father's condition remaining fairly stable when a call from the clinic, advising me that he was rapidly failing, put me on the next flight to Amsterdam. I met Mother in the lobby of her hotel. "Father may not make it," she said. I was surprised by her composure. I saw then that she, like Nora (like all women?), possessed a hidden strength. I thought of Nora in times of crisis in our life—during the war when she alone brought the children from Italy, and coping with our various moves with grace and good humor—nothing seemed beyond her ability to cope.

The next morning, Mother and I went to the clinic. "You have a stubborn husband," said the nurse in Father's room. And then, turning to Father, who had given no sign of recognizing us, she said, "Don't you say hello to your son?" "I feel fine," Father responded testily, with a touch of arrogance. It was obvious that the world around him had long ago turned to stone.

The two hours I spent alone with Father the next morning, the hours before his death, hang in my memory like an exquisitely embroidered flag at half-mast. It was the first warm day of spring. I sat in an armchair by the window breathing in the scent of freshly cut grass. The blackbirds in the clinic's park were chirping, and Father turned to look at me. He was crying. I had never seen him cry. "What's the matter, Dad?" He screwed up his face and tried to speak, but nothing came out. Then suddenly the word *lente,* Dutch for "spring." He said it twice, clearly and cleanly, like flowers in spring. "It hurts," he added as an afterthought. Then he let his head fall back on the pillow. Father died of a bleeding ulcer.

My father appears in my memory like a Marino Marini sculpture of a man whose features echo the taut logic of his mind. He was known and respected for his sharp and clear intelligence, but I took pleasure in his impeccable taste and sense of measure. He knew and honored the exact place and form that the Muses had assigned to each object in our house. And with his little pocket ruler he could draw the perfectly straight lines for the charts on his Wall Street *"cyfertjes,"* from which he expected not only secret financial insights but aesthetic pleasure as well.

One would have expected Mother to be the taste bearer in the family. Far from it. Despite the fact that she was an indirect product of the newly born artistic middle class with a potpourri of Bohemia and vaguely defined socialist ideals, Mother's talents were totally concentrated in her music. Unlike Father, she had no feelings for the visual world. Every creative shade in her personality seemed directed to making her a truly great singer. Yet hidden in some dark fold of her destiny, a secret anger was lying in ambush. She feared and knew it well. And one day it struck, destroying in one sweeping gesture what she had so passionately built to perfection, note by note. And many years before old age would have affected her vocal cords, she simply reverted to what had been her familial roles: the oldest sister, the head of the family, the authoritarian decision maker. But we all knew that once in a while, without notice, she would occupy (I mean this almost in the military sense of the word) her place next to the piano and reveal her formidable talent, her profound understanding of music, of the human voice, and of the demands of style. Those were the truly impressive qualities that had mysteriously defined her.

I often wonder what had given her the unfaltering insight and power to free the sounds of music from their physical source and allow them to take flight. I ask myself who or what in the hidden history of my elders could have handed her the little DNA spiral responsible for her ability to nurse a particular sound to the very end of its audible presence, a gift which I had hoped so desperately to inherit in its visual version. But Mother, whose art by all standards ranked so high above average musicianship, had been unable to place herself among those who could boast a full schedule of performances. Though I do remember the occasional visit of some great opera stars, like Toti dal Monte or Gilda della Rizza, who would come to our house to hear Mother sing, and so far as I know she never refused to perform for them. She was close to seventy when she told me the story of her "great failure."

The story began in the Amsterdam Concertgebouw at the time my parents were considering emigrating to America. When Mother heard that Willem Mengelberg, the conductor of the Concertgebouw Orchestra, was going to be in New York at more or less the same time for a series of concerts at Carnegie Hall, she asked him for advice. He admired Mother's voice and promised that he would help her lay the groundwork for an American career. When Mengelberg arrived in New York, Mother, who had been anxiously awaiting him for several weeks, received a personal message from him requesting her presence at a rehearsal at which the

Metropolitan Opera star Frances Alda was to sing. It was a part that Mother had sung under Mengelberg's baton in Amsterdam. Mother was incredulous. "Somebody's joke" was her first thought, but she recognized the conductor's signature, identical to the one that adorned the photo that had stood in its heavy silver frame on her piano for so many years. What did Mengelberg want of her? Was it to hear Alda's interpretation? Did he want Alda to hear hers?

When she arrived at the hall the next morning, it was still empty and dimly lit. After a long, nervous wait she was ushered into Mengelberg's room. "You are late," he said with Dutch sarcasm. "How is your voice these days?" Her heart missed a beat. "I like it," she said, trying to be clever. "Alda has refused to sing the high C at rehearsals," he continued. "If she refuses today, you get the part. It will be hard work. Can you do it?" Mother held her breath in a long silence. It was a moment of total lucidity. I had heard the story before and yet felt my body tense in expectation. "Why didn't you give it to me in the first place?" she said. Mengelberg didn't say a word. He got up and walked out of the room. And that was the end of Mother's career.

Mother stayed on in Amsterdam after Father's death until her legs would no longer carry her. She could be seen every afternoon sitting at her little table at the American Café, reading. I've heard people say, "See that lady there? She was once a famous singer, but I can't remember her name."

Mother suffered from arthritis and finally was happy to come and stay with us in San Bernardo, in the sunny little guest room which I had designed with her in mind. When her pains got worse and X rays revealed a spreading cancer, we moved her to a private clinic in Lavagna, where in 1968 she died while I held her hand in mine.

From the sixties on, the quality of my recollections has undergone some drastic and surprising changes. As they come closer to the tangible, noisy present, the time spans seem shorter, events are bathed in a disagreeable light that is neither day nor night, and the sounds of words are sucked up into a black silence. The screen of my memory grows uncomfortably large, and the simplest happenings cover great distances and long, tedious periods of time. It takes me hours to cross my room. I see the world through new, unfamiliar lenses. I had always thought that recent events must be denser, livelier, and more precise than those of a distant past, but the opposite seems to be true. Like tiny objects brought close to the eye, they become larger and larger until at the touch of an eyelash they wrap themselves around us and disappear. How steady and easily lit, how pleasurable to observe were the little worlds of my early youth!

Sometimes I wonder if image makers are endowed with a special memory stage. Do others, as I do, see their mothers mostly at great distances, quite small, not much larger than a mouse or a salamander as on a podium that seen from the center of the sixth row vanishes at an imaginary horizon? Or smaller still, somewhere in a distant town, unreachable as a dream within a dream?

I am sitting now in a compartment with five unknown fellow voyagers on my way to Bologna, the first stop after Milan. The Watershed is already many years behind me. I am nearing a moment of my life where past, present, and future seem to converge. The sixties, seventies, and eighties, once a future, are now zooming by, flickering like small abandoned railway stations in the void of night. Now we are nearing Bologna, and the usual panic grabs my heart; I never know for sure whether to get off or stay onboard.

San Bernardo

We had asked our friend Goffredo Palazzi, a real estate broker who lived in Chiavari, to find a house for us in the hills above Chiavari and Lavagna. Less than a month later, while we were on a Mexican vacation, we received a cable from him triumphantly announcing that he had found a beautifully located old villa in a four-acre olive grove with a splendid view. It was incredibly cheap, he thought, but since others had already made an offer we should decide immediately, sight unseen. With the letter was a brief but ecstatic note from Paolo, who was in Italy at the time and had seen the house. After a restless afternoon on the Zocalo, Nora and I decided to gamble, and a week and a bundle of cables later we owned a villa on the Italian Riviera.

The first time we saw San Bernardo was the very day we arrived in Genoa on our definitive voyage "home." We both cried when we saw the view, and although we were exhausted we didn't sleep all night, questioning each other's recollection of details of the house, whose entire eastern wall threatened to collapse at any moment.

San Bernardo was nestled in the midst of dense olive groves halfway up the hills that rim the Tigullian Gulf from Portofino to Sestri Levante. The view of that arc of the Ligurian coast, dotted here and there with an occasional chapel and villas similar to what we now proudly called "our house," was breathtaking. Fortunately, the towns of Lavagna and Chiavari, charming from within but ugly when seen from above, lay hidden behind a chain of smaller hills below us.

The house was a typical Ligurian middle-class villa, a simple cube enriched and enlivened by trompe l'oeil marble details painted in the old fresco technique around the windows and doors. What was pretentiously called "the villa" had been built by an uncle of the Lanatas, the farmers who lived in the stone farmhouse in the olive grove. Like many retired people in the region, he had emigrated to South America toward the middle of the nineteenth century, to return rich at the beginning of the twentieth. Chiavari and Lavagna are full of retired emigrants in whose houses you can find, among the endless varieties of overornamented silver monstrosities from Peru, small collections of precious Aztec or Mayan vases. And in many families the language is still what the more sophisticated locals disdainfully call Itagnolo, a fusion of Italian and Spanish.

We appropriated the name San Bernardo from that of an ancient nearby chapel. Although the house seemed so unsuited to our style of living, we loved it instantly. But then we had approached every house we had lived in with this peculiar enthusiasm. We were learning the challenge of adapting a house to fit our tastes and needs; no matter where we lived, we always seemed to end up in the same house.

The transformation of San Bernardo into a Lionni house began five months after our return. Walls came down and bathrooms went in. With Mannie's help we redesigned the ground floor to give us a large living room with a cozy dining alcove and a spectacular kitchen, for which I had made the ceramic tiles at Albisola. There wasn't a detail that hadn't been obsessively discussed, and when we finally moved in we knew we were home.

The one exterior alteration we all agreed on was to tear down the stable that had been added to the back of the villa to house Lucy, the Lanatas' only cow; for the time being she could be brought to the small barn below the chicken coops. The question was, Could Lucy walk? Would she walk? Since the day, sixteen years before, when they had brought her from the yearly cattle market in Chiavari, she hadn't moved a hoof. It took close to an afternoon to get Lucy to her new home. And a fortunate thing this move proved to be! One week later, the whole stable, which was leaning against the house like a drunken bum, collapsed from the vibrations of a tractor engine into a heap of rubble. We could now redesign that part of the house, and months later I triumphantly mounted the steps to my brand-new studio.

Mannie and Paolo shared our passion for San Bernardo, and in no time it had become our family house. Being on the tourist route from France to Italy, it was an easy place for our friends to visit us, but our love affair with San Bernardo only reached perfection with the arrival of Chica.

In Philadelphia we'd had a briard, a beautiful beast, an enormous black, curly pup who burst into our life and ruled it for a while. But he vanished from my memory with the arrival of Chica at San Bernardo. Chica was a pastore Bergamasco, an Italian version of the French briard. She was a one-month-old pup when I went to fetch her at a farm on the outskirts of Milan, but it didn't take her long to become a large, woolly

Chica (and me)

bundle of a dog, with solid loyalties, imposing manners, and a strong ego. She developed into an authoritarian eccentric who managed to keep the mongrel gang from the neighboring farms at a considerable distance from our gate with no more than a grunt.

We had never met the Lanatas, but they knew who we were through Papà Maffi, whose politics they shared, and Goffredo, whom they had known forever. When we finally met, there was some awkwardness on both sides, but after a few outbursts of laughter, some good solid swear-words on the part of Remo, the farmer, and a few glasses of *our* wine, we all felt comfortable and well disposed toward one another.

For the first time in my life, and in conflict with my most sacred Marxist principles, I was now a *padrone,* a boss. Naively, I proposed that I be called *Baccan,* Genovese for "Boss," but a lighter, more gentle word, and because it was dialect and I had proposed it, it suggested a certain degree of self-irony. Remo laughed and shrugged his shoulders, but after some awkward trials the word stuck. Nora automatically became the *Baccana,* and even in Tuscany, where we now live and where the word is foreign, we are the *Baccani.*

Thinking that I had brilliantly subdued my sense of guilt, I lost my inhibitions and felt at peace with my conscience. But no sooner had the house been finished and the last American crates unpacked than the class problem reared its head once more. Near the foot of the stairs to the studio I discovered a small flagstone platform shaded by two old apricot trees—a perfect place for my after-lunch siestas. It had probably been the base for a piece of agricultural machinery or the dumping place for harvested olives, or perhaps it had been the foundation for a large birdcage. I grabbed a beach chair from the garage, and as I walked back with it I thought I saw Remo working in the vineyard below. I stopped. There was no one there. But by now the vision of Remo busily at work a few meters from where I would be napping on the terrace had settled in my mind. At the mere thought that it *might* be so, I took the deck chair into the studio, and before you could say *Das Kapital* I was sound asleep.

A few weeks later, when the hot desert wind from Africa had been blowing for days without reprieve, I woke up with one of those headaches which make your head seem to burst with every step you take. As I staggered slowly to my studio, holding my head in my hands, Remo came toward me, carrying an enormous bale of hay on his back. I stopped to let him pass, and to explain the expression of pain on my face I said, "I have an atrocious headache." Remo looked at me from under his heavy load, smiled gently, and said, "That makes sense. You work with your head and get a headache. I work with my back and get a backache." That took care of my sense of guilt and soon of my headache. And later that very same day I helped Remo replace the broken flagstones of the platform and re-move the dead weeds around it.

Swimmy

Probably one of the most important events of 1963 was the arrival of the first copy of *Swimmy,* my fourth children's book. When I began unwrap-ping the package, my hands were so shaky that Nora took the package and the scissors I was brandishing, and in no time at all produced what in a single glance I recognized as my best book to date. I placed it with my three others, side by side against the wall, dragged the armchair to the center of the studio, and sat down.

The need to compare what I was doing now with what I had done be-fore, and to recognize the direction in which my work was moving, was a habit I had inherited from Leon Karp. With my paintings it had become an interrogatory practice, but evaluating the continuity of content and style in the books required years. Since I had an agreement with my pub-lishers not to do more than one book a year, this annual event had taken on an importance in my life that I would never have predicted. And, in-deed, when I sat down to look at the four books, I was fascinated by the differences and the similarities.

The first thing that struck me was that no group of books by one au-thor could possibly look as different one from another as these four. Defy-ing all the rules for building a reputation, a personality, a trademark, they seemed to have very little in common. *Little Blue and Little Yellow* was the most aggressively modern and the least bookish of the four; it had bro-ken all the rules and was a real invention. *On My Beach* did not look like a children's book at all and probably wasn't. Yet it contained many mem-ories of my childhood vacations on the Mediterranean pebble beaches: the close-up look, the endless search for "special" pebbles with the discovery of hidden images and unusual shapes. Impressed by the success of *Little*

Blue, Fabio had asked me to produce a comparable book for the following year. Logically my first efforts had been directed at *Little Blue Two,* but the more I tried to find a viable idea for a sequel, the more I realized that *Little Blue* was a unicum that should not be exploited or imitated. I decided that if I made more books, each one should have a character of its own. After toying with the tempting idea of Little Blue goes to the zoo (another identity quest), I decided to go in the exact opposite direction: black and white instead of color, drawings instead of collages, sharp-focus realism instead of abstract shapes, spreads instead of single-page illustrations. But while I was working on the drawings for *On My Beach Are Many Pebbles,* I had another idea which, because of its autobiographical implications, slipped to the foreground, the story of an inchworm, which became my second book, with the title *Inch by Inch.*

And now, with a slightly mysterious cover, low key in color and composition, here was *Swimmy,* my first real fable, which in no time became the role model for most of the books that were to follow. It contains all the principles that have guided my feelings, my hands, and my mind through my long career as a children's book author.

Swimmy was the book that for the first time led me to consider the making of books as, if not my main activity, one that was no less important than my painting and my newly discovered sculpture. In my relentless involvement in the invention of new forms and new ideas, I had never thoroughly examined what had made the old ones satisfying and successful, nor had I found enough distance from the process of making to realize how complex the production of these four books had been. The ethics of art not only as a pleasurable but as a useful activity was clearly the moving force in the book. The central moment is not so much Swimmy's idea of a large fish composed out of lots of tiny fish but his decision, forcefully stated, that "I will be the eye." Anyone who knew of my search for the social justification for making Art, for becoming or being an artist, would immediately have grasped what motivated Swimmy, the first embodiment of my alter ego, to tell his scared little friends to swim together like one big fish. "Each in his own place," Swimmy says, suddenly conscious of the ethical implications of his own place in the crowd. He had seen the image of the large fish in his mind. That was the gift he had received: to see.

Different as the four books were, they were linked by characteristics: the rhythm, the simplicity of the action, the logic of the sequencing and positioning of the protagonists on the page. All of these qualities had their origins in the hundreds of pages I had manipulated in putting together

Nora

Lavagna, 1964

the many issues of *Fortune* that had been produced under my art direction. I must admit that even in an activity as new to me as the making of a children's book, in many ways I was a pro before I began, and I no longer feared an inability to maintain the variety, the originality, and above all the passion and the fun with which I had initiated this new profession. Foreign editions of the books began to multiply, and the mailman started bringing me a fan letter now and then.

For the first time in all my work, I found myself confronting a tangible audience. Along with the fan mail came invitations from schools, and these awakened in me a need and a desire to understand my audience. I found myself digging deeper and deeper into the memories of my childhood, and I learned to distinguish within myself that which was peculiar to my own feelings and experience and that which was universal to children everywhere. I became ever more conscious of the problems children face and the importance of the messages we send to them. It is often said—and I think somewhat too easily—that to write for children you must be the child, but the opposite is true. In writing for children you must step away and look at the child from the perspective of an adult.

A Busy Year

Shortly before Christmas of 1966, I received an invitation from the University of Illinois at Urbana to spend three months at its Institute of Advanced Studies. The invitation assured me that I would be free to use the time and the institute's research facilities for whatever project I chose to undertake, my only commitment being the delivery of at least two public lectures.

I was very excited by this prospect, and although I was already committed for three months with my friend Giuggi Gianini to set up a state-of-the-art animation studio for the National Institute of Design in India at Ahmedabad, I couldn't resist this exceptional opportunity to deepen and extend my knowledge of recent developments in linguistics and phenomenology, which I felt could shake the foundations of our inherited assumptions about communications.

Ever since Sartre, Bachelard, Lévi-Strauss, Foucault, Robar Caillois, and other French philosophers had taken center stage at the Sorbonne, I had been captivated by their revolutionary theories on semiotics, phenomenology, and structuralism. As a logical aftermath of Sartre's existentialism, their works had fascinated me to the point of becoming an essential aspect of my thinking. For some time, in fact, I had been toying with the idea of writing on these new methodologies in terms of a clearer understanding of our visual environment and hence of the visual arts.

The invitation to Urbana triggered a whole new set of ideas, which I felt would be perfect material for this occasion, and after endless trials and transformations they reappeared in a totally new form, far more convincing than the one I had vaguely envisaged. That day I wrote in my notebook: "For Urbana: 4 public lectures on the Human Face: the Face Observed; the Face Remembered; the Face Disguised; and the Face Compared." And that was the proposal I sent with my letter of acceptance.

Me with an imaginary portrait on the easel

Imaginary (and one real) profiles

A few days later, I received a letter from Hedley Donovan inviting me to be *Time*'s guest at the Montreal world's fair, Expo '67, where *Time* had an apartment in Habitat, the architectural experiment designed by the Israeli-Canadian architect Moshe Safdie, whom I had met at one of the Aspen Conferences. Bucky Fuller would also be there with his U.S. pavilion, the largest geodesic dome ever built, and Sandy Calder with an enormous stabile.

Nineteen sixty-seven was going to be quite a year! I began to ask myself, as I consulted my notes, how I could possibly deal with these various projects around the globe. Luckily, as I went over them one by one in my mind, I realized that they did not in any way interfere with one another, since each one had its own schedule built in.

The Ahmedabad job, which sounded like the most demanding of these commitments, was first of all a technical undertaking, and thus primarily Giuggi's problem and only indirectly mine. In his letter, Gautam Sarabhai, the Indian industrialist who was greatly responsible for the creation of the institute, had warned me that the equipment, which had been donated by the Ford Foundation four years before and which was supposed to have been kept dust free in an air-conditioned environment, had been stored in crates in an improvised shack somewhere in a remote corner of the institute's grounds. My work would be only the last phase: to produce some actual animation sequences with a group of five or six students. But this by its very nature was a problem of improvisation.

And as far as Urbana was concerned, the only real work was going to be the research for the four lectures and, of course, writing them. To accomplish this, given the extensive research facilities at my disposal in an atmosphere that I expected to be as serene and inspiring as we, the self-taught, always imagine Academia to be, two months would be more than sufficient.

Meanwhile, in the San Bernardo studio I had just finished the illustrations for *Frederick,* my newest fable. Carefree at last, I was eager to get back to the profiles I had recently started—half a dozen plywood silhouettes ready to be painted. But creativity has its own unpredictable and perverse little whims, and before I knew it I found myself surrounded by a chaos of sheets of paper of all dimensions, thicknesses, and colors from Italy, France, and the local butcher—pieces of cardboard, samples of fabric, tin, silver, brass, chunks of clay, and even a few thin slices of ivory and tortoiseshell. Not to speak of pencils, brushes, jars of colored inks, watercolors, and an impressive array of shears and scissors.

It was an orgy. I drew profiles, painted profiles, cut, traced, tore, folded, polished, sawed profiles with an intensity, an urgency I had seldom experienced before. I don't know how many profiles left my hands nor how long the frenzy lasted, but when finally, a few weeks later, exhausted, listless, and lonely, as if a spirited lover had just left me, I found myself avoiding the door of my studio, I knew that, as with my obsession with the small Fayum-inspired portraits that had preceded them, and the challenge of the "fat and white" peony petals, and—long before that— my infatuation with the spiraling forms of the futurist rhetoric, the profiles too had run their course and finished their cycle in a wild flourish of my imagination.

After days and days of dolce far niente on the beach, when I was finally able to turn the handle of the studio door, determined to clean up the mess and get back to the six blank silhouettes that stood patiently waiting for the colors of life, I was astonished to find enough material for a large show. Much of it, in fact, ended up at the Galleria l'Ariete in Milan, in an exhibition for which Ben Shahn wrote an introduction. By that time I had gone to Venice to make some glass and crystal profiles in Murano, and there I found an artisan who was able to translate some of the smaller, more carefully executed drawings into tortoiseshell combs and ivory medallions, which were included in the show.

Panorama and Un-American Activities

If this were a novel, the last thing the author would think of would be having a large American publishing company ask our hero to take on the editorship of a new Italian magazine. No wonder that Giorgio Mondadori, the Italian partner with Time & Life in this particular venture, was shocked when he heard the proposal. It is possible that he had heard my name before, for the names of Italians who "make it" in New York are bound to come up in Italian publishing circles. But this would make the proposal even more absurd—wasn't this Lionni a graphic designer and artist, a layout man? And yet this is what happened in real life when Hedley Donovan, Time & Life's editor in chief, a job he had inherited from Henry Luce himself, suggested me as editor of *Panorama.* It was not a stunt—we had worked together when he had been appointed editor of *Fortune,* during the time I was art director of the magazine.

Giorgio Mondadori and his group were not enthusiastic, but whatever the reasons for their surprising assent may have been, they agreed, and one June afternoon Nora appeared at my studio out of breath with the news that Hedley was going to call me later for a phone conference. Now it was my turn to be shocked. When I heard the details of the proposal, I could hardly believe it. In one day our lives were turned topsy-turvy, and a few months later I sat in my office in Milan, a few blocks away from a furnished apartment we had rented, as if my life in San Bernardo, my studio, exhibitions, new friendships had been only a dream.

For a monthly magazine that was supposed to deal in depth with Italian and international news, the status of the arts and sciences, political commentary, cultural events, and great national and international problems of the times, we had a ridiculously small staff. We did, of course, have total access to the articles that appeared in *Time* and *Life,* which were to amount to about half the contents. Luckily, my new teammates included some intelligent young journalists and a managing editor who not only was experienced and creative but in a short time became a close friend.

In February 1962, just about the time my first issue of *Panorama* was to be published, I got a surprise call from Jack Masey, whose boisterous, enthusiastic voice I hadn't heard since the Brussels Fair in 1958. Jack, in charge of exhibits for the United States Information Service, asked me if I would be interested in accompanying a graphics exhibition to Russia in the fall. The exhibition, the first of its kind, was scheduled to tour four cities, accompanied by a small group of American designers as hosts: Ivan Chermayeff, Robert Osborn, Norman Rockwell, and myself. Jack said that he hoped I would choose Moscow, but, good friend that he was, he warned me that although the Soviet capital had many obvious advantages, the conferences, discussions, and endless public visits would generate a heavy presence of the KGB, a drawback I might not like to cope with. As an alternative, Jack proposed Yerevan, the capital of Armenia. At the mere mention of the name my heart responded with a quiver of excitement. Because of my lifelong passion for Byzantine mosaics and architecture, I was familiar with photos of the extraordinary churches in the region. The opportunity to see them during a leisurely stay in the Armenian capital was enormously tempting. Even so, I had never set foot on Soviet soil and was depressed at the prospect of facing the squalid reality of the physical and moral decay of the country that during the dark years of Fascism had held high our beacon of Utopia.

Nora's reactions were quite different. Generally cautious and, despite all our exotic travels around the world, fearful of the unknown, she was full of joyous excitement when I told her of Jack's call. She told me each little detail she remembered of her father's two trips to Moscow when she was a little girl and Moscow was on another planet—once in his capacity of lung specialist when he had been summoned by the Soviet government to treat Lenin, and the other time, historically more important, when he and several other Socialist members of the Italian parliament went to Russia to join the recently founded Italian Communist party.

Obviously, this was an opportunity I could not ignore. Two weeks later I received an official letter and the usual FBI forms to fill out, and we began reading all we could to prepare ourselves intellectually and emotionally for an adventure that deep in our hearts we both desired and feared. If I hadn't had my hands full with *Panorama,* my upcoming show at the Naviglio Gallery in Milan, and the gestation of a new book, the long wait for a cable or a call from Washington would have made my life miserable, but the busy days rolled by until one morning there was a call from a gentleman I'll refer to as Harry Springer, the chief security officer of the American Embassy in Rome, who asked me to meet him as soon as possible at the Genoa Consulate in connection with our trip to Russia.

We met there a few days later in a long, barren conference room that smelled of wax and cold smoke. Harry Springer was a small, modest-looking, tight-lipped Southerner in a dark gray suit a bit shiny at the elbows. After he had slowly emptied his briefcase and stacked its varied contents neatly in front of him, he took out a notebook and looked at me as if I was supposed to speak. When I didn't, he changed the rimless glasses he was wearing for a heavy-rimmed pair and without raising his head, his eyes glued to the writing pad, he said, "Name?" "Leo Lionni." "Lionni two *n*s?" "Yes." "Born?" I told him. "Name of father?" "Louis." "Mother?" And when he had finished asking he shoved the pad away from him, leaned back in his chair, crossed his arms, and with the steel voice of a federal prosecutor said, "In 1939 you were a member of an organization called For a Free Greece. Is that right?" For a moment my mind went dead. I tried to produce some kind of image, but nothing appeared except that funny shape hanging from the belly of Europe—Greece. "Look," I finally said, "I have belonged to a great number of organizations, but I swear that although I have always been for a free Greece and always shall be, I remember nothing about a committee For a Free Greece. I really don't know what you are talking about or driving at." "You were on the board of directors," Springer said firmly, his eyes sharp as needles. "All I want to know is, who else was on that board?" I was dumbfounded, but after a moment of total confusion I recovered my bearings and knew exactly what to say. I leaned forward and looked the man straight in the eyes. "Listen," I said, "if I remembered belonging to that Free Greece organization I would tell you, but I don't even remember what the Greek government was like in 1939. Let me make one thing very clear: I will tell you anything you want to know about me, but I will not talk about anyone else."

There was a long silence. Then Springer took the papers that lay before him, opened his briefcase, and while he was slowly tucking them away he said, "Well, in that case it is of no use continuing." "That's your problem," I said. Neither of us budged. Then suddenly he looked at me as if in deep thought and said, "OK. Let us check your public record," after which he pulled the papers out of his briefcase and we went through them one by one. I was astonished. Every important political meeting I had ever attended was there. Every organization I had belonged to was listed. When at a certain moment he read a short article in the *Daily Worker* about Ben Shahn, Leonard Boudin, and I having founded the Emergency Civil Liberties Committee, a flash of nostalgia came over me, and I could hardly control my tears. Toward noon we decided to call it quits. By now

Springer must have understood that after some innocent revolutionary leanings when I was still in my teens I had been only a few degrees left of the typical well-meaning liberal New York intellectual, and I, on my side of the table, had realized that Springer was only a minor government employee doing what he was told to do.

When we were about to part I took him by the arm and said, "Mr. Springer, you can be frank with me. Do you think that I will go to Russia with that show?" He thought for a moment and then said, "Frankly, my personal opinion is no. If it were for Paris or Berlin, perhaps yes, but Russia is too sensitive a post. But don't forget," he added smiling ironically, "I am only what is called a data gatherer. The decisions are made by an evaluator." That very evening I wrote a long note to Jack Masey telling him that it was probably because of my stupid refusal to answer a few questions on the FBI questionnaire that things had gone the way they did. I asked him to forgive me and wished him well with the project. That, I thought, was that.

The first issues of *Panorama* had appeared; I had redesigned the experimental dummy, and the magazine was now slowly taking shape. With a more relaxed, more open layout, larger but with fewer illustrations, and a slower rhythm in the flow of the articles, the magazine was beginning to look the way a monthly should: discursive, substantial, a readable commentary on what was happening in the world; up-to-date and yet at a healthy distance from the frenzy of the "just happened" syndrome of the weeklies. And the exhibition of thirty of my "imaginary portraits" at the Naviglio Gallery in Milan looked good. The opening had been celebrated with many old friends, some new friends, and all the relatives. It was a festive evening. The very first day, an old gentleman who no one in the gallery knew walked in and bought two paintings. When I met him in the gallery the next day, he told me that he collected only nineteenth-century paintings. I was too startled to ask him why he had bought mine.

In the beginning of September, when we were to celebrate the twelfth issue of *Panorama,* I received a call from Hedley on vacation with his wife, Dorothy, in Paris, asking if Nora and I could meet them in Seville to discuss some urgent *Panorama* matter. Despite the impending arrival of guests and other minor complications, we flew to Seville, and two days later we all met in the Moresque lobby of the Palace Hotel. Shortly after we had settled at a table on the patio, Hedley showed me a letter from Mondadori, proposing in terms that practically amounted to an ultimatum that I, whose task had been "honorably fulfilled," now be replaced by Alberto Sechi, the highly intelligent and experienced Italian editor who was ready to take over the editorship. Hedley then told me that he had consulted with his staff and the people at our Paris Bureau, and the general consensus was that in that case Time Inc. would pull out of the partnership. He added that he had wired Mondadori that he was meeting me in Seville and would let Time Inc.'s decision be known. He then showed me a rough draft of his answer, in which he stated clearly that, if I were to leave, so would *Time*.

After a first moment of dismay, greatly assuaged by Hedley's affectionate humor, it didn't take me long to realize that what was happening was nothing more than our original understanding that my involvement with the magazine was to be temporary. The letter came as no surprise. Through the grapevine I had sensed that something was going on, but I had been too busy to speculate on the rumors that flew around the Mondadoris' offices like houseflies. Apart from my affection for my young staff and the close friendship with my second in command, Fabrizio Dentice, without whom I would have never succeeded in putting the magazine together, I felt immensely relieved. I could finally return to the life I had decided to live, giving all my time and energy to painting and the other things that really mattered to me. As the balmy evening in Seville progressed with a fantastic paella and ended in a superb *tablao flamenco* in the hotel lobby, I was assailed by a euphoria I hadn't felt since walking out of the Time & Life Building three years before. I had looked forward to a short Andalusian vacation, but now, eager to retake possession of the lifestyle I had temporarily sacrificed for an experience that I thought would root me firmly in Italian soil, we returned two days later, I to Milan to say good-bye and pack my things and Nora to San Bernardo to prepare herself and the house for the return of the prodigal husband.

It was a bright, clear day when I left Milan, but I was too involved with the "operational" details of my departure from the publishing scene and surprisingly unaware of the symbolic charge of the moment. True, I had lived through all of this a few years before, only to betray my new life at the first temptation. But now things were different. What I was taking with me this time were a few books and magazines and some matter-of-fact recollections of insignificant episodes that had not touched my feelings. Then my decision had caused an upheaval of enormous proportions—my entire past, my emotional life, my style of living, the language I had grown into. Now, with my foot on the accelerator, I was ready to wipe clean what I had absentmindedly soiled. It was very simple: the scent of turps was waiting for me and I was on my way.

Toward the end of September, the time of the year when I would be assailed by sudden unbearable waves of nostalgia—not nostalgia for a particular place or sound or smell but an undefinable urge to be somewhere else or someone else, in a distant but recognizable past—I received a letter from Jack Masey saying that we had been cleared for our Russian trip by the FBI but that the Russians had turned down our request for Russian visas. Who was masterminding my destiny?

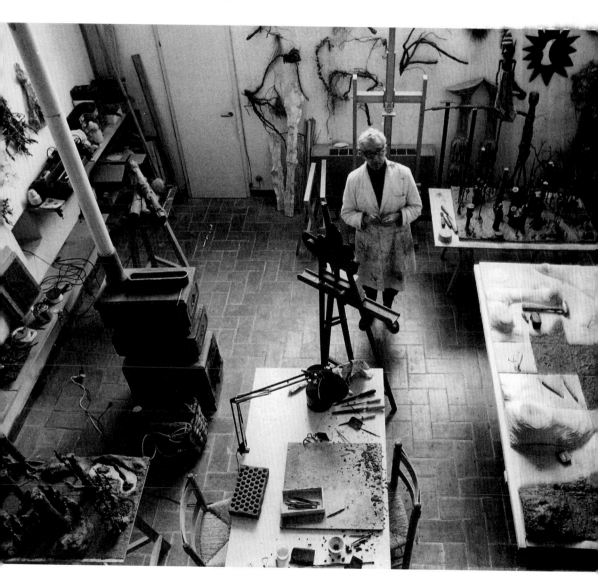

In the Porcignano studio

Botany

The many profiles I had painted in the previous few years had freed me from the stiffness, the maniacal repetitiveness, the obsessive frontality of my earlier imaginary portraits. No longer were my protagonists staring at you from the center of their allotted space with identical remote expressions. The profiles, with their greater compositional freedom in an extendable space, not only allowed more variety of composition but encouraged the use of canvases of different sizes and proportions. I had also explored all kinds of media and materials, from wood and glass to ivory and tortoiseshell and even gold. Now, although I dared not confess it even to myself, I was nostalgic for an average-size canvas and eager to start working on a "normal" painting.

To my great surprise, in the cellar I found one brand-new, 80-by-200-centimeters Belgian linen canvas mounted on seasoned prewar

Working in clay

stretchers; since it had been placed horizontally against the wall behind stacks of smaller canvases, I had failed to notice it before. Looking more closely, I remembered that I had mounted it years ago, at the time of my first New York show, when I had tried my hand at some large, semiabstract figure compositions. I brought it to the studio and placed it vertically on my easel, inclined it slightly forward, took a chair, and sat down in front of it.

In those first moments the canvas felt frighteningly large, as large as the screen of my memory, on which slides of celebrated nudes were being projected: Rubens's "nude in the fur coat," almost indecent in her provocative nakedness, at the Munich Museum; the Uffizi's Goya, with her disconcertingly beautiful gray silk dress; Cranach's bony Eve that I saw at the Philadelphia Museum; the Woman in Bath by Bonnard I saw at the Museum of Modern Art. That was the last image that floated across my memory; then the canvas stood there naked, very white, waiting.

I believe that hands have a memory of their own, for it was in my empty, brushless right hand that the urge to paint was most acutely felt, and despite my loyalty to the human image, I found my mind's eye forming meaningless shapes to fill the empty vertical space. My strong ideological commitment to the human image had always prevented my occasional flirtations with abstract expressionism from affecting this basic belief. So far as I can remember, this was the first time I was seriously tempted to let an imagery develop freely from the inside of the painless process out rather than from a carefully planned scenario. And before I knew it, following the natural rotation of my arm, I had drawn a large green oval which occupied the top two-thirds of the canvas. I sat down and looked at it for a long time. The roughly sketched shape had a strong frontal presence, but it suggested nothing except a symmetrical ovoid flying or floating unconnected in an endless space. To stabilize this primitive missile I chose the most banal solution: I traced a thick black line that ran from the center of the shape straight down to the center of the canvas's edge.

I didn't know where to go from there—perhaps there was nowhere to go—and so I left it on my easel and returned to the drafting table, where I was working on a book. But every time I looked around the studio I couldn't help noticing the shocking contrast between the small, modest portraits that were lying, leaning, hanging everywhere, each with its own identity waiting its turn to be seen, and the large, aggressive, green blob that was standing in a flat white nothingness like a message from outer space.

Then one morning a small black speck in the green ovoid caught my eye. Looking more closely, I saw that it was a fly. I whisked it away with my hand, and then I saw a tree. It was not a fleeting idea—it was a lasting vision. It existed. It was there—clear, hard, definitive. It left no choices. It had to be painted. Now.

I prepared my palette and went to work. I worked until the sky I had painted in the background was the only light remaining in the studio. It was a distant, luminous sky with a slight hue of orange above the cool horizon—the sky of Hobbema, of Ruisdael, of all the Dutch painters who at this time of the afternoon grouped their cows and sheep around the fat, knobby stem of a tree whose name I never learned.

I now sat down and saw. And then for the longest time I sat without seeing and just looked. And I recognized a feeling I had had once as a child when I had ventured beyond the second corner into the P. C. Hoofd Straat, where the shops had mannequins in the windows and the trolley rolled and people with hats rode on bikes looking straight ahead. I had run away.

Had I run away this time, too, but never to return? So it would seem today, twenty-three years after that first ambiguous adventure with a tree that was conceived neither in reality nor in the imagination but in some undetermined no-man's-land in between, where things somehow seem to invent themselves.

This was a period when once in a while I would drive up the coast to Albisola and work at some ceramics. Although it was barely a two-hour drive from Chiavari, I had been there only once since we had returned from the States, and I had found the center of the small resort shamefully degenerated; it was full of little shops that sold nothing but ceramic junk. To profit from the increase of automotive tourism, amateur artisans had flooded the market with the silly, kitschy, overcolored products of a craft that had always tottered dangerously at the fragile borders of sculpture and painting but had now fallen to an unprecedented level of bad taste. With the lucky exception of my friend Mazzotti, now quite old, and a few artist-friends like Lucio Fontana and Wilfredo Lam, who had their studios in the countryside nearby and worked for the sophisticated art markets of Paris, Milan, and London, the state of the craft presented a grim picture.

But luckily there was Lele Luzzati, the eternally active and optimistic set designer and illustrator from nearby Genoa, who still had intact his great gift of exciting his friends with the inexhaustible outpourings of his multimedia talents. And above all there was still Bianco and his quaint old ceramics studio at the Pozzo della Garritta, a semienclosed piazzetta, a veritable Casbah corner with its accumulation of small whitewashed houses, each with a different style and shape of step, where nothing had changed since the end of the last century.

Bianco's studio consisted of a small house that was a labyrinth of tiny rooms, where each of us could work alone with the cozy illusion of striving together in a common pursuit; where conversations mostly consisted of shouted questions and answers flying back and forth from one little room to another, as if they were independent from us ceramicists, who were immobilized by our concentration on our craft.

After a few ill-fated attempts at making ceramic profiles, I had thrown some large, hollow, pear-shaped forms, each of which held a single loose ball perfectly shaped and smooth but somewhat larger than the slit through which this symbolic seed was visible. The effect was quite mysterious; the question everyone asked was, How did you get the seed inside without breaking the shell?

Most of these magic pears were painted with a thick, grainy magnesium, a technique I had learned from Lele. The magnesium comes out of the oven an earthy and ambiguous dark violet with flashes of silver. It was perhaps these metallic flashes that gave me the idea of making a few of these pears in bronze. They seemed to have the right dimensions for objects that could lie in the grass in the garden under a tree or on a large coffee table. I enjoyed playing with the more frivolous sides of art now and then—a sin that Picasso, Miró, and their friends had taught us to respect. Not to speak of Calder.

I knew nothing about metal sculpture. I had never set foot in a foundry and very seldom in a sculptor's studio. It was one of those holes that autodidacts often stumble into in their careers. I decided to ask Arnaldo Pomodoro, one of Italy's most famous sculptors, for advice; since he had a studio in Milan and I knew him, it was easy. One day I went to see him and showed him my pears. To cast a loose ball enclosed within the fruit form seemed an impossible undertaking. "Why don't you take these things to my foundry near Verona? Fausto has a solution for everything." So one morning I drove to Sommacampagna, on the outskirts of Verona, one of my favorite north Italian towns, and met Fausto Bonvicini in his office. Pomodoro had alerted him, and he was expecting me. When I showed him the pears, he said simply, "What is the problem?" I showed him that I wanted the seed to roll around freely, yet be impossible to remove from the hollow of the fruit. Fausto gave me a reassuring smile. "That's easy," he said. "We cast them separately, then we cut the fruit open, put in the seed, close, solder, and that's it." And then he added an embarrassed "Would you like to see the foundry?"

Fausto was a powerful, stocky man with a calm self-assurance in his speech and gestures, and a slow, steady determination in his movements. That first time we met I noticed that he immediately put me at my ease, and as we walked toward the *sala dei gessi* I felt a sensation that I would never fail to recognize each time I worked there over the next thirty years. It was a feeling very much like the surprising sensation of serenity I feel each time I am being rolled into the operating room of New York Hospital. Then, too, an inexplicable (and unreasonable) sense of well-being comes over me, no doubt from having delegated to my surgeon all responsibilities for whatever is going to happen. I knew that as long as he or Fausto was around, nothing could possibly go wrong.

My discovery of the foundry—of bronze—of working with intelligent, sensitive workmen on what I naively assumed to be an equally shared

In the foundry with Fausto Bonvicini

Working at the foundry

Three moonflowers in Venice

level of dignity, commitment, and happiness affected my life in many important ways. Besides the thrill of acquiring knowledge and deftness in a new field, I had discovered in collaborating with the foundry workers my private little Marxist paradise, the pleasures of frequent periods of temporary celibacy and aloneness, the beauties of Verona and the Lago di Garda. And new friendships. But over and above all these unexpected blessings, the discovery of one of the most fertile and beautiful provinces in the kingdom of Art: sculpture. A lifetime after my masterpiece *Three Little Mushrooms on a Base,* I had discovered a new play and a new role both more demanding and more rewarding than any I had acted in before. When in Verona I was introduced with the customary Maestro Lionni, I realized that while paintings have to work for a living, sculptures by the mere fact of being sculptures are treated with respect and admiration.

Several months had gone by after my first visit to the Bonvicini Foundry when I realized that during all that time I hadn't touched a brush. The colors on my palette had hardened, the turps had evaporated, the easel—supreme symbol of my commitment to painting—had been pushed into the darkest corner of my studio. But I had not been idle. The drafting table I had bought in Chiavari shortly after our return from the United States showed signs of great activity. It was covered with hundreds of small pen-and-ink drawings on the pages of a leather loose-leaf notebook which had become my steady vade mecum; I never left the house or the studio without checking my pockets for fear of finding myself in a café in Mantua, a restaurant in Milan, or even home in San Bernardo with a sudden idea for a sculpture but without a decent piece of paper to commit it to.

The drawings were mostly of what from a distance might have looked like ordinary shrubs, flowers, cactus leaves, and branches or parts of these, but at closer range they revealed the telling details of organisms that could have grown only in the soil of the imagination. They looked as if they had been drawn ages ago; the subtle shading, the brownish afterhue of the black ink, and the unfinished edges gave them that eighteenth-century look of suspended immobility which the surrealists and dadaists had so cleverly appropriated. Perhaps it was no coincidence that it was in Zurich, the birthplace of dada, that I had bought an expensive ballpoint pen with an ink that can take on the color of old etchings, the dark gray shade that rests in the folds of centuries-old robes. My visual memory is still as perfect as Mother's musical pitch was when she was well over sixty: she would sing a high C, walk to the piano, and there it was. With my new ballpoint pen I could draw and shade any imaginary object so convincingly that not only would you be sure that it exists but you could guess, with reasonable chances of being exactly right, its intended dimensions. Paradoxically, for me, whose studio was never large enough, the 2-by-3-inch pages of my notebook are the ideal dimensions for representing an imaginary object from five to six feet away. A larger sheet would demand unnecessary detail, while a smaller one would be too small to evoke its identity.

Someone who has never experienced the feeling of becoming, of being, of existing, or who has never witnessed the birth of things would never believe that the spaces where our imagination takes us need be no larger than the page of a small notebook. My work was becoming an obsession, to such an extent that in the first excitement of being at the foundry, I would have moved to Sommacampagna were it not for my dependency on Nora and my need of her presence. To let work shape my lifestyle would have been nothing new; I had done it before—lightly, almost imperceptibly, following the difficult paths of conformity and compromise. But this time it was different. The choice was one not so much of adopting a new style of living but of living a new style of feeling. My discovery of sculpture had not happened because of my exposure to a new medium, a new subject matter, or a new technology. It came about because of a total change of vision. It was as if my vaporous dreams had suddenly solidified, and the center of my being, the nucleus of my creative energies, had moved elsewhere, far from the comforts of inherited traditions. The metaphor that had been the sustaining column of all my realities was suddenly unrecognizable: from *standing for* things, from *representing* things, the images had become things themselves. The shadows had solidified, the world was no longer *about* something—it *was*. Painting was no longer what it once had been, the making of magic. I saw it now as a shorthand for sculpture. The new technology was my notebook, the little soul of my now solid dreams. The solitary tree had been the last of my imaginary portraits. Now another "possible" nature, *une nature autre*, was rising on the other side of the lake.

The weeks, the months flew. There were days of poetry and days of prose, but the fantastic forest whose real dimensions had ceased to exist, where a giant cedar could be no taller than the hair of a lichen, became richer and denser by the day. By the summer of 1972, the studio, the storeroom, and the garden were worlds filled with botanical oddities waiting for their patina to age so they could join the festivities of the living.

I spent months at the foundry, and in October of 1972 I had my first exhibition at Il Milione Gallery in Milan—one room for the paintings and

In the foundry

bronzes, the other, much smaller, for drawings and prints. Two years later, the result of this three-year body of work, three years of concentration and elaboration of a theme, was shown at the Baukunst Galerie in Cologne, and a slightly reduced version five years later, in 1977, at the Staempfli Gallery in New York. The large bronze *Three Moonflowers* was on the campo in front of the Hotel Gritti as part of the international sculpture exhibit that spread throughout the city of Venice. I had invented a new game for myself, perhaps the most exciting game of all.

Since I was also responsible for one of the exhibitions of the Biennale Experimental Graphics, together with Erberto Carboni and Albe Steiner—both, like me, designers of the old guard—I felt a great need for a rest, and since I had learned that the only way to rest was to find a total change of scenery, I decided to go to Spain for two weeks of flamenco.

Flamenco

The Finca Espartero is a simple three-story building in the narrow valley that runs between the hilly olive groves a few kilometers south of Morón de la Frontera and seventy-five kilometers south of Seville. In the years I went there for two- or three-week flamenco workout sessions, the owners were Don Pohren, an American amateur guitarist, and his Spanish wife, a ballet dancer who taught flamenco dancing. What attracted me and four or five others to the *finca* was that Morón was the center of what I would call hard flamenco, the flamenco as yet unspoiled by jazz and by South American melodies and rhythms.

Don had made the finca the headquarters for hard flamenco, whose undisputed czar was a *gitano* my age, a good-looking gentleman who might have been the director of the local branch of the Banco de España but whose name, Diego el del Gastor, would send a shiver up the back of any well-informed flamenco aficionado. I believe that Don was something like an agent for the *gitanos* who lived in Morón, most of whom were professional musicians. He would arrange for records to be made, articles to be published, and concerts to be organized. For me, his paying guest, he would arrange lessons, organize *juergas*—parties with flamenco performers—on the *finca*'s terrace and trips to Jerez, where, near the slaughterhouse, there was a room in the back of the café in which, by appointment, two old singers in the hard flamenco tradition would perform, accompanied and encouraged by the *tocador* Diego el del Gastor. Nothing in the whole world was more exotic than the exclusive privilege of sitting for several hours in the small room above the only bar in town, watching and listening to Juanito, one of Diego's nephews, practicing a *falseta* on his guitar until his fingertips bled. The most important thing I learned in Morón was that so-called improvisation is mastered with the same dogged discipline and hard work as any other musical form.

I never really understood what made me study flamenco, what brought on this passion that had me nailed to an uncomfortable chair for hours at the time, kept me anxious about the condition of my fingernails, and on which I spent almost as much time as on painting. I never heard anyone explain his flamencomania rationally. Perhaps what all passions have in common is that their cause is never clear. While I can give a dozen reasons for each of the minor hobbies that has lightened the burdens of my daily life, I am at a loss to explain rationally my love for India, my love for flamenco, my love for fly-fishing. It was Ed Zern who opened my ears to flamenco, yet I can think of no one less likely to teach me the rudiments of that severely disciplined art than he. Neither could I have ever foreseen that flamenco would be the great life passion of Ed and Evelyn's son, Brook, whose flamencomania reached professional levels. What is perhaps more curious is that Ed was also in a way responsible for my passion for fishing. I wonder if my admiration for him in my early Philadelphia days when we were close friends might not have played a part. There was something enormously seductive about Ed—about the style of his intelligence, his daring egocentrism, his humor, and his disclosures of his vulnerabilities, all of which were so different from my own character traits. There was a civilized macho quality about him that I envied. Suddenly I am reminded of my feelings for Uncle Piet—the same sense of gratitude that from the throne of his strength and independence he would hand me the most graceful flowers.

Paolo

I cannot remember when Paolo died. Was it five years ago? Fifteen? I can hardly remember the place. Florida? California?

The moment I ask myself these questions my mind freezes up. I have tried to write about him before, but each attempt ended in failure and futile pain. The fragmented tale of his sudden departures and unexpected returns to and from his secret worlds has left Paolo unreal, illegible, an abandoned manuscript ripped to shreds.

Downstairs in the storeroom there is a small metal trunk full of his things—proofs, postcards, poems, pictures, pamphlets. Paolo would say, "You see? Look at all those words beginning with *P.* These things happen to me all the time." In a world of logic and conformity, he always saw weird connections in his invented universes. He believed in miracles—in his unsummoned visions. And because he was a poet, he believed in words as yet unnamed.

I have tried to organize the things he left, clean them, get them into some kind of order, but without their little private chaos, their smell of dust, smoke, and mold, they too, like my memory, freeze up, lose their point, lose him. On the twentieth of June, I shall burn them and place the ashes close to his grave under the cypress trees.

And someone perhaps will read this letter I wrote to his family and friends about the days before his last, definitive departure.

I have just returned from Clearwater on the Gulf of Mexico, one of the many popular vacation resorts on the coast of Florida, blessed at this time of the year with a marvelous climate, white beaches, an ultramarine sea, an extraordinary light, and the flights of seagulls, pelicans, and herons. Unfortunately, this natural paradise like so many others around the globe has been spoiled by the unruly proliferation of bungalows, restaurants, parking lots, pizza parlors, hotels, motels, and gas stations.

Paolo and Jane are fortunate to have found an apartment in one of the few quiet, orderly parts of town, owned by friends who rarely go there. It is elegant, comfortable, and on the sixth floor, with a fantastic view of the gulf and the mainland all the way to the crowded beaches of the island where we stay while we are here. Paolo and Jane can stay in the apartment indefinitely. What luck! In these tragic circumstances it makes everything so much easier and a bit more bearable.

Paolo's condition has deteriorated at a faster pace than had been expected. Since a few weeks ago the right lung has also been invaded by the tumor. This makes his breathing dif-

Paolo

ficult and painful. He has reduced his conversation to a few essential words, but when his mind is clear he is as eager as ever to confront philosophical, literary, and political problems. He is aware of being ill, but he believes that it is only a temporary infirmity and that in the month of June he will be in Porcignano, or in Philadelphia for a big project of the Center for Medieval and Renaissance Studies, or in New York. Often he asks Jane if the Philadelphia apartment is ready, and when she says yes he is satisfied. He lives in a no-man's-land between reality and fantasy, with unpredictable excursions from one to the other.

All this has a profoundly tragic side, but it does make life with him easier, since it is the proof that he suffers less than one would expect. His face has not changed, but he is unbelievably thin.

Although we have no illusions and the pain is unchanged, we are less anguished than we were a year ago. Most of the time he sits in his bed with his head resting on his knees—this evidently is the position that makes his breathing easier. He coughs continuously. This is what is most upsetting to those who come to visit him, but after a while you become aware of the surprising fact that it causes no pain. What bothers him most, I believe, is his restlessness.

When we arrived he hadn't shaved for a few weeks. He was very handsome. A few days ago he shaved, and now his face is more or less the way we remembered it. His eyes are perhaps less lively, but this is the effect of the codeine he's given to help him sleep. The doctors obviously do not make a prognosis. It can last a few weeks or a few months, but we all agree that his life should not be unnecessarily prolonged but made as comfortable as possible.

Jane is an astonishing young woman and has all our admiration. Paolo, like many seriously ill persons, is very demanding and wants full attention. Jane has become his slave. She doesn't have a second to herself. When we arrived she hadn't left him for a moment for several weeks. She never leaves home and rarely the room, and she looked like a rag. Now that we are here, especially Nora, things seem somewhat easier. We made Jane understand that she had to take care of herself. They bought a hospital bed and a wheelchair, and from tomorrow there should be a nurse for three or four hours a day.

Mannie, who is in Clearwater today, is of great help to us. Before we saw Paolo in this condition, our anguish was even greater. It was worse when we were alone in New York with our imaginations. The fact that he is not in pain and that he is not aware of the seriousness of his condition is for us a great relief.

Forgive me if I did not write to each of you, but the reasons are obvious. You know that we think of each of you personally and that is how we love you and embrace you.

Tho other day in a moment of lucidity Paolo said to us, "I have won two great battles, the one against heroin and the one against cancer." He is very much helped by his faith, and we are grateful for this too, even if as atheists we see it as very exotic. Every day someone (the Scientology version of a psychologist) comes to speak with him, and that apparently helps him a lot.

He feels strongly attached to the family and often asks

about each one of you. He always mentions his love for Europe in general and for Italy and Porcignano in particular. We shall bring him there to the little cemetery of Coltibuono, where together we shall put him to rest.

All my love.

When we lived on McCallum Street in Philadelphia a woman came twice a week to do the cleaning. Her name was as round and big as she was: Beulah. Beulah was enormous; she must have weighed three hundred pounds. Although she was as black as mahogany, she reminded me of Oma. They had in common the even-paced slowness, the elemental rationality, and with the children, the light-handed authority exercised by merely straightening out the massive bulk of their bodies.

Beulah loved the boys, and they both loved her, but her feelings for Paolo were special. When she talked about him, she hushed her voice slightly, as if she had discovered deep inside his soul a secret frailty that no one but she could have suspected, a worrisome wound that she secretly treasured like a black, worm-eaten totem.

One morning, after breakfast with the kids, when we mounted the stairs to finish dressing, we found Beulah waiting for us on the landing. "Look," she said, holding a crumpled piece of paper with what looked like cigarette butts, "I found this in Paolo's room behind the aquarium." I was shocked. "Cigarette butts?" Paolo couldn't have been more than six or seven at the time. "That's what they are, Mister El." "You mean to say that Paolo smokes?" said Nora. "Let's not be hasty—kids pick up all sorts of things." "Mister El, there were ashes on the floor."

I took the butts, and we went to the bedroom. Nora threw herself onto the bed. I fell into the armchair and in a daze listened to her sobbing. Suddenly I remembered. "My God!" I shouted. "What?" said Nora, drying her tears. "This is incredible! Last week Paolo asked me if he could smoke. I had just heard on the radio or read somewhere that it's no use prohibiting children from smoking. 'Let them try,' they said, 'they'll be sick as dogs and never want to smoke again.' Armed with this magic remedy, I told Paolo that it was his problem. 'If you want to get good and sick, go ahead and smoke.' "

A few weeks later I was driving to the garage to have the brakes checked when I thought I saw Paolo and a friend behind a tree across the street, lighting cigarettes. I talked myself into believing that it wasn't them and said nothing.

A foreboding? Things are easy to predict in retrospect.

Paolo died on April 6, 1985.

Porcignano

Perhaps it had been a mistake to call San Bernardo our "forever house" without providing the customary *scongiuri*. In countries where every flattering remark must be exorcised, certain centuries-old rites must be respected. Touching wood where most houses are made of stone is simply not trustworthy. True or not, in 1966 the news began spreading that our Riviera would soon be blessed by a super autostrada that would bring undreamed of prosperity to the region. Subtle items of propaganda began to trickle from official sources: the road would be a fragrant ribbon of exotic flowers flanking the sea from Genoa to Naples. Noise? New building materials had been developed that would not only absorb all noise but, having absorbed and digested it, expel it in the form of music. And the excitement was high among shopkeepers when they learned that every village along the coast would have its own exit, so that the Milanese pale-faces, still wet from the fog and rain, could stop and load up their Ferraris with local goodies. Pessimists were dangerous nihilists, and the lessons developed during twenty years of Fascism were once more considered dangerous defeatism. No one fought the project seriously. We, a small group of ecology-conscious architects, and the local left-wing parties joined in a group suggesting a far cheaper and ecologically more correct inland route that would have brought work to underdeveloped areas and spared the coast. The final upshot was a compromise: the autostrada would pass halfway between the projected coastal route and ours, placing it right through the middle of our property. That was the end of San Bernardo.

We were very depressed, unaware that, as with so many other events in our lives, fate was preparing a spectacular revenge. It happened a few years later in Paris, when in the hall of a Saint-Germain hotel we met some Milanese friends, the Stucchis, who owned an important estate with a dozen farms and the famous medieval abbey Coltibuono between Florence and Siena. When we told them of our predicament, they suggested that we spend a weekend with them at Coltibuono, where they had some abandoned farms for sale with ancient farm buildings that, once restored, would make wonderful homes in one of the most spectacular landscapes in Italy.

• • •

The Porcignano studio and the house

I well remember the first time I saw Porcignano, a month or so after our Parisian encounter with the Stucchis. "Let's begin with the most beautiful," Piero had said as we left the abbey in the worst thunderstorm I had ever witnessed. "You don't believe in crescendos?" I ventured. "Not in this case," said Piero as he turned into the road to Radda and soon slowed down at the entrance of a path that descended toward the high part of the valley. He parked at a wooden cross there and began walking, curved against the whipping rain. I followed him, concentrating on holes in the path and an occasional stone.

"Let's stop here, where you can see the whole valley," he said. "The entire property comes to about twenty acres of woods and those three

At our window

hills there with the vineyards." The rain had stopped, and several blotches of bright blue sky hung above the hills, shifting shape as new, darker clouds accumulated. Stucchi shouted, "Farther down where that small cypress stands you get the full view, including Radda, six miles from here." Finally my eyes embraced the whole property. It lay there, calm like an ancient garden now an abandoned landscape, an island anchored in a fjord. Suddenly the sun appeared teasingly, slowly, from behind a cloud, with all the glamour of a diva. I kept looking for the buildings, but dark, hard-edged shadows moved swiftly from one bush to another. In my search to locate the buildings, memory shifts to the next time we saw Porcignano, and the third time—when we were with a small group of people, among whom was the notary from Siena, who was preparing the maps for the contract.

Kukai

In 1981 I was granted the Japan Foundation award for the Japanese edition of *Parallel Botany*. It consisted of three weeks' unlimited travel in Japan with Nora and a guide, who, to our great joy, turned out to be our Japanese friend Mie Uchida, who had studied in the United States and spoke fluent English. It was she who had discovered the American edition of the book and had it translated into Japanese and published under her supervision by Kowsakusha, the unpronounceable publishing firm for which she worked and which had been founded and was headed by the young philosopher Seigow Matsuoka.

I vividly remembered my first meeting, on an earlier visit to Japan, with this eccentric intellectual, who always provided startling connections between the aesthetic aims of the Western avant-garde and the ancient Oriental traditions. I had been waiting half an hour in his office before his secretary came in to announce that Matsuoka-san had called to say he was on his way. Ten minutes later an assistant brought the message that he had just entered the building and would be with me shortly, and after another five minutes, preceded by a big commotion in the corridor, Matsuoka slowly made his grand entrance, bowing deeply. Without saying a word he walked vaguely in my direction until he stood facing me.

Then he straightened, gave me an expressionless look, and threw himself straight at my feet, arms stretched before him, remaining motionless and without breathing in that position for a worrisome and embarrassing minute before quickly standing up, smiling, shaking hands, and in the most cordial, informal American way saying, "Welcome to Japan! What a pleasure to see you!"

This time we met as old friends and had lunch in his office from an unforgettable set of very large trays holding endless small edible mysteries. And it was during lunch that he proposed two days of uninterrupted conversation with me. "There are so many interesting things to talk about with Reo-san!" he said to Nora. Had news of my inability to say no reached the shores of Japan? The upshot was that before we left on our trip south, Matsuoka kept me in front of a microphone for two entire days; the transcribed conversation appeared in a book titled *The Book of Ma*. There are several photos of the two of us talking, plus some scribbles that must have some bearing on the subject. Although the concept of *ma* is

In Japan—Matsuoka is across from me.

close to unexplainable to a Westerner, I proudly thought then that I had gained a slight inkling of its meaning, but now I must confess that I really don't know what this book, which I coauthored (and cherish, of course), is all about.

Mie had made appointments with various important personages in the Japanese cultural firmament whom she thought I might be interested in meeting. We had tea with an eighty-year-old avant-garde poet honored with the title "National Treasure" who had read *Parallel Botany* and wanted to show me his amazing collection of eight thousand varieties of cactus. We watched another "National Treasure," and "Great Brush," one of Japan's most famous calligraphers, teach a young, frail woman how to build up enough angry energy to decapitate an entire Western alphabet with one portentous brushstroke. We met with the architect Isozaki and his sculptor-wife, whom I knew from her exhibitions at the Staempfli Gallery in New York, where she showed her elegant, airborne calligraphy, steel shapes miraculously thin and delicately balanced. And of course we had dinner with Shuntaro Tanikawa, the foremost modern Japanese poet and translator of some of my children's books, whom we knew from a previous trip. It was a happy and a fascinating week.

I have no recollection of the exact itinerary of our trip, but I know that we spent many leisurely days around the Kyoto and Nara area, revisiting the temples, palaces, and local curiosities that, although familiar to us, produced some new, unexpected discovery each time we returned. On this, our third visit to Japan, I had decided to concentrate primarily on the traditional forms of Japanese architecture, which had survived so strongly in my visual memory and now could be studied in greater depth. But my good intentions were once more shattered by my enthusiasm. I was so overwhelmed by the beauty of buildings I had not seen before, so moved by the potency of their poetic charge, that I returned home richer in memories and nostalgia but as ignorant as ever.

I shall always be grateful to Mie for having included Koyasan in our itinerary. It is a village at the foot of Mount Koya in Wakayama's mountainous hinterland, which prides itself on having close to one hundred temples and the greatest cemetery in Japan. But its most important treasure is Kukai's grave—Kukai, founder of Japan's version of esoteric Buddhism, a saint, scholar, painter, architect, hermit, inventor, and great calligrapher. I find it extremely difficult to describe and explain my fascination with Kukai, who alone would have sufficed to make my visit to Japan memorable for the gifts, both light and heavy, which he gave me and for the mysteries he revealed.

The San Bernardo studio—the door of memories

Don't ask me what esoteric Buddhism is. I suffer from a congenital incomprehension of spiritual phenomena and know little about their presumed power, their metaphoric meaning, and their moral function. But fascinated by the words and rites of all religions, I am easily touched by the pain, the angst, and the passion of imploring crowds. Because of my fables I feel at ease in the worlds of the imaginary, of the once-upon-a-time, and when sometimes I suddenly recognize an invisible force guiding my writing or my painting hand, I faint away into a lightness of being never known otherwise. And so I have listened for a message from Kukai, from the height of his hermitage on Mount Koya, which may one day bring the sound of the one true word, mantra, Shingon.

At the end of our month of meandering through Japan, there was a round table to discuss my reactions to our trip. When Tanikawa asked me what my religious beliefs were, I answered, without thinking, "I am a mystic atheist." I expected some of the participants to be shocked, as undoubtedly some of my American and European friends would have been, but here no one raised an eyebrow. After all, wasn't the early Buddha an atheist and a mystic? To feel and recognize the embrace of a Universal continuum does not necessarily involve belief in a God—to me it happens when, totally absorbed in the work, I may experience that rare moment of thought and will and memory and feeling and the muscles of the body seeming to melt into one harmonious flow of energy, one chord of perfections—the moment of the lightness of being which my Gypsy friends call *duende*.

part five
Letters to Bob

Bob Osborn and I met in Philadelphia fifty years ago. During all those years he was my closest friend, and despite his recent death he still is. We rarely encountered each other except in our letters. In his short messages—often three or four a week—he let his writing pen or worn brush sum up his momentary rages or pleasures by thundering them onto his beloved Arches paper. My writings were less frequent but usually dense and wordy, typewritten. We always agreed, and we always knew it was because we were so different and because distances in time and space forced us to sharpen our vision and understanding. Some of my letters I never sent; some lay on my desk for months, until edited by the violence of living and the reality of a phone call they had lost all reason for being saved. Others, more recent, are eternalized willy-nilly in that miraculous instrument my computer, which contains the voice of my aging fingers.

Bob Osborn

Dear Bob,

Someday I shall count the letters you've sent me during the last years of our bizarre friendship. In Porcignano there are several cardboard boxes full, and in our New York apartment they fill a filing drawer. Five hundred? A thousand? I don't have the slightest idea.

You ask me how the Book is coming along. It's funny how that question splashed right into the murky pool I was wading in, trying to find an answer to the same question. Did you feel that I was in some sort of crisis?

There are times when I am so tensely inside the process of dressing up my memories that I don't realize that in the "real" world time moves forward. Accustomed as I am to thinking of fables in terms of a beginning, a development, a crisis, and an end, I seem to have been working on the story of my life pretty much along this same scheme, only to discover that as I am moving toward the end, events are seen in a new light. Eliminating the hypothesis of a happy ending by you-know-what, I seem to lack the arrogance of proposing a moral to my story. Am I a man or a mouse?

Peep! Peep!

Dear Bob,

I don't believe I ever told you that toward the end of last summer I had a visit from a Dutch journalist who had asked to interview me for Dutch radio. We talked for more than two hours. It was all in my old-fashioned Dutch, which miraculously I still speak without the trace of an accent but with a "house, garden, and kitchen vocabulary" reduced by the wear and tear of time to a child's babbling. At the end of the session we were both exhausted. I stretched my legs, and he was packing away his recording equipment when he suddenly stopped, looked at me in desperation, and said, "Oh my God, I forgot to ask you the final question." I couldn't believe we had left a single episode of my life unexplored, but he handed me the microphone once more, fussed with the wires, and said, "OK, here we go!

"Are you afraid of death?" He threw it hard, and the question sailed toward my bat with a nasty curve. It caught me totally unprepared. My mind went blank. And then I heard myself say, "No, I am not afraid of death. I just think it's a terrible waste of time," and we both exploded in a fit of laughter. It was a perfect ending.

Dear Bob, *Mon Cher,*

Even if they come in those long American envelopes with our name and address written across them like neon signs, *letter* is surely the wrong term for those things that make the girls at the Radda post office talk about hiding their faces because they're not supposed to giggle at their customers' mail. It's lucky that your envelopes are sealed tightly, for if the girls knew what goodies there are inside, I would never see another one of them. Those things you make with words that dance across your pages like young snakes in love would never be delivered and would vanish in the Chianti air or into someone's drawer the way Nico Tucci's box of postcards did some eighty years ago. I don't believe I ever told you that story.

Did you know my friend Walter Cohrssen? Walter was a young German composer whom I met in Milan in the thirties and who stayed with me in Philadelphia for a few weeks before Nora's arrival. You may have met him at our house in Greenwich during the fifties. He was then teaching music history at Seton Hall, and we saw him and Carla, his adorable wife, from time to time. What I know about music I learned from him. He even taught me to hate Brahms—for a while—but despite his hairy disposition and his irritating arrogance, I loved him for his subtle intelligence and for letting me share his passion for chamber music. Carla was Walter's opposite. While he saw himself as a brilliant polemicist, Carla, modest, reasonable, generous, and even-tempered, worked hard to become a psychoanalyst without ever telling their friends. But only a few years after starting a practice in Newark, she died of cancer. Her death was a great tragedy for Walter, and we didn't hear from him for several years. After we returned to Italy, he wrote me some strange, angry letters in response to the catalog of a show of my little portraits. In three or four pages of vile invective he accused me of betraying my principles by giving in to a cheap modernity and to the fashionable slang of pop art, and of catering to the taste of collectors and museums, et cetera. We heard nothing more from him until

about six years ago, when we received a letter in which he announced that he had remarried. He had moved to Miami,
where his bride, a successful real-estate agent and investment
banker, owned a villa, a Lincoln convertible, and a white poodle. Shortly thereafter we got a telegram announcing that
they would be in Florence on their way to Rome for a congress
on investments in the Iron Curtain countries and could they
spend a few days with us in Porcignano? Faithful to our old
friendship, I answered yes, we would be delighted. And so on a
Friday morning, alerted by the shrill barks of a neurotic white
poodle and the deep aristocratic horn of an expensive automobile, we ran to the entrance of our garden just in time to
see a silver Lincoln convertible with a Florida license plate
roll down our driveway and stop before us without so much as
a shiver. A petite, purple-haired, heavily made up, recon-
structed Southern lady in her early seventies was at the
wheel. Next to her, sunk deep in his soft leather seat, was a
small gentleman with a vague resemblance to Walter, all
wrinkles and dark glasses, dressed in a blue cashmere jacket
with gleaming brass buttons.

I shall not bore you with a detailed description of the
longest and most painful weekend we have ever experienced.
Walter, unrecognizable, barely opened his mouth, and the conversation hardly ever rose above the degrading level of Miami
small talk. Walter's only recognizable gesture was wanting to
see the Piero della Francesca frescoes in Arezzo on their way
south. I foolishly proposed meeting them there at the café in
front of the Church of San Francesco for a collective visit to
the recently restored frescoes and a final espresso together.

It was the first Sunday of the month, the day of the great
Arezzo street fair, where anything more than ten years old is
called an antique. When we took leave of our antique newlyweds, we walked them to their car, which was parked near the
post office, where the fair began. Exhilarated by our regained
freedom, we decided to take a look at the fair, something we
had always avoided. I reached for a shoe box full of postcards
in the midst of stacks of old issues of the *Domenica del Cor-
riere* and some badly damaged parchment-bound books, probably stolen from a country church nearby.

At first sight, the postcards, fifty or so, seemed to be addressed to the same person, but judging from the stamps they

came from different countries. And then I suddenly realized that the name of the person had a familiar ring to it, and as I began reading them at random it dawned on me that the person must have been the mother of Niccolò Tucci, whose beautiful stories about his childhood in Italy, which frequently ran in *The New Yorker* in the fifties and sixties, you surely remember. In fact you probably met him at openings of exhibitions or at Del Pezzo, of which he was a steady habitué.

Noting my obvious interest, the woman who ran the stand stepped forward and shocked me when she declared with superb nonchalance that the price was two thousand lire each. Outraged, I chose five, including one dictated by Tucci to his older brother when he was five, and one in Russian. It was only when we got home that I realized what a stingy fool I had been—I should have bought them all. But now it was too late. If I'd had Tucci's address I would have sent him the cards right away. A month passed before it occurred to me to call Nico's agent in Milano, Eric Linder, who was also my agent for *Parallel Botany*. It is from him that I learned that Nika had been staying with our neighbors the Stucchis at the Badia de Coltibuono for more than a month. That very evening, in the frescoed refectory of the abbey, I handed him, without explanation, a sealed envelope with you-know-what.

Bob,

Your brilliant and touching letter burst in with the question "And the Book?" You caught me off guard at a moment when I was feeling threatened by all sorts of unresolved doubts about the validity of what I had written so far and what I had planned to write here in Chianti. And it was easy, as always, to muster a hundred excuses for not writing at all.

This problem is not new. It happens regularly every six months, when I leave New York for Porcignano and vice versa. Even if I have no immediate commitments it takes me a good month or so to find my bearings in the luxuries of space, light, and mood of the studio and in "the other room," where I have my computer and the fax. In New York I am not less conscious of my surroundings. Even in the modest corner of the New York living room, I feel disoriented the first weeks after our return there, for the city is always throbbing with new and unfamiliar energies.

From where I now sit at my computer, surrounded by folders, sheets of paper, dictionaries, and a carafe of water, I can see through the open passageway my beloved easel carrying an old semiabstract painting. Were I a real professional, would it matter to me where or how I have been writing or painting? It is ridiculous. I have been working at "the Book" close to four years now, and I still worry about having the *physique du rôle* of an author.

It is part, I guess, of the ambiguous nature of the beast. After all, I am writing mostly about myself, and the reader expects a reasonably accurate portrait. But how can I, the author, be trusted if I am also the protagonist? I may want to be perceived in a certain way. Should I warn the reader in advance? As author, I have the tricks to manipulate appearances, it's part of my business, and no one can deny me the right to devote part of my talents to help you the reader form an image of me that is partly fictional. In autobiography we are all together in this same Pirandellian boat.

But that is not the real problem. There have been too many distractions, and I have been too eager to fall into their traps. I even had the unsolicited cooperation of an exceptionally beautiful spring, with the brush and forsythia splashing the slopes of our valley with their heavy, buttery yellow and the chestnut trees exploding their silver blossom stars in the new blue sky. I danced with the winds of spring, naively certain of finishing the Book in a few weeks once I got at it. It was getting at it that was the problem. I was sure I would finish toward the end of July. There were only two chapters left and some conclusions, and it should have been easy and even fun to close with the party after the opening of my retrospective at the Museum of Modern Art in Bologna. In more than one way the exhibition was a rehearsal of my present attempt at autobiography. But seen in the light of the entire narrative, writing about my life from the late sixties on has been surprisingly difficult. Not that there was a lack of interesting and even entertaining events. After all, the '70s were the years of the parallel botany. Had it not been for Bologna, Heaven knows where my flowers would have flourished. But there were shows everywhere. The Venice Biennale of '72, the magnificently mounted show at the Baukunst gallery in Cologne, the Staempfli Gallery in New York, and the Galleria Giulia in Rome.

All these exhibitions led to the Bologna retrospective in 1991 and the publication of *Arte come Mestiere* by Electa, a 180-page catalog of my life's work with separate essays on each of my various activities: painting, sculpture, drawings, photography, design, film animation, and children's books. It was the first time that I was handed the opportunity to display the whole spectrum of my activities, without fear of being judged superficial or amateurish. For the first time in Bologna, I myself got an overview of my total output. There was, indeed, a constant urge to make things regardless of their importance—the game was to make them well.

Dear Bob,

Last night I woke up at three a.m., lay in bed fantasizing, and finally—it is now a quarter to seven—I got that old, sick body of mine out of bed, grabbed hold of my walker, and pushing it slowly, painful step by painful step, I managed to reach the corner of my New York studio, where I am sitting now facing the screen of my computer and you.

I should finish the rough editing of my forever unfinished autobiography, fill in the holes, and find an appropriate ending, but these last two months have been hell, and for one unreasonable reason and excuse after another I have postponed even looking at it until I realized that, yes, I had those excruciating pains in my right hip and leg, and, yes, for a week or so I had that weird combination of hiccups and vomiting, and, yes, I felt nervous about returning to Porcignano. . . . But the real reason was an attack of angst—fear of writing, of failure. I guess all of that, encouraged by Mr. Parkinson (I presume), added up to a minor depression.

I snapped out of it the day before my eighty-fourth birthday, suddenly feeling great and creative and triumphant for no special reason at all. I enjoyed the next day's party with twenty or so friends for drinks and in the evening had a long chat with Jean Michel Folon and Paolina, who had arrived that very afternoon from Monte Carlo. I even mustered the chutzpah to have June Dunbar read some pages from my manuscript, the ones about my room in Amsterdam when I

was eight or nine. It was the first time I had given it to anyone to read other than Nora, my editor and friend Frances,
our cousin Mario, who I hope will do the Italian translation,
and wonderfully wise Mannie, whom I consulted on the parts
about politics. I am not ashamed to say that I was impressed
and even moved on hearing it.

Writing is a funny business. Over the years I have produced forty fables, all in print in twenty or so languages, including Chinese and Hebrew, and in braille. In 1976 I wrote
Parallel Botany, which was translated into Japanese, English,
French, and German (I wrote it in Italian). I have written and
published short stories and endless essays and articles for
newspapers and magazines, edited an Italian monthly . . . and
yet I feel embarrassed when someone calls me an author or a
writer, and even when in odd moments I think of myself as
one, I lower my inner voice to an embarrassed whisper.

I have always considered myself an artist—first, with
all the turbulent, romantic overtones of the word; later, with
the smooth serenity that comes with having mastered a craft.
I am a painter who also does graphics and sculpture. This
definition may have seemed difficult at one time, but I no
longer have a problem with it. But writing is a different story.
Although I have done a lot of writing—perhaps more than
painting—I have never considered it my profession. I've perceived it as a kind of bonus for living well, like talking, eating,
and walking.

Do you know what I mean, Bob? I believe that you too
must feel this way, even if our ways of doing art and writing,
like our talking, are quite different. I know that we both love
words, but while my games with words are elaborate, and I
often risk being pompous and overemphatic, you play with
words like a large puppy. You throw them around, pick them
up and shake them, but when you find a juicy one you put it
aside for tomorrow's breakfast. We both feel deeply about our
writing, and the two of us have published more stuff than
many professional writers, but even when you wrote *Osborn
on Osborn,* did you think of yourself as an author?

As a writer, I have had to invent my education. In school
all I learned was how to write an Italian business letter—not
a mean feat, but useless for an essay, a novel, a children's
book. Or an autobiography, for that matter. I began writing

with serious intentions when I was seventeen with the wild urges and the fragile means of a heart and a mind in full Sturm und Drang—and love. I have a folder of short stories written during those years. The style is what I would call Strictly Adolescent, but it betrays secret literary ambitions.

The first serious criticism I ever had was when Persico read an article I had written for *Casabella* and said, "You should always try to lift the end with an important word like peace, humanity, freedom." That was in Milan during Fascism. In those slippery years I wrote a few articles now and then. I needed the money and liked to see my words and name in print.

Fate, as you know, had other plans for me. Judging correctly that I was a thing-person and more specifically one that has the urge to *make* things, He/She saw to it that during the twenty years that followed my long adolescence, I would have neither the urge nor the energy to write professionally. Yet in the little I wrote now and then I can recognize the rudiments of a basic personal style, somewhat romantic, declamatory, and emphatic, with clear traces of Dylan Thomas and James Joyce.

It was not until the sixties, when under the charisma of Sartre and his Existentialist circle, that I discovered the four-dimensionality of the written word. This happened to be the period when I was editing *Panorama,* spent an unforgettable afternoon with Lévi-Strauss in Paris, and had friends like Giorgio Soavi, Raffaele Carrieri, and other Italian poets. I became more ambitious about the text of my fables. Writing one fable a year was very little writing, but it kindled the ashes that lay still warm in my memory. I also began reading again. First, parts of the *Recherche,* natch! and then Bachelard, Foucault, most of the writers of the Editions de Minuit (le nouveau roman)—Claude Simon, Michel Butor. Later came the South Americans, especially Borges and Márquez, single odd volumes like *Hadrian the Seventh* and *Under the Volcano,* forgotten masterpieces like *Archy and Mehitabel;* and, weaving their way through it all, Joyce, Kafka, and Genet, and whatever else was politically and intellectually correct at the time. Did you ever read the *Hadrian* and *Under the Volcano*? They've gone out of fashion, like *Archy and Mehitabel,* but to me they're still as magnificent as ever.

How did I get here? Oh yes, I was trying to tell you how I feel about writing. A few years ago, when *Chelsea,* a New York–based poetry magazine, had just published some memories of my childhood, I asked my friend Brian Swann, who was then the dean of humanities at Cooper Union, how he would classify my writing style, if indeed there was such a thing. Was it simply "old-fashioned"? Brian was taken aback. "Well, you could say postmodern, I guess." It was my turn to be taken aback, for the term *postmodern* raises all the hair on my forearms. As you well know, there is no architectural style that I despise as much as postmodern. Was my writing that bad? That contrived? That reactionary? When I finally had the courage to ask Brian why he considered me a postmodern writer, he said, "Did I say that? I meant high modernist." Although I didn't know what that meant, I felt better—proud, as a matter of fact. Please, Bob, will you tell your friends that I am High Modernist?

But the question of style raised another important question more pertinent to the Book and one that perhaps explains the reason for my short period of depression. I had reached the early seventies when I got hopelessly stranded in a jungle of indecisions. I reorganized my library; transferred all my photographs and transparencies to another drawer; cleaned out all the drawers of my desk; rewired the computer; read and studied the entire instruction booklet—translated from Japanese—for my new fax machine, and even relettered all the labels on my files. Every day I had a sensible new excuse for not touching my manuscript. And when one evil day I returned to my computer, the images I found in my narrowing memory were little more than an inventory. The closer they came to the present, the more they evoked the banalities of the heavy parallel world I seemed to be confined to. Unpleasantly hard and assertive, they were pressing embarrassingly close to the skin of my history, leaving no room for fictional reinforcements. I was now caught in the web of my own words winding tighter and tighter around me.

I then sat down with the first hundred pages of the manuscript to reread the chapters on my room in the Amsterdam sky—"the temple of my aloneness"—when, in a sudden, dramatic moment of self-confrontation, I realized what had happened. I had lost the voice I had been writing in—the mode, the sound, the rhythm, the character of its emphasis, and the melodies of the familiar songs behind the words. Why couldn't I recapture it now and finish *in gloria?* Gradually a few important considerations began to emerge. The memories of recent events are still too brightly lit, too large for the field of vision, too smelly of the reality they have shed, and too shifty and restless to be contemplated, judged, and understood. No fictional underpinning is clever and sturdy enough to steady them into a believable image.

Autobiography is by its very nature and definition open-ended. But as a painter and sculptor I have the inborn habit of enclosing my vision—real, imagined, or remembered— in two- or three-dimensional rectangular spaces, a habit I've unconsciously adapted to writing as well. All my fables have the classical structure, and as in Greek drama their protagonists wear the masks of their fates, from the very first gesture when the line of action begins to move inexorably through the pages from left to right, parallel to my writing. I cannot think of organizing them in any other way. The habit implies a stylistic unity within each book, guiding the fluctuations of text and images through the intricacies of telling to the conclusion, the Great Magnet END, whose cosmic appetite sucks up and swallows whatever comes in his direction.

I knew all of this before. I had talked about it in my lectures, discussions, and seminars. I know I've talked with you about it. It has defined the form of all the things I've made. Even the hidden skeletons of my largest and most complex bronzes were conceived as rhythmic underpinnings of outer shapes that were apparently free and alive. No wonder that after these years of intense commitment to the writing of my autobiography, the discovery that I had been walking to nowhere on an endless road caused a major shock. I went to pieces and disappeared for a month into the dark recesses of a full-fledged depression.

Great God, Bob, that I have been sitting here at my computer for hours putting these considerations together is understandable, but to have pulled you through this *Via Crucis* is unforgivable.

Dearest friend,

Being a precious four years your junior in this, our over-eighty era, I cannot invoke old age and all the physical difficulties I have experienced these last three or four years as an excuse for not writing. As a matter of fact, the substance of my complaints is not much different from that of those which have preceded them except that the *grande maladie* is now more pompous, more operatic, more manipulative than its predecessors. I realize that. And I must immediately add that what is extraordinary is that what, according to the books, should be a period of remembrance and contemplation and of coming to terms with the statistics of living and dying has been and still is as hectic, creative, exhilarating as things have ever been. Perhaps now that the great gamble is at its greatest, the excitement of existing is also at its peak.

I never told you the details of this more sordid aspect of my life not so much because of *scaramanzia* but because an organ removed doesn't cease to exist. Rather like the underlying charcoal sketch that has been erased, it will forever be hovering over the finished painting, waiting for another chance. But so are the ghosts of all living things that die. Neither the removal of a large polyp in the upper part of my colon, nor the loss of my gallbladder, nor the deletion of a fist-size tumor from my stomach has affected my life to any great extent. And yet I know that their ghosts are there, waiting in ambush. I must confess, however, that the diagnosis of Parkinson's depressed me. Probably because it is a disease of the brain and therefore affects the very essence of being human. It was made a few weeks before I was to give the keynote speech in 1987 for International Children's Day at the Library of Congress. Nora accompanied me, and I remember vividly a slow, serene walk we took through town after a visit to Philip Johnson's most poetic little building for Dumbarton Oaks and our meal at a pleasant Japanese restaurant. I remember the large room where I spoke and had to warn those ladies who had brought books for me to sign that because of Parkinson's I was unable to write, but that my tremor had considerably improved my flamenco guitar playing. After that event I practically ceased to exist for a whole year. I could not button my shirt, did not remember how to get in and out of bed, had practically lost the use of my left hand. Then one sunny morning I decided to see if by adopting a rigorous, step-by-step method I could get a button through a button-hole. Seated on the edge of my bed, I made a schematic analysis of the motions of the right and left hand and counted twelve distinct motions that must now be learned. Occasionally when buttonholes are slightly too small or the button too big I need Nora's help, but ever since that day I have been able to come to the breakfast table completely dressed. Writing is still a great and painful problem that has been partly resolved through the use of my computer. My handwriting has become so small that I can barely decipher it, and then only with the help of a very large and strong magnifying glass.

Things are much better now. I am busy organizing our New York social life, planning a program for Public School Nine in the Bronx, trying to get Bob B. interested in an idea I have for large universal exhibitions to be held simultaneously in twenty or more world capitals on "The Moment of Genius." This would be a celebration of the peak moments in the creative process throughout the ages, the great leaps of the imagination, sometimes banal, sometimes sublime, always mysterious, impersonal, thrilling—the universal *duendes* not only in the arts, sciences, and professions but involving for once men, women, and children of all walks of life. A celebration of the Imagination. I wish I could find someone with the vision, the courage, and the ability to sell this idea when the human race is at the lowest moment of its self-esteem. The deep silence before the lone violin in the *Nutcracker Suite,* Morandi defining all of art with an endless series of small, modestly painted bottles, Mallarmé's *Un Coup de Dés,* the Eiffel Tower, and the inventions of swimming, whistling, making love. Of the dog and the cat. Of words like *yes* and *no.* The last page of *Ulysses.* Yes? The Slinky!

On one of our trips abroad when time was still scaled to human limitations, we encountered a fellow passenger who owned a department store. "You know where I got the money that put me in business?" he asked me. "During the war I was in the navy. I was standing on the deck of a destroyer when an enemy shell hit us. It exploded a piece of machinery not far from me into a thousand pieces. Untouched but transfixed by fear, I was standing there stupidly watching some rounded pieces of metal roll here and there when a ten-inch metal spring, 'walking' down the stairs, contracting and expanding to tumble from step to step, caught my eye. 'I've got to remember that,' I said to myself, and when the war was over I had it patented under the name Slinky." A Moment of Genius.

Bob, even if it is less and less likely that we shall see each other in the near future, I keep thinking how terrific it would be if we could see the Matisse show together. Mannie's Barbara, who when she went had felt crowd sick, advised me not to go, because looking at four hundred Matisse fragments through a tunnel of shoulders is so frustrating and tiring. When a few days before our return to Porcignano I called Bunny Rose in the drawing department of MoMA to say good-bye, she told me that if I wanted to I could come and see it from a wheelchair the next day before the doors opened to the public. How could I refuse? I called Sylvan, Paolo's son who is twenty and studies painting at the School of Visual Arts, and told him to pick me up the next morning at nine and be prepared to take the whole morning off. Bunny was at the museum's entrance waiting for us with a wheelchair, and we saw the Matisse show *alone*.

It was one of the most important art experiences in my whole long life. From one vantage point you could see several walls by just shifting your eyes. You could compare and trace ideas and mannerisms, but above all you could witness, detail by detail, the creative process as it developed from canvas to canvas, from year to year. And what a joy to be able to do this with Sylvan, who is at that magic time in his life when each day brings a new revelation and a new revolution. I often think of those last rooms of the show, where you can see the echoes of the very first paintings painted once more but now polite, measured, pretty but without the fury of impulse, the guts of doing it. Without the flames of passion. You move slowly through this room meditating vaguely about old age and death and then *wham!!* there is the explosion of life and vitality, of the joy of making and doing—the walls with the giant cutouts, the collages. A celebration.

Amsterdam

Dear Bob:

    Life is not open-ended. It coils, and at the end it bites its tail. This is why we are here. I have been working hard on the book, now mainly to pull things together as tightly as possible. I want it to make the complete circle. So we came to Holland, where it all began—as if I had found an old return ticket never used. We arrived two days ago, and had it not been for the mechanics of arrival—luggage, cab, et cetera—I would have cried. Did I do the right thing in coming here? Is it a ritual? Is it theater? Is it real? Is it a form of self-emulation? Is Amsterdam the last of my parallel universes? Is this my last game?

    We are settled in a modest hotel carved out of some uninteresting ancient houses in the historic center, close to the museums and not far from the American Hotel, our Amsterdam Deux Magots. Nearby are my canals and some of the streets of my youth, and we're not far from Oma's house. Our room was intended to be cozy, like everything else in this town. Coziness glues it together. But there isn't a horizontal surface in the room except for the top of the TV and the bed. Where am I going to work? Why do interior decorators hate shelves and tables?

    Everything is so low in this flat city that you have the feeling that when the day is ended they roll it up and unroll it for breakfast in the morning. Don't think that my sarcasm means I am disappointed with Amsterdam. Sarcasm is the first reaction of every native Amsterdammer to whatever he is told. Nora, who doesn't know the differences between sarcasm and irony, thinks that both were brought to Amsterdam by Jewish immigrants in the sixteenth century. Amsterdam Jews are even sarcastic about their sarcasm. Still, what a beautiful, civilized town it is. A metropolis that never swallowed anyone, where even the few new skyscrapers at the edge of town have human scale. Like the pigeons.

    In many ways Amsterdam is really a more interesting and moodier city than Venice, with which it has always been compared. Although Amsterdam was planned and Venice had a natural base, Venice is the more contrived and Amsterdam the more natural of the two. The difference is probably that Venice is way beyond our means, whereas here I could imagine

myself and Nora living in that ugly royal palace with no difficulty at all. Cities, like people, must have a kernel somewhere
that defines their essence. New York is gritty—grit is the secret
kernel of its soul. A tough, chutzpah-ruled, gritty city. I like
that quality. Amsterdam could be the grittiest city if its inhabitants weren't so obsessed with cleanliness. Perhaps one could
say that Amsterdam has the cleanest grit in the world. A grit
that smells of soap and cologne—soap for the sidewalks, cologne
for the bedrooms. In between hangs the scent of cigars and
cabbage, a smell that brings tears to my eyes—the scent of
Oma's house. Yesterday we went to the museums—to my
museums, the Stedelyk and the Ryks. My great surprise was
their new dimensions. The Stedelyk of my memory was
smaller than the one I saw yesterday. This is perhaps due to
the fact that when I was a young boy the rooms were filled
with familiar paintings, while now you can expect to see three
pebbles and a piece of string in one, a door handle in the
other. The surprise of discovering the beauty of a painting you
had never noticed before seems to be gone forever. Why are we
killing the image? But will the word be our savior?

In the Ryksmuseum no one was killing the image, but I
had the feeling that the paintings I loved had stepped further
back in history. Or could it be that when we were young we
didn't know what history was and that those pictures, like
everything else in the world, are part of our collective knowledge now?

If it could be arranged for one day only, wouldn't it be
nice to live in a two-thousand-year time span telescoped into a
veil of time in which all things are contemporary and all
events simultaneous?

Bob,

Forgive my long silences. I didn't want to bother you
with my struggle to produce some decent English prose so
long as the Book is proceeding more or less on its planned
course, and from time to time it looks as if, far, far away, the
word End is in sight. But generally the going is rough, and the
problems are many and always unexpected. Two months after
our return to Porcignano, I had a minor setback, a linguistic
incident, that has led to strange repercussions and has slowed
down my writing quite a bit.

I'm sure I must have told you that ever since I started working on this project I've had great difficulties sleeping the steady eight hours I was used to. I usually go to bed around midnight, get up around two or three, work until five, and then return to bed to sleep another two hours. Often I lie there wide awake with my eyes closed, trying to solve a particular writing problem. But mostly I get up around two and with my pocket light tiptoe through Nora's sitting room to the guest room, which this year, for the duration of what probably are my last literary efforts, has been transformed into a temporary night studio.

Let me tell you what happened one night a few months after we had arrived in Italy when I'd been unsuccessfully struggling with the opening paragraph for a new chapter. Awaking after two hours of deep sleep, my body had found its perfect balance, and my mind was clear and swift. Smoothly and with great elegance of thought I defined the idea, shaped the phrases, chose the words that would invite the reader to join me on a voyage through the intricacies of a problem that I intended to explore. I worked until all the possible alternatives had been exhausted, and I had produced a paragraph so clear in its intentions and yet so subtle in its implications, so strong in its structure and harmonic in its sound, that it would surely be quoted for centuries to come as an example of perfect English writing. I didn't dare move and kept my eyes closed for fear that this short masterpiece might vanish forever from my mind. Then I worried: suppose I fell asleep and lost what I had so artfully created? No, I'd better get up and put it down on paper. I slid out of bed and made my way to the guest room, sat down in front of my new Olivetti laptop, turned on the power switch, and began writing, conscious of each precious letter. When I had completed the first sentence, I stopped to read what I had written. The piece I had elaborated in my mind with such extraordinary lucidity was in Italian.

For most people, being bilingual is simply knowing a foreign language as well as one's mother tongue. I, however, am bilingual in Italian and English, but neither one is my mother's tongue, which was Dutch. Yet although I speak Dutch fluently, I cannot consider *it* my mother tongue. Since I left Holland when I was twelve, my vocabulary is limited, and because of radical changes in the language during the last half century, I can't even spell it correctly, let alone read the newspapers, which are the first to exploit idiomatic novelties in their headlines. Now, "*Huis tuin an keuken Hollands*" may be fine for general small talk and more than sufficient for my tourist needs, but it is grossly inadequate for more sophisticated conversations or writing. One could say that I have no mother tongue; linguistically speaking, I am an orphan.

I became aware of this during our recent stay in Italy, when I realized that my writing English had begun to deteriorate noticeably. Surrounded as I was by Italian, I found myself thinking in Italian, which then had to be translated into English. This was a sure way to lose the immediacy and stylistic coherence I was aiming for. My friends say, "Oh well, write in Italian and have it translated." They don't realize that the elaboration of ideas happens in a world of symbols, of rules and conventions where substance and form are so tightly interwoven that the slightest oversight, intervention, or infraction threatens the solidity and the beauty of an entire fabric. Luckily we came back to New York just in time. Now, fanatic zapper and couch potato that I am, I live, at least during the evening hours, totally immersed in a language that may not be English but comes close to it. We have been here only a few weeks, and already Nora and I automatically speak English together and invariably we have to stop from time to time to hunt for an Italian word. I bet you that between the two of us we squander more than two hours each day trying to remember words or the names of authors, movie stars, and friends.

Native English or American writers have a great advantage over linguistic latecomers like myself. They have at their immediate disposal a great choice of idiomatic expressions, many of them acquired in early youth. These natural "turns of phrase" are important to a writer because they enrich the language and help to establish between writer and reader a degree of familiarity (I could dare say gemütlichkeit) that we foreign-borns will rarely achieve.

There are many more subtle difficulties for the linguistic outsider like myself. For example, in English-speaking countries repetition is appreciated when it is used for rhetorical effect. In France and Italy it is considered pompous and banal.

But these are what my friend Alfredo's grandmother used to call "problems with sugar on them," an editor's delicacy.

In giving you this very long preamble to a chapter I never wrote, I am simply begging for your sympathy and indulgence in a moment when, from a writer's point of view, I feel fragile and terribly insecure. Bodily speaking, I am even worse off. Parkinson's may have improved my tremolo on the guitar, but for eating soup it's a disaster.

Carissimo Maestro,

I hadn't seen a *ramarro* since we came back from New York, but this morning when I staggered to the studio, I saw two. The *ramarros* are not trapeze artists nor are they an Ecuadorian folk group. They are those large green lizards that because of their luminous color and their size scare the hell out of the playful little lizards that we have here by the hundreds around the house, the pool, and the studio. They are not rare like the gigantic orange salamanders, but when you see one on your road you stop. Seeing two in one walk from the house to the studio must be a good omen, and since I had vaguely considered writing a long letter to you today, here I am.

In Siena I have a lawyer-friend who, when he visits my studio, always asks if I ever thought of doing the Palio. And each time I explain to him that the few times I tried to climb on a horse I fell off the other side. I didn't know, as I do now, that doing the Palio means painting the large banner that is the trophy that goes to the winning *contrada* of the wild three-minute race that twice a year attracts some fifty thousand Sienese to the ancient city's central square. At the end of the historic parade that precedes the race, the Palio banner is carried on a cart pulled by four white oxen. It is a thrilling moment, especially for the artist who created it, when the fifty thousand people who fill the campo stretch their necks to get a glimpse of the banner as it slowly circles the square. After the race it will hang forever in the winning contrada's museum. To be asked by the city council of Siena to paint the Palio is the greatest honor that the city can bestow upon an artist.

I assure you that I never expected to qualify, since our life in nearby Radda has been quiet and I had no reason to believe that as an artist I had great recognition here. Nora and I had only seen the Palio twice, and I was unaware of the fact that the banner for each race was painted by a different well-known artist until Andrea Rauch, a young graphic designer–friend of mine, who lives near Florence and has written about my work, told me that he had proposed my name to the council. It was while we were still in New York that I received a copy of the council's deliberations, in which it was laboriously spelled out that I was to paint the banner for the July Palio.

It was not an easy job. The banner was to be painted on a piece of silk eight feet long and three feet wide. It had to contain the Madonna, who sponsors the race, the shields of the ten *contrade* whose horses were competing, the shields of the city of Siena and the mayor, among others. It also was to celebrate the date when Siena was freed from the occupying Germans in 1944 and, naturally, the race itself. Toward the end of June I asked Paolo's son Sylvan, my grandson who is graduating from art school next spring, to come and help me, especially with the shields, which needed to be very carefully painted.

There were moments when I wondered what I had gotten myself into. You are lucky that you had the strength to decide many years ago to draw only what you chose. Unfortunately for me, the word *no* has dropped from my vocabulary. But I shouldn't complain—I have had luck on my side for a long time.

As it turned out, the whole affair was a fantastic adventure, more than worth the work. I shall never forget the ceremony of the presentation of the Palio one week before the race, the dinners in the streets of the various *contrade,* and, naturally, the moment the cart with the white oxen entered the square and very slowly, accompanied by flag throwers, made the round of the campo. Yes, I shed some badly concealed tears. Report has it that my Palio banner was liked—an important detail for my status in Radda, where I have always been considered an enigma. Leo Lionni? Who is that old gentleman who claims he is a painter, makes strange bronzes of plants, draws or prints books for children, and must be rich because he drives that big Lancia and before that a green MG, and lives part of the year in America and the other part here? The mystery is finally solved. It took almost twenty years, but now they know. Lionni? He is that old American eccentric who lives in Porcignano and painted the 1994 Palio.

Mon Cher Ami,

We left Paris three weeks ago, and I can't get it out of my head. The light now is sheer magic from where I am sitting facing the stupendous view of the Radda valley before sunset.

My memories of Paris, even the most recent, possess a corporality so convincing that little more than a postcard of the church of Saint-Germain, a bill from the Hotel des Saints Pères, a glass of Kir, or a ticket for the Métro will set off an irresistible temptation to go there. And when early in the morning I don't want to wake up Nora, I will lie motionless next to her and imagine climbing quietly out of bed, getting washed and dressed, ready to board a plane to Paris. Grossly overrating my strength, I then walk for hours with the crowds through the narrow streets between Saint-Germain and the bookstalls of the Rive Gauche, or along the Champs Elysées or around the Place des Vosges, recognizing with a smile every store, every café, every "Défense d'afficher" sign, and every straggly little tree. Rue de Seine, rue Jacob, rue de l'Echaude, rue du Bac, rue Vaugirard, rue du Dragon . . . names that have colors and smells that never fade. Paris still has that magic of living in our memory whole, unscathed by the rust of time.

It has not changed very much since the last time we were there, except at the periphery and the Louvre, both affected by the French dreams of grandeur. But, as I mentioned to you over the phone, my mood was not steadily happy the week we were there. Without apparent reason it would jump from unmotivated spleen to sudden, equally unreasonable elation.

We spent delicious hours with Pippo (Mannie's son) and Sophie and their two little ones. I met with my French publishers, who at a pleasant little luncheon in a bistro in the rue du Dragon, where I had once eaten with Miró, raised their glasses of Beaujolais Nouveau to the news that the previous day they had sold my millionth children's book. Nora and I had a fine dinner à deux at a restaurant behind the Church of Saint-Sulpice, and a three-hour lunch with André and Margaret François in an Italian trattoria on the Ile de la Cité, and an even longer breakfast with Jean Michel Folon and Paolina at the Café Flore. And one evening we helped Philippe Costagrande, Sophie's brother, celebrate the happy end of his struggle with the life of Pontormo, which will be published by Skira. Last but not least, we went to see the recently inaugurated new wings of the Grand Louvre, where a wheelchair was waiting for me at the Pyramid when we arrived. "Not bad for a week in Paris," you will say.

And yet much of the time I was not happy. My legs hurt and so did my right shoulder as I sat for long hours uncomfortably sloped in a small, straight-backed armchair of pink velvety rayon trying to decipher *Le Monde* with a magnifying glass. A melancholy mist coated the images I tried to exhume from my previous visits to Paris. The ancient paradise I found in my mind was one of peeling wallpaper, creaky floors, the scent of urine, and the scratchy sounds from a radio in the suite next door. I found a cold, empty loneliness. *"Monsieur Lionni? Je regrette. Je ne le connais pas."*

Had I never been in Paris before? Or had I simply been the protagonist of someone else's dream? A Parkinsonian hallucination? No, I decided, I was not that far gone. But then what was it? My aging soul? It is as if I had gone through all of this once before, I said to Nora one morning while we were sipping our cappuccinos. I was thinking of the time I had gone to Paris for the inauguration of an exhibition of Sandy's stabiles in the early '60s. There I had met Paolo and Nancy, a budding actress with whom he was then living, young Folon, and Titina Maselli, a beautiful and gifted Roman painter with a futurist vision. Then, too, I was suffering from some sort of desperation *au rallenti,* an emotional void I had diagnosed as the obol I had to pay for pushing my energies and feelings beyond the border of reason. The party was a *dîner dansant—* there must have been two hundred people. We had a table to ourselves in a dark corner of the hall, backed with palms. Most of the guests were dancing wildly when the music suddenly stopped and a voice announced that President Kennedy had been shot.

There was a loud collective gasp, and for a few seconds the dancers remained frozen in the position in which the news had caught them. The Americans who were present hurried back to their tables or to the telephone. Then the five-piece or-

chestra started to play again, picking up where it had left off.
Paolo spared no words in saying how upset he was by the fact
that no one had proposed halting the festivities as a sign of
mourning and solidarity. Sandy, zombieish, was in an advanced state of drunkenness. There was nothing else to do but
leave, and so we followed Paolo, walking slowly with him
toward the Place Saint-Germain, where small clusters of people were listening to the radios of parked cars. There were violent discussions, and in less than ten minutes we had met the
few Americans who were there. We knew that we shared each
other's pain and anguish, and with them we convened on the
dark Deux Magots terrace and, seated on chained chairs at
chained tables, we talked till early dawn, when I suddenly
felt, with an inexplicable sense of elation, that I had witnessed the end of the romantic illusion.

Je t'embrasse.

Hi Bob,

These last days I have been brooding a lot about architecture for various ill-assorted reasons . . .

. . . because in a book put together by Steve Heller there
is a spread on Van Nelle graphics in the twenties, which
brought me back to the first article I wrote for *Casabella,* in
the early thirties, on the Van Nelle factory by Brinkman and
Van der Vlugt . . .

. . . because of the catalog Charles Correa sent me with a
touching personal note, which put the pressure on my nostalgia for India . . .

. . . because I owe you something more intelligent about
I.M.'s new Louvre than what I said to you too schematically
over the phone . . .

. . . because I owe I.M. something intelligent . . .

. . . because my little Morandi flowerpiece has a lot in
common with Mies van der Rohe and nothing in common with
F. L. Wright . . .

. . . because of Gehry's museum in Minneapolis and Lou
Kahn's in Fort Worth . . .

. . . because I believe that the Isu temple in Japan is as important a masterpiece as Chartres or the Rheims cathedral . . .

. . . because we are badly in need of an honest definition
of what a museum is . . .

Dear Bob,

   Your last letter arrived this morning. Your brief out-
cry of pain moved us to tears as we sat in silence in the car,
in front of our ugly, "modern" little post-office building halfway up the hill to Radda surrounded by vineyards and vegetable gardens. It is difficult for me not to translate your
lonely suffering and anger into an easily imagined scene, a
concretization of my fear of being soon in a similar situation
here—I taking care of Nora or she of me. We do live through
more and more moments of that sort of reality, but we can
still muster enough illusion to be able to claim with a firm
voice that, yes, we are in good shape. But I, especially, have
frequent Parkinson problems that plunge me into shameful
outbursts of self-pity. Luckily, I am still too strongly motivated by my love of life and its pleasures, especially my work,
and too tempted by an irrepressible *mot d'esprit* or an un-
avoidable pun to let my personal little tragedy take command. But when I see Nora, eighty-one, despite her back
troubles, moving swiftly from one room to another, carrying
things to the kitchen, running upstairs, I cannot believe the
decay of my own body, now ill-supported by my cherrywood
cane with the silver band in which I've engraved, in illegible,
tiny letters, my name, address, and telephone number in case
I should be found lying unconscious on a New York sidewalk
or in an auto wreck on the road that swerves through the
woods from our house to Castellina.

   Today, Marcello and Veronica, my assistant, packed all
the black-table paintings for the Rome show. I was very self-
confident until yesterday, when I showed them to a little
group of friends and noticed that several canvases, seen from
the side, showed opaque blotches in the black backgrounds.
This will probably go unnoticed once they hang in the well-lit
gallery, but I did feel a pang of guilt at the sight of my sloppy
workmanship. Now that I am writing to you I feel more relaxed—after all, what a privilege, as you would say, to still be
able to pick up a pencil and place a line of exactly the right
weight in exactly the right place on a sheet of paper.

   This morning I showed Veronica how to tear mouse bodies and cut mouse ears and mouse tails and mouse legs.
Otherwise a sweet young woman, she seemed to enjoy doing

these things enormously. I may have enough mouse parts for five or six children's books. It occurred to me that arriving in New York with a briefcase full might encourage me to produce another book. I have some ideas limping through my mind. But what will customs say?

Ciao!

Bob died on the twenty-second of December 1994. We had a short phone conversation a few days before. His voice was husky, and he spoke only a few terse words, like his last letters. Our friendship lasted half a century, a season borrowed. The weather was beautiful all the way. The light we shared was the varnished light of old paintings, the light of the Amsterdam sky.

Nora is in the kitchen preparing breakfast. Mannie and Barbara will have lunch with us on their return to Burlington. My incoming basket is filled with unpaid bills, unwanted offers, unanswered letters. The Book is practically finished. All I need now is a good ending.

A Note on the Type

The text of this book was set in Century Schoolbook, one of several variations of Century Roman to appear within a decade of its creation. The original Century Roman face was cut by Linn Boyd Benton (1844–1932) in 1895, in response to a request by Theodore Low De Vinne for an attractive, easy-to-read typeface to fit the narrow columns of his *Century Magazine*.

Century Schoolbook was specifically designed for school textbooks in the primary grades, but its great legibility quickly earned it popularity in a range of applications. Century remains the only American face cut before 1910 that is still widely in use today.

Composed by North Market Street Graphics,
Lancaster, Pennsylvania

Printed and bound by Berryville Graphics,
Berryville, Virginia

Designed by Iris Weinstein